Strange Good Fortune

T0336321

Books by David Wojahn

Poetry

Spirit Cabinet (2002)
The Falling Hour (1997)
Late Empire (1994)
Mystery Train (1990)
Glassworks (1987)
Icehouse Lights (1982)

Edited

The Only World: Last Poems of Lynda Hull (1995)
A Profile of Twentieth-Century Poetry (1991, coeditor)

Strange Good Fortune

Essays on Contemporary Poetry

David Wojahn

The University of Arkansas Press
Fayetteville 2000

Copyright © 2001 by The University of Arkansas Press

All rights reserved
Manufactured in the United States

05 04 03 02 01 5 4 3 2 1

Designer: John Coghlan

⊗ The paper used in this publication meets the minimum requirements of the American National Standard for Permanence of Paper for Printed Library Materials Z39.48-1984.

Library of Congress Cataloging-in-Publication Data

Wojahn, David, 1953–
Strange good fortune : essays on contemporary poetry / by David Wojahn.
p. cm.
Includes bibliographical references and index.
ISBN 1-55728-708-2 (pbk. : alk. paper)
1. American poetry—20th century—History and criticism. I. Title.
PS325 .W65 2000
811'.509—dc21

2001000487

For Noelle Watson

Acknowledgments

I would like to thank the editors of the following journals and anthologies in which these essays first appeared, often in earlier versions:

Crazyhorse: "Some Kind of Statement, One Ear Showing: Social Poetry and Its Problems"

Denver Quarterly: "Without a Deep Delight: Neo-Narrative Poetry and Its Problems"

Everything Human: On the Poetry of W. D. Snodgrass (University of Michigan Press): "Snodgrass's Borrowed Dogs: S. S. Gardons and 'Remains'"

Green Mountains Review: "Large Air: A(Millennial) Notebook"

Kansas Quarterly: "Like a Rolling Incognito Lounge: Rock and Roll and American Poetry"

Missouri Review: "Generations 'I': The Future of Autobiographical Poetry"

New England Review: "The State You Are Entering: Depression and Contemporary Poetry"

The Notre Dame Review: "Illegible Due to Blotching: Poetic Authenticity and Its Discontents"

Shenandoah: "Ferality and Strange Good Fortune: Notes on Teaching and Writing"

Verse: "Weldon Kees: A Photo and Two Afterlives"

The Writers' Chronicle: "'Mad Means Something': Anger, Invective, and the Period Style"; "John Flanders on the Anxious Highway: First Books and the Politics of Poetry"

The James White Review: "A Cavalier and Doomed Lot: James L. White, a Memoir"

Writing It Down for James: Talks and Lectures from Writing Conferences (Beacon Press): "Mercantile Eyes: Travel Poems and Tourist Poems"

I am also grateful to the following for permission to use extended quotations from the copyrighted works of these poets:

Craig Arnold, *Shells* (Yale University Press, 1999). Copyright © 1999. Reprinted by permission of the publisher.

Elizabeth Bishop, *The Complete Poems: 1927–1979* (Farrar, Straus, and Giroux, 1983). Copyright ” 1979, 1983 by Alice Helen Methfessel. Reprinted by permission of the publisher.

Jimmy Carter, *Always a Reckoning* (Times Books, 1995). Copyright © 1995. Reprinted by permission of Times Books, a Division of Random House.

"Language Mesh" and "So Many Constellations" from *Poems of Paul Celan,* translated by Michael Hamburger. Copyright © 1972, 1980, 1988, 1995. Reprinted by permission of Persea Books, Inc. (New York).

University of Chicago Press, for permission to quote from *The Greek Papyri in Translation,* ed. Hans Dieter Betz (Second Edition, 1992). Copyright © 1992.

Mark Doty, *Bethlehem in Broad Daylight* (David R. Godine, 1991). Copyright © 1991. Reprinted by permission of the publisher.

Austin Flint, trans. *Selected Poems of Wislawa Symborska* (Quarterly Review of Literature, 1982). Reprinted by permission of the publisher.

Thom Gunn, *Collected Poems* (Farrar, Straus, and Giroux, 1994). Copyright © 1994. Reprinted by permission of the publisher.

Mark Halliday, *Little Star* (William Morrow, 1987). Copyright © 1987. Reprinted by permission of HarperCollins Publishers.

Robert Hass, *Human Wishes* (Ecco, 1989). Copyright © 1989. Reprinted by permission of HarperCollins Publishers.

Richard Hugo, *Making Certain It Goes On: Collected Poems* (W. W. Norton, 1984). Copyright © 1975 by W. W. Norton, 1984 by The Estate of Richard Hugo. Reprinted by permission of the publisher.

Lynda Hull, *Star Ledger* (University of Iowa Press, 1991). Copyright © 1991. Reprinted by permission of the publisher.

Robert McDowell, *Quiet Money* (Henry Holt, 1987). Copyright © 1987. Reprinted by permission of the publisher.

Charles Martin, trans. *The Poems of Catullus* (The Johns Hopkins University Press, 1989). Copyright © 1989. Reprinted by permission of the publisher.

Susan Mitchell, *Rapture* (HarperCollins, 1992). Copyright © 1992. Reprinted by permission of the publisher.

Sharon Olds, *The Gold Cell* (Knopf, 1987). Copyright © 1987. Reprinted by permission of Alfred A. Knopf, a Division of Random House.

David Rivard, *Torque* (University of Pittsburgh Press, 1989). Copyright ©1989. Reprinted by permission of the publisher.

Theodore Roethke, *Selected Letters* (University of Washington Press, 1968). Copyright © 1968. Reprinted by permission of the publisher.

David St. John, *Study for the World's Body: New and Selected Poems* (HarperCollins, 1994). Copyright © 1994. Reprinted by permission of the publisher.

Mary Joe Salter, *Unfinished Painting* (Knopf, 1989). Copyright © 1989. Reprinted by permission of Alfred A. Knopf, a Division of Random House.

Armand Schwerner, *The Tablets* (National Poetry Foundation, 1999). Copyright © 1999. Reprinted by permission of The Estate of Armand Schwerner.

Frederick Seidel, *These Days* (Knopf, 1989). Copyright © 1989. Reprinted by permission of Alfred A. Knopf, a Division of Random House.

W. D. Snodgrass, *Selected Poems 1957–1987* (Soho Press, 1988). Copyright © 1988. Reprinted by permission of the publisher.

Bruce Weigl, *The Geography of the Circle: Selected Poems* (Grove Atlantic, 1999). Copyright © 1999. Reprinted by permission of the publisher.

James L. White, *The Salt Ecstasies* (Graywolf Press, 1982). Copyright © 1982. Reprinted by permission of the publisher.

David Wojahn, *Glassworks* (University of Pittsburgh Press, 1987). Copyright © 1987. Reprinted by permission of the publisher.

David Wojahn, *Mystery Train* (University of Pittsburgh Press, 1990) Copyright © 1990. Reprinted by permission of the publisher.

David Wojahn, *Icehouse Lights* (Yale University Press, 1982). Copyright © 1982. Reprinted by permission of the publisher.

James Wright, *Above the River: The Complete Poems* (Farrar, Straus, and Giroux, 1990). Copyright © 1990 by Anne Wright. Reprinted by permission of the publisher.

Araki Yasusada (Kent Johnson), *The Double Flowering: From The Notebooks of Araki Yasusada* (Roof Books, 1997). Copyright © 1997 by Kent Johnson. Reprinted by permission of the Segue Foundation.

Adam Zagajewski, *Canvas* (Farrar, Straus, and Giroux, 1991). Copyright © 1991. Reprinted by permission of the publisher.

Thanks is also due to the National Endowment for the Arts for a fellowship during which certain of these essays were written; to the trustees of the Estate of Amy Lowell for the receipt of an Amy Lowell Traveling Poetry Scholarship, which was invaluable to me during the time in which these essays were composed; and to the Illinois State Arts Council, which awarded me two fellowships.

Contents

Preface

Earlier this summer I gave a poetry reading at one of the convention centers at Chicago's McCormick Place, a locale which is more typically the province of auto, boat, and electronics shows. But there I was at the American Library Association Convention, in the middle of the exhibit hall, surrounded by Scholastic's behemoth display of the new Harry Potter opus; by software companies peddling programs that they claim block access to online porn; by makers of futuristic-looking library carrels and scratch- and stain-proof tables; and by large-size clothing companies whose lines were aimed at "today's New Librarian"—and, if these companies are to be believed, the New Librarian favors a kind of sixties retro look, floral print muu-muus being the norm. Books, however, seemed not to be the norm, Harry Potter notwithstanding: there weren't many books in evidence, even in the displays of the big commercial houses, which seemed more eager to peddle their audio books and ancillary products than something as oldfangled as printed words between covers. Books aren't very sexy anymore, and the librarians know this, the publishers know this, and even the makers of tables know this, no doubt anticipating that the wear and tear on their products will come not from ink stains made by people underlining passages of Pascal but from folks who spill their double lattes.

Yet within this muu-muu and software bazaar stood an exhibit sponsored by Poets House, a Manhattan-based arts organization which seeks simply to be "a place for poetry." One of its missions is to promote among librarians a greater interest in contemporary poetry, and thus the Poets House exhibit consisted of twelve hundred books of recent verse, all published during the previous year. The offerings of the big New York houses and the university presses were represented, as well as those of the better-known small presses. It was an impressive display, to say the least. After the librarians had browsed the exhibit, they could sit down before a nearby podium, where over the course of the convention some dozen poets would read from their work. Several of them were writers whose work I much admire; others I'd never heard of before. I watched a Latino poet read his bad poems very well, an African American poet read his good poems badly, and a slam poet read bad poems very badly, but with considerable enthusiasm. Like almost everything that has to do with poetry today, the event was both splendid and silly at once. At a time when books seem destined to go the way of the dodo, before me stood over a thousand collections of work in a little-regarded but often-practiced genre; yet no more than a few of these collections will likely find more than a thousand readers. But at what other period in human history have so many books of poetry been published during a single year? And in a place where the librarians could easily have been tempted by the complimentary champagne and freebie T-shirts emblazoned with witty sayings that some of the exhibitors provided, a stalwart few chose instead to spend several hours listening attentively to poets read from their work. True, a good percentage of the books represented in the exhibit were dreck, and many of the poems that the live readers presented to the librarians were similarly awful. But many of the books and several of the poems were not. Some people still need poetry—need to read it, to study it, to write it, and to hear it read aloud. The essays of this collection proceed from that very simple premise, and they attempt to appraise both the splendidness and the silliness of present-day American poetry. There is never enough of the former and always too much of the latter, but to truly appreciate the richness of our era's verse we are required to examine both.

Recent poet-critics seem little able to perform this double task. Some seek mainly to examine the essential silliness of much of today's verse, and they can easily be identified by the glib titles which they employ for their critical studies—*My Way, The Castle of Indolence, All the Rage,* and *The Cure of Poetry in an Age of Prose* being four recent examples. The writing in these collections tends to be hectoring and monochromatic. On the other hand, poet-critics who seek to extol the essential healthiness of recent American verse can veer into a rather embarrassing solemnity or gush, both in their writing and in their choice of titles. A respected poet in midcareer recently offered up a study called *How to Read a Poem and Fall in Love with Poetry,* and it is ironic that some of the most fervently upbeat tomes about the state of contemporary verse bear the most self-serving and apocalyptic titles: thus we have *The Fate of American Poetry* and *Can Poetry Matter?* As a poet who writes criticism, I want to align myself neither with the wise-ass party of poet-critics nor with the earnestly apocalyptic crew. "One writes poetry because one must," said Stevens, and the best criticism of poetry tends to arise from a similar sense of inexplicable necessity. Yet poet-critics have an odd and somewhat rarefied mission to undertake when they turn to prose: they have to preach what they practice, and this means that each of their forays into criticism is to some extent designed to help them better understand their own poetry and to better understand the forces—both within the tradition and within their own era—that have shaped their personal aesthetics. But personal aesthetics are by their very definition highly eccentric; they cannot be straitjacketed into theory, nor can they be reduced to simplistic bromides.

Almost all good poet-critics follow in the line of Sidney and Shelley, offering to the reader their own versions of a Defense of Poetry. But they also know that poetry ultimately should need no justification and that its best defense comes in poems themselves and not in prose—and especially not in the exposition of whatever Party Line of the Imagination happens to be fashionable among critics and scholars. Critics and scholars are likely to tell you that they *know* what poetry is or what it should be; poets and poet-critics are wary of such claims. As Randall Jarrell, the poet-critic whom poet-critics most admire, put it, "We should love explanations well, but the truth better, and often the truth is that there *is* no explanation." Jarrell's best criticism, like his best poems, begins in astonishment, and its wisdom comes from understanding that criticism—like poems—must end in astonishment as well.

I first started writing about contemporary poetry twenty-five years ago, as a book reviewer. Since then I've written about hundreds of collections of poetry, but none of these reviews are included here, and only a few of the essays are pieces commissioned by magazines. Instead, most began as lectures I presented to my students and colleagues in the MFA in Writing Program of Vermont College. The essays thus arose from ongoing discussions about the state of American poetry as it pertained to a community of poets and would-be poets. I found myself writing about topics which happened to be in the air at a given time—for example, the legacy of Confessional verse as it affected American poetry in the 1990s or the revival of a particular kind of narrative poetry in the late 1980s—but I also had the freedom to explore topics in which I had a more personal stake, such as in the essay on depression and the memoir about James L. White. I was also drawn to subjects that seemed to me insufficiently explored by other critics; the Yasusada hoax, for example, raises issues about representation and authenticity which resonate far beyond the limited audience for contemporary poetry. The links between literary politics and social politics are sometimes hard to identify in an era when poetry has become so marginalized, but several of the essays seek to speculate about how these links are formed and about what they mean for poetry today. This is not to say that the collection has a specific agenda or aesthetic program: I think of it as a species of autobiography. But I also feel that the book's concerns are representative ones. Collectively, the essays attempt to create a profile of American poetry at the start of a new millennium. And in them both the sublime and the silly can be identified.

I would like to extend my gratitude to the editors who published earlier versions of these essays in journals and anthologies and to several friends who commented upon them as they were being written. The late Lynda Hull, who coauthored the essay "Mercantile Eyes," was the most gifted reader of poetry I have ever known, and she has influenced these essays in innumerable ways. I would also like to thank Tony Whedon, Bill Olsen, David Jauss, Roger Mitchell, Jim Harms, Brian Teare, and Dean Young. And to Noelle Watson I owe the greatest debt of all.

The date following each essay indicates its year of composition, not its year of publication.

Bloomington, Indiana, July 2000

I.

1.

Generations "I": The Future of Autobiographical Poetry

"When I speak of keeping the human image, I am speaking of keeping, not selves, but the value of selves."

—*Allen Grossman,* The Sighted Singer

Robert Lowell, circa 1962 or '63, and looking at the camera with the sort of fixed intensity that's displayed in so many of his photos. He's wearing the black owlish horn-rims that were the uniform of the myopic early sixties, a time when the rose-colored glasses of the Byrds' Roger McGuinn and John Lennon's oval wire-rims, shading acid-dilated pupils, were still unknown. In this particular photo Lowell looks uncharacteristically calm, his hair neatly brushed; there's none of the eerily disheveled gawkiness of his more famous photos; no Einstein-wild hair; no sense that he possesses a body always shambling and awkward, too large to fit within the room the photo contains. When the photo was taken he'd recently released *Life Studies,* possibly the most influential book of American poetry published in the last half-century. I don't know the name of the photographer, for the photo was rescued by a friend of mine one day while she worked as a secretary at Harvard, when she was asked to clean out and throw away some files. On the back, in faded pencil, are the words *Mr. Robert Lowell.* The photo came in the mail a few months ago and now occupies a space on the wall above my desk, along with various other icons—Akhmatova, Louise Brooks, Bob Dylan, Stanley Spencer, Frank O'Hara, Miles Davis. And of course the family photos: of my father in his corporal's stripes, circa 1944; of my mother waving from the Perisphere of the '39 New York World's Fair; and the photo which would eventually find its way to the jacket of my wife's posthumously published book of poetry. In profile, with a drop earring and a scarf pulled half-way back, turban-like, she looks uncannily like Akhmatova; profile to profile, they face each other as I look from them to the leafless March trees beyond and back to Robert Lowell. The living have no place here, it seems. The mothers and beloveds dead. And the fathers: when my father posed for the photo before me—somewhere halfway up the boot of Italy—it was nine years before my birth. And when Robert Lowell looked up from the podium at the Woodbury Poetry Room, facing some unknown photographer's flash while reading, perhaps, his new poem "For the Union Dead," I was nine years old. It would be another decade before I would hear of Lowell or read his work.

But clearly Lowell is the other dead father, as he is for so many of the poets of the last two or three generations. And, as it must be with any dead parent's—or even dead grandparent's—legacy, he has bestowed upon us a complex and often troubling influence. He has been both model and pariah, and certain of his tics and mannerisms have been incorporated into our psyches so fully that we are scarcely aware of their presence. Without *Life Studies,* the careers of as diverse a list of poets as Sylvia Plath, Anne Sexton, James Merrill, Philip Levine, Seamus Heaney, Frank Bidart, Robert Pinsky, Louise Glück, Robert Hass, C. K. Williams, Sharon Olds, Frederick Seidel, and Charles Wright would be impossible to imagine. And one could also make a case for Lowell's considerable but less obvious influence upon writers such as Jorie Graham, Paul Muldoon, Carolyn Forché, and Allen Grossman. Lowell's impact on these writers manifests itself in many ways—in a prosody that mixes various elements of traditional and free verse, in a sense of public history's intricate connections to personal history, and even to some degree in use of imagery. But it goes without saying that the most crucial aspect of Lowell's influence has been his creation of a particularly influential form of autobiographical lyric. The self in the world and the self in relationship to its past are Lowell's principal concerns after *Life Studies,* and most of the significant movements in contemporary poetry can be seen as deriving from Lowell's approach to such concerns. The intensely introspective lyrics of neosurrealists such as Merwin and Wright owe their existence in part to Lowell's attentiveness toward the self; similarly, though less clearly, the quirky subjectivity of Ashbery and his disciples nods to Lowell in this regard. True, the sort of autobiographical lyric that *Life Studies* contains was also being practiced in the fifties by several of Lowell's immediate contemporaries—one thinks of *Howl* and of Snodgrass's *Heart's Needle,* as well as of the jaunty nervousness of O'Hara's *Lunch Poems.* But *Life Studies* spread its influence everywhere, far beyond the cliques of would-be Beats and New York School followers who modeled themselves on Ginsberg or O'Hara. And the influence can still be felt today—though in ways far more curious and problematic than the obvious ones which I have outlined here.

What has *Life Studies* wrought? Most significantly, American and British poets of the last four decades have found permission, for the first time in our literary history, to speak in unalloyed and unguarded terms about their own lives—the self who speaks in the typical contemporary poem is considered to be the poet him/herself, not a persona, not a character. While fringe movements such as Language poetry have rightfully questioned the aesthetic presuppositions of the autobiographical lyric, there is no question that it is the prevailing period style, both among established poets and among aspiring ones. A recent issue of *Poetry* might serve as example, for its poems' subjects are ones which would have been impossible to imagine before 1959. This particular issue's twenty-five poems treat a familiar litany of personal subject matter, many times the speaker's woes: one miscarriage, three dead parents, three unhappy childhoods, one husband on his deathbed, and one contentious divorce.[1] The poems are all quite competently written and are clearly deepfelt; their authors range from well-known poets such as W. S. Merwin and William Matthews to writers publishing for the first time. I note that two of the issue's poets are former students of mine, which means that I at least have some ability in teaching—if teaching means successfully conveying the rudiments of the period style. The thirty-five-year-old computer programmer from Decatur, Illinois, writing of his bitter divorce in a community-college poetry workshop, and the twenty-year-old undergraduate, trying to confront the memory of, say, her mother's death or her uncle's repeated incestings, each owes something to "Waking in the Blue" or "Skunk Hour" or "Man and Wife"—even if these tyro poets may never have read Lowell. One of the reasons why poetry's audience has expanded greatly in recent years—but not in such a way as to much affect the sales of poetry books—is that several generations of aspiring writers have emerged who seek, simply and often poignantly, to write about their lives. And poetry seems to offer them an opportunity to reach this end, one which other disciplines in an age of shrill media culture cannot claim. For whatever reasons, Robert Lowell, posed with his locked razor at McLean's or "tamed by Miltown" on his marriage bed, has proven the most enduring model for this horde of scribblers. The situation is certainly not Lowell's fault, for the effect of any period style, once it has been widely disseminated among writers, is a dilution of its virtues, which turn into mannerisms.

The following poem appears in a recently published collection and serves as a particularly interesting example of this process:

Of My Father's Cancer, and His Dreams

With those who love him near his bed
seldom speaking any more,
he lies too weak to raise his head
but dreams from time to time.

In one, he says, he sees his wife,
so proud in her white uniform,
with other nurses trooping by,
their girlish voices aimed to charm
the young man lounging there.
Then eyes meet his and hold.
A country courtship has begun.
They've been together thirty years.

Now, she watches over him
as she tries to hide her tears.
All his children are at home
but wonder what they ought to say,
or do, either when he is awake
or when he seems to fade away.
They can't always be on guard,
and sometimes, if his mind is clear,
he can grasp a whispered phrase
never meant for him to hear:
"He just seems weaker all the time."
"I don't know what else to cook.
He can't keep down anything."

He hears the knocking on the door,
voices of his friends, who bring
a special cake or fresh-killed quail.
They mumble out some words of love,
try to learn how he might feel,
then go back to spread the word:
"They say he may have faded some."

He'll soon give in to the rising pain
and crave the needle that will numb
his knowledge of a passing world,
and bring the consummating sleep
he knows will come.[2]

I make no claims for this as a particularly notable piece of writing, but it has some modest virtues. The deathbed portrait of the father is at times sharply observed; the snippets of dialogue spoken by the relatives and friends have a certain authenticity as well. The speaker, through his title and through his occasional adoption of the dying father's point of view, gives the poem a spirit which might be characterized as autobiographical—as testimony. The ironies of the "dream" conceit also possess a certain effectiveness. True, the handling of the meter and the inconsistency of the rhyme scheme strike us as a bit awkward, and the final stanza, although it attempts to be a taciturn and Hardyesque evocation of oblivion, comes very close to sentimentality. But this is a thoughtful and sensitive effort, by no means doggerel verse. But two other aspects of the poem are worth pointing out and are more remarkable. First, the author of the poem is a former U.S. president, Jimmy Carter. Second, readers familiar with contemporary poetry will hear in the poem distinct echoes of two of Lowell's best-known *Life Studies* poems, "Terminal Days at Beverly Farms" and "My Last Afternoon with Uncle Devereux Winslow." Carter of course lacks Lowell's biting wit and hugely inventive metaphors (think of the "animated, hierarchical" Uncle Winslow, dying "like a ginger snap man in a clothes press"), but we should remember that Carter's forte as president was earnestness, never wit or imagination. When ex-presidents mimic *Life Studies,* and in their efforts achieve reasonably passable results, we have reached a curious situation. Surely President Carter's choice of a retirement activity is a more admirable one than Gerald Ford's and George H. W. Bush's choice of the golf course as a vale of soul-making, but are we to read Jimmy Carter's poetry as an indication of his sensitivity or as an example of the utter exhaustion of a particular style of autobiographical verse, one which even ex-presidents can learn? How, as the century draws to an end, can autobiographical poetry be seen to have a future—as I believe it does? Is a poetry focused upon the self and its struggles in any way timely in a era dominated by post-structuralist skepticism, which calls into question the very concept of the self as knowable and consistent? Today's critics are apt to think of the self in the manner of William James, who whimsically defined it as "peculiar motions of the head between the head and throat." Such critics would no doubt see as quaint J. D. McClatchy's definition of contemporary poetry as an act of "the self against *everything*—ideology, history, nature, time, others, even against the self, and especially against 'cultural force.'"[3] But most contemporary poets would readily concur with McClatchy's definition. Perhaps we no longer view the self as heroic in a Wordsworthian sense, but that the self exists we have no doubt. How the self can express itself in a fashion which is rich and complex in an era of mere self-disclosure and self-indulgence is another question.

That we are living in an era during which many poets are primarily concerned with self-disclosure there can also be no doubt. And it means that sometimes poetry seems merely another one of the various self-therapy movements that have had such a huge vogue in recent decades, ranging from traditional psychotherapies to Paxell and Prozac, from Eastern religions to twelve-step programs tailored to address a seemingly infinite number of addictions and maladies; there even exists a twelve- step program for survivors of autoerotic self-strangulation victims. Some would say that such movements foster a kind of substitute dependency just as imperiling as any of the addictions that prompted their creation, but I am by no means one of these critics; the value of the self-help movement seems to me considerable. And who is to argue that poetry does not sometimes serve to give the very sort of specific personal solacing offered also by AA, Al-Anon, Rolfing, Zoloft, or Sufi dancing?

Where does this leave poetry, however? Three of our more astute critics of contemporary verse— Marjorie Perloff, Mary Kinzie, and Alan Williamson—have all recently addressed this question. The members of this trio have little in common. Perloff is a champion of the avant-garde tradition deriving from Stein and Cage, and her sometimes tiresome cheerleading for this camp once prompted a friend of mine to label her "Language Poet Ninja." Kinzie promotes a sort of neo–New Criticism, lots of close readings and an exasperatingly obtuse style which derives from Blackmur and to some degree from premodern critics such as Arnold and Hazlitt; in fact she shares with these latter figures a rather schoolmarmish and moralizing tone. Williamson, a student of Lowell (and a good poet himself), practices psychoanalytical criticism, although he is by no means a Fruedian party-liner. Perloff and Kinzie view the contemporary state of autobiographical poetry with a fair degree of alarm; Williamson takes a more balanced approach but acknowledges the problems inherent in the "peculiarities" of a situation in which it has grown "very hard to draw a clear line between work whose main value is therapeutic or inspirational and work which really addresses, and expands, the possibilities of the art itself."[4]

Perloff's argument against autobiographical poetry is essentially a Marxist one; predictably, she regards mainstream poetry's involvement with self-disclosure as an example of social commodification, and her method of illustrating this is witheringly effective. In a fascinating essay entitled "The Changing Face of Common Intercourse: Talk Poetry, Talk Show, and the Scene of Writing," Perloff argues that the "packaging" of the self on television talk shows such as *Oprah* and *Jerry Springer,* with their emphasis on intimate disclosure (usually centering upon what were once called shameful secrets—infidelities, transvestitism, drug addiction, various sorts of criminal activities, etc.), differs little from the similarly ritual gestures packaged as the self in contemporary poetry.[5] She is especially concerned with debunking what she sees as the myth of "authentic speech." The tearful and handwringing confessions of secret lives and shortcomings among talk show guests represent the media's crass commercialization of human suffering; the confessions become merely a formal device, a component of the package, and "authentic" only insofar as they facilitate the needs of programmers and sponsors. A similar packaging, both of the author's sense of selfhood and of a language meant to convey that sense of selfhood through a transparent free verse diction, is seen by Perloff as a major component—and shortcoming—of contemporary mainstream poetry. She builds her case by debunking certain neo-Wordsworthian notions about "primacy of feeling" and "earnestness" as expressed by Louis Simpson in defense of poetry. And later, in a merciless reading of Philip Levine's "To Cipriano, in the Wind," she performs her coup de grace. Unfortunately, Language Poet Ninja Perloff, in true Samurai tradition, is better at fighting battles than at anything else. Once she has sheathed her sword and surveyed her smoking battlefield full of dead "talk show poems" and poets, she introduces us to the new emperor and his court, which seems to be made up of Language poets Steve McCaffery, Susan Howe, and Leslie Scalapino—a trio of interesting writers, but Perloff is not a convincing apologist for them. Perloff offers us some standard Language poetry bromides: word-consciousness over self-consciousness, the questioning of self-referentiality, and so on. Towards the end of her essay Perloff admiringly quotes a passage from a long poem by Susan Howe which begins, "Posit gaze level diminish lamp and asleep (selv) cannot see" and continues on in a similar vein.[6] It makes one wonder when Oprah or Jerry will devote a show to recovering Language writers. ("I've been there! A graphomaniac! An addict to syntax!")

What Perloff terms talk show poetry Kinzie defines as "applied poetry," a term she borrows from C. S. Lewis's characterization of certain minor Elizabethan poets, who cast advice about crops and animal husbandry in verse form. But where the age of Wyatt had its couplets describing beekeeping and bull-neutering, we now have Anne Sexton, whose failings are seen as representative of a trend to "supplant other notions and kinds of poetry with an exclusivity of therapeutic discovery."[7] Although Sexton strikes me as a somewhat better poet than Kinzie regards her as, Kinzie's description of Sexton's baneful influence is instructive: Kinzie derides Sexton's "enormous reputation as a victim-seer"; her protofeminist concern for invective, in which "anger is a curiously over-valued enterprise"; and her partial responsibility for an atmosphere in which "a *persona* extrinsic to the making of poetry has been mistaken all the way around for an excellent *poem*."[8] Thanks to Sexton, Kinzie implies, there has been a kind of dumbing-down of autobiographical poetry, a loss of the aesthetic gravity which it possesses in the work of writers such as John Berryman and Robert Lowell, who of course was Sexton's teacher and major influence. Self-exploration is replaced by a tedious and unevenly written litany of victimhood. Although Kinzie makes these observations in a fashion both simplistic and alarmist, she has a point. And she sees "applied poetry" not so much as an approach to subject matter as a form of environmental disease, the poet's version of black lung, afflicting us all to varying degree: "The legacy of this turn is not only much bad verse, but also the production, even in good writers, of uncertainty. Even when poems today are very good indeed, the false sparkle of application flickers around them, so strong is the drive of emotional shortcut in an age of applied art."[9] It is easy to regard this passage as unintentionally comic, partly because of Kinzie's cumbersome metaphors and partly because it characterizes self-disclosure more as an involuntary tic than as an accomplishment actively sought-for: autobiography becomes a kind of prosodic Tourette's syndrome. And yet anyone who has attended or taught a graduate poetry workshop knows that one of the most common critiques—deriving from both teachers and students—is that student poems are not "personal" or "self-confronting" enough. We do not *intend* to teach talk show poetry and applied verse. But, for better or for worse, they have become our major product line, the jug wine that keeps the vineyard solvent. But the vintage stuff is there as well—or so we hope.

Williamson, in a groundbreaking essay entitled "Fictions from the Self," describes an alternative to talk show and applied poetry and sees among certain younger poets the emergence of a new sort of autobiographical verse. Like Perloff and Kinzie, Williamson is aware of the problems inherent in most contemporary autobiographical lyrics, but he knows that our better young poets are aware of these problems as well. "All the negative attention," he writes, "may have stimulated poets to approach the self's story with a tact, a self-awareness, an eye to exclusions and the thematic 'figure in the carpet,' fiction writers have taken for granted for generations. . . . One reads the best of the newer narrative poetry with a sense of point of view, of strategic timing and delayed exposition, that makes the great poems of Lowell and Plath seem raw lyric by comparison."[10] Williamson, like Alan Shapiro in a similar essay entitled "In Praise of the Impure: Narrative Consciousness in Poetry," sees the new autobiographical poetry as essentially narrative, but neither writer defines storytelling in a simplistically linear fashion. Williamson instead describes a narrative verse fractured by flashbacks and flashforwards, by cinematic jump cuts and ruminative asides. It differs from the Confessional lyric of a generation or two ago in part because it emphasizes the speaker's actions with a more expansive regard for the play of consciousness over time. More so than Confessional writers, the new autobiographers are concerned with the meaning of memory, and thus we have the long and troubled meditations on adolescence and young adulthood which comprise C. K. Williams's *Tar* and the yearning and disjointed struggles with family history found in Frank Bidart's *Golden State.* Williamson would add to this list younger poets such as Tom Sleigh, Brenda Hillman, and Shapiro himself. Such poets enact, in Shapiro's words, "the complicated drama of perspective between a recollecting and experiencing self."[11] It goes without saying that this stance toward structure also affects prosody: hence, the immensely long but often highly spondaic lines of Williams and the idiosyncratic lineation and use of italics and boldface in Bidart, both of which can be seen as attempts to more acutely render the elasticity of consciousness. The new poetry of self, in other words, is seen as expansive and inclusive in ways which Confessional poetry decidedly was not; Shapiro goes so far as to claim that the new autobiographical writing is therefore more socially and politically aware than was Confessional verse, a claim somewhat puzzling in light of Lowell's *Notebook* or even parts of *The Dream Songs.*

In examining some work that seems to me representative of this new autobiographical poetry, I want to explore some issues that Williamson and Shapiro only touch upon. Specifically, what is the new poetry's stance toward self-disclosure and how does it differ from the often self-lacerating aspect of talk show and applied poetry? How does the truth of self differ from factual truth? This final question may seem to us a simplistic one, more pertinent to sophomore philosophy courses than to discourse about poetry. But one of the mysterious legacies of Confessionalism is the reader's implicit belief that poets tell the truth about themselves and that this activity is not only good but sufficient in itself to create a good poem. If anything divides the realm of applied and talk show poetry from the realm of the new autobiographical writing, it is differing attitudes toward the purposes and possibilities of truth-telling. For example, the following poem by Bruce Weigl treats a subject which is sadly fashionable on the talk show circuit; there are reasons for classifying it among talk show or applied poems as well.

The Impossible

Winter's last rain and a light I don't recognize
through the trees and I come back in my mind
to the man who made me suck his cock
when I was seven, in sunlight, between boxcars.
I thought I could leave him standing there
in the years, half-smile on his lips,

small hands curled into small fists,
but after he finished, he held my hand in his
as if astonished, until the houses were visible
just beyond the railyard. He held my hand
but before that he slapped me hard on the face
when I would not open my mouth for him.

I do not want to say his whole hips
slammed into me, but they did, and a black wave
washed over my brain, changing me
so I could not move among my people in the old way.
On my way home I stopped in the churchyard
to try to find a way to stay alive.
In the branches a redwing flitted, warning me.
In the rectory, Father prepared
the body and blood for mass
but God could not save me from a mouthful of cum.
That afternoon some lives turned away from the light.
He taught me to move my tongue around.
In his hands he held me like a lover.
Say it clearly and you make it beautiful, no matter what.[12]

There is much to admire in this poem, as there is in all of Weigl's work. One of Weigl's virtues is the elegant precision of his writing, and here this quality is abundantly displayed in the uncomplicated syntax and relative lack of enjambment, which give the poem a reportorial insistence that nevertheless permits several shifts into a more formal rhetoric—for example, the liturgical echoes of "That afternoon, some lives turned away from the light" and the heightened diction of "so I could not move among my people in the old way." The transparency of Weigl's language is especially successful as he relates the specifics of the speaker's recollection of the sexual abuse. The horror of the scene is neither downplayed nor sensationalized, and this furthermore permits Weigl to perform the delicate task of characterizing the speaker's abuser as believably complicated in his ambivalence: Weigl refuses to demonize him. The man tenderly holds the speaker's hand "as if astonished." And yet, "before that he slapped me hard on the face / when I would not open my mouth for him." The immediate aftermath of this trauma for the child is also well-rendered, with a straightforwardness that effectively conveys the young boy's point of view: "In the branches a redwing flitted, warning me."

The main shortcoming of the poem, however, is one typical of many contemporary poems, especially autobiographical lyrics: the poem refuses psychological perspective in favor of mere rhetorical substitutes for it. In the beginning of the poem, Weigl's speaker chooses not to explore the compelling question of why he has chosen a particular moment in which to recall his trauma, and one would imagine that the circumstances prompting the setting down of the recollection might be as significant as the memory of the incident itself. But we are instead given a kind of plain-style telegraphy: "Winter's last rain and a light I don't recognize." Suddenly the memory holds the poem completely at siege—until its final lines, which are equally disappointing. What are the consequences of the speaker's sexual trauma and of his need to relive it in his poem? Merely that on the day of the event "some lives turned away from the light." The final line is a regular-guy rewrite of Keats—"Say it clearly and you make it beautiful, no matter what." What is troubling about this statement is not merely its logical dubiousness but also Weigl's apparent belief that we are to read the poem's narrative as a form of fable, to which the writer has amended this moral. Of course, art has always strived to make the unbearable beautiful and therefore "truthful"—the irony of this project may be to some small degree implicit in Weigl's title, but nowhere is it acknowledged within the text of the poem. The poem fails at its moralizing purpose in part because of an inherent contradiction within many recent autobiographical lyrics: art may make experience "beautiful," but the form of the contemporary autobiographical lyric seems more frequently designed to convey the illusion of reportorial *fact* than to emphasize the complexity of psychological truth—or beauty, if we are to assume that beauty is more than meets the camera's or the journalist's eye. (Lowell himself bemoaned this problem in his "Epilogue" to his final collection, *Day by Day:* "sometimes everything I write / with the threadbare art of my eye / seems a snapshot, / lurid, rapid, garish, grouped, / heightened from life, yet paralyzed by fact. . . .")[13] The desire for transparent and "clear" writing, one of the main goals of the plain style, brings with it the problematic notion that clarity *is* truth, just as the various gurus of pop psychology have told us that to remember a repressed event clearly can, in many cases, in itself affect a *cure* for one's ailments rather than mark a step towards a cure. Weigl links himself in "The Impossible" to applied poets and talk show poets in part because he appears to operate within an aesthetic that in subtle ways confuses self-disclosure (nowhere in the poem does Weigl imply that we are to see his speaker as a persona) with the more resonant sort of poetic artistry which Wiegl's best efforts display. "The Impossible" is a good example of Kinzie's contention that the applied art "tic" affects even our better poets—and who can say whether the poem is hobbled by the poet's personal stance toward self-disclosure or by a period style that mandates a sort of unvarying reportorial earnestness?

Susan Mitchell's "Leaves That Grow Inward" makes for an interesting contrast to Weigl's poem. Mitchell seems to me one of the better representatives of the new school of autobiographical writers that Williamson and Shapiro have identified, both because of her inventive approaches to narrative and for a linguistic richness—deriving from High Modern sensualists such as Crane and Stevens—that is exceedingly refreshing in an era of dressed-down minimalism. Rather than build her poem around a single emblematic anecdote as Weigl does, Mitchell braids several narrative strands and imagistic leitmotifs. And, as we will see, her method of self-disclosure—and by extension her very stance toward memory and catharsis—differs significantly from Weigl's. Like Weigl's poem, "Leaves That Grow Inward" centers upon a memory from childhood, but it focuses upon this memory only after some circuitous meditation. Here is the poem's first stanza:

> So you see, it was my favorite time
> for walking, toward evening, when the lights came on
> all together like candles on a child's cake. I would yawn, as if just leaving a
> movie.
> The better part of the day was over, no longer
> the chance of doing anything worthwhile.
> The relief of it. This was the hour
> I took a bath as a child,
> not always alone, sometimes with a friend, Clara,
> whose left arm ended abruptly at the elbow,
> as if she had managed to draw up
> inside her the hand, its fingers, even
> a small object the fingers had been holding
> at the time this miracle occurred. If
> I had known Holderlin's poem about the leaves
> that grow inward, I would have recited it
> to her, *hangen einwarts die blatter,*
> as she splashed water in my face
> with that budding stump of hers. Once
> at this hour my mother plucked a snail
> from watercress, a black glistening that sweated
> across my palm. Clara held it too
> with her eyes, the way I held her
> in the school playground until all at once
> I heard the train, still far away, that brought

my father from his office, its wind
blowing on the lights of our street.[14]

Around the core memory of the speaker and the crippled Clara, Mitchell builds a more elaborate narrative structure; the opening, with its in medias res address to a "you" who may be a specific individual or may be the reader, conveys both the sense of intimacy and the relentless pace that will characterize the poem. Yet the speed of the poem's narration does not preclude a lavish and strange attentiveness to detail—for example, the almost baroque description of Clara's misshapen hand, or the snail as a "black glistening that sweated / across" the speaker's palm. And if these descriptions possess a hugely charged eroticism, so too do the similarly strange images of the father's commuter train's return convey a sinister repressiveness.

And this sense of the repressive continues in the poem's second stanza, with its description of the speaker's childhood as "burning like a fever" and of the speaker's mother urging her to practice the piano obsessively, as if drinking "the music like blood." The act of memory, which in the initial stanza had seemed bucolic and sensuous, is here likened to a fever, a cry, to "pulling hairs from the tenderest parts of the body." These menacing descriptions, in contrast to the specificity of those in the initial stanza, seem amorphous and free-floating, until suddenly the speaker makes a startling confession:

Only, to tell the truth, there
never was a Clara, a point I might confess
to a psychiatrist. Instead,
I confess it to myself, waiting
for illumination, eyes closed,
but still as if through leaves, through the sap
of my cells . . . At school, there was
a girl like her, but her arm
terrified me. I withdrew
from it. Which is quite another thing,
isn't it? Though in the safety of my bath
she sometimes entered my life as a possibility
of future loss. So, you see,
I am not the person you thought I was,
the one you had grown comfortable with, maybe
even liked a little. . . .

More is happening here, of course, than Mitchell simply playing the old "I'm lying—do you believe me?" game. What makes the passage impressive is the rigor of the speaker's self-analysis, her insistence on exploring the contrast between the authentic recollections and the wish fulfillment of the imagined ones. And the essential point is that this contrast troubles and even frightens the speaker. To explore it, she must jettison several of the period style's more familiar methods of seeming to tell poetic "truth," methods so ingrained into our sensibilities as readers that Mitchell can slyly play with them. But Mitchell is not merely being coy. Autobiography, she implies, is a chronicle of the inner life—of the "leaves that grow inward" and are shaped by psychological forces—more than it is a truth which can be captured by mere description and anecdotes, which, as Mitchell has reminded us, can easily be false or misleading. A further sense of uncertainty is conveyed by Mitchell's stance toward audience. Despite her initial insistence upon intense intimacy with the poem's "you," Mitchell reminds us in an aside that even her "you" does not exist: "there / never was a Clara, a point I might confess / to a psychiatrist. Instead / I confess it to myself. . . ." Mitchell's narrative drive and urgency do not permit her to merely leave things here, however; post-structuralist notions of slippage and of the exploded self, which the Language poets embrace, are nodded to by Mitchell but have little to do with the self-transcending romanticism that the poem's final stanzas bring forth. Now that Mitchell has established her goal of eliminating the line between truth and fable in order to achieve self-knowledge, the poem can grow expansive and Whitmanesque. The speaker describes herself waking to hear "the high rise in which I live / talking to itself like the sea / or like someone stumbling in and out of sleep. . . ." This does not, however, mean that Mitchell is about to "contain multitudes"—not yet, at least: "The grief of my neighbors, the grief of all / the neighbors I have ever had is / another story. . . ." And first she must return to Clara:

What
would it have been like to be the one who played
with Clara, whooping down to the neighborhood
bakery, mouth stuffed with strudel, not caring
if my tongue scorched and blistered? What would it
have been like to hold
the sticks of dog shit, the purified chalk
they scrawled their names with? At the edges
of memory, Clara glimmers, beckoning
as if into a forest. Striped with desires
more bruising than prison bars, she leans out of herself. . . .

This symbolic figure of Clara is a memorable embodiment of the id's capacity to be liberating and self-annihilating at once. But to cast the meaning of

Clara in such baldly Freudian terms does a disservice to the passage's fluency and mystery. And the poem's final passage builds upon these qualities, removing them from fantasy and placing them in the real world, a world, moreover, that is now charged with a sort of intense sensuality, a visionary landscape more reminiscent of Norman O. Brown or Wilhelm Reich than of Freud—"polymorphous perversity" incarnate:

> Well, life
> is better now and sometimes I consume
> four movies in a day, surprised, as I drift
> to the street, it's dark outside too, surprised
> to see people waiting to see what I have just seen.
> This is the hour when two men
> kiss in the elevator, a long kiss
> which stops only when an old woman gets on,
> then they hold hands. Half asleep,
> I hear them kissing and the sky
> darkening, washing out to the Hudson
> where the freighters kneel in the sailors' shadows
> and the kids tripping on acid come to watch the men knotting
> and unknotting in their ecstacies.
> Even from here I follow their brief spurts
> of pleasure, the tides of clouds, until I feel far
> as someone drifting in a boat
> or waving from a train a paper
> hat, while the dark snails of my flesh slide
> toward some heaven of their own.

The conclusion of Mitchell's poem is convincingly exultant, yet it also refuses—in contrast to Weigl's poem—to reduce the struggle between the self and the world to a well-intended truism. And it furthermore refuses to draw from its examination of the speaker's inner conflicts the implication that these struggles have now somehow been solved. Mitchell instead opts for a panoramic intensity, a landscape we read as an enactment of the speaker's self-interrogations. And fittingly, these self-questionings do not resolve themselves in a rhetorical flourish but in a vivid recapitulation of the poem's motifs, imbuing the landscape *with* the self rather than claiming to define or map the nature of selfhood.

It is this stance, highly exploratory, eschewing the easy reductiveness that has too often become the norm of contemporary poetry, and obsessive in its urgency, that has created a new sort of autobiographical approach. And it seems to me that a small but growing number of younger poets share with Mitchell these concerns, among them Mark Halliday, Mark Doty, Deborah

Digges, Rodney Jones, Dean Young, and Brigit Kelly. But of course the values I have identified here are not new ones and are in fact the values which have continued to attract me to the searching and flawed heroism of Robert Lowell—not the Robert Lowell whom even retired presidents can ape but the Lowell who will continue to look down on my desk, who questions unrelentingly, and who sees the self in all of its tricky complexity—and in all of its elusive preciousness.

(1995)

2.

Some Kind of Statement, One Ear Showing: Social Poetry and Its Problems

Many people would like to know who killed Gerald Bull, but his murder will probably remain unsolved. There are suspects, however. Some say it was the Mossad, some the CIA, others agents hired by Iran or Iraq. Clearly, Bull had made a good many enemies before he was shot in a Brussels apartment in 1990, and for good reason. Bull was an arms salesman, one of the best, eventually peddling his merchandise to any government or group willing to pay the price, many of them international pariahs such as South Africa and Iran. One reason why the Iranians may have wanted Bull out of the way is because he worked both for them and for their enemies in Baghdad. He seems to have been the principal designer and procurer of parts for what became known as the Iraqi Super Gun, a cannon which, had it been put into operation, would have been capable of delivering a nuclear or gas warhead from Iraq to Tehran, Tel Aviv, Mecca, or any of several dozen Middle Eastern cities that happened to be on Saddam Hussein's shit list. Bull's knowledge of Iraqi armaments might have prompted Iraq's enemies to eliminate him. Or perhaps the Iraqis themselves did him in. The occupational hazards of arms dealing must be legion.

Yet I fear that I have done a disservice to Bull by characterizing him merely as an arms merchant. He was first and foremost a scientist, and a brilliant one by all accounts. The story of his transformation from precocious boy genius to arms dealer is nothing less than Faustian.[1] In the 1950s, the young Canadian engineer and physicist proposed the notion that satellites might be launched into orbit from large cannons, in the manner described in Jules Verne's *From the Earth to the Moon.* Bull believed the technology for such ventures was already available, and at a considerably smaller cost than was needed for a missile launch. His initial goal was altruistic: to find a cheap way of making satellite launches available to small and Third World countries. The Canadian armed forces, feeling that they might have a rare chance to scoop the Americans in the development of a new technology, poured a good deal of money into Bull's project through grants to McGill University, Bull's nominal employer. Of course, research as promising as this couldn't escape the notice of the Americans for long, and American government money and university support was soon coming Bull's way as well. (For a short time Bull was given funding by one of my own employers, Norwich University, in Vermont.) Within a few years Bull was able to build two impressive research facilities, one in the Caribbean and one in New England's Green Mountains, the latter a uniquely situated complex which straddled the American-Canadian border; this enabled Bull's facility to officially exist in no country at all.

Bull's story takes on elements of the tragic (and Faustian) when McGill and the American and Canadian governments began to question the usefulness and expense of the projects they were funding. Bull's government money dried up at a time when his facilities had become most impressive: some three hundred scientists and employees were at one time working in Bull's little principality in the mountains. Why did the funders pull the plug on him? There are many possible explanations, ranging from Bull's personality, which, according to many accounts, was difficult, to the simple cynical fact that super cannons seem rather unglamorous to militaries during an era of star wars and smart bombs. Thus began Bull's transformation to arms designer and merchant, and he began to serve new masters; how different these new patrons were from Bull's former ones is of course a matter of opinion. But before long Israel, South Africa, and various Arab states had filled in the gap left by McGill and Company. The Americans tolerated these activities for a time, and probably tacitly supported them, but in 1980 Bull wound up serving a few months in an American prison for his activities, and his Green Mountain proving ground/laboratory was abandoned. Bull eventually conducted his business from Europe.

A Faustian story, but it has nothing to do with art. Or does it? I first heard of Gerald Bull last year, during a visit to the cabin of my friends the writers Tony and Suzanne Whedon, who live in northern Vermont. We had driven into Quebec on a rather bizarre quest to find a Mexican restaurant that had just opened in the town of Sutton, right across the border and the nearest town to Bull's abandoned laboratory complex, which Tony pointed out to me on route to the eatery, a rustic affair in a one-gas-station town. But our food was very good. The owners were a Guatemalan woman, who did the cooking, and her Canadian husband, who acted as our host and suddenly grew very animated when we asked him about Bull and his laboratory. It turned out that he had worked at one time for Bull and had traveled around the Middle East on missions for him. The life of an arms merchant didn't sound glamorous, though. One of his more time-consuming tasks turned out to be purchasing sheep and goats from Jordanian shepherds; the animals were then killed in demonstrations of a new artillery shell of Bull's design. Our host was a good raconteur, conjuring up a scene of a short and pudgy King Hussein, weighed down in the regalia of a field marshal, poking at dead ewes with his riding crop, a row of bodyguards and generals looking on approvingly. We were eating outside, on the restaurant's porch. It was one of those summer evenings in the north during which the light lingers until ten o'clock. There was still a bit of sunlight left, and as we left our host suggested we take a drive up to Bull's laboratory for a look around.

We passed scores of small buildings, each tucked to the side of the winding mountain roads, all of them boarded up save for the largest building at the very end of the road, which our host at the restaurant told us had served as the foundry where the barrels for Bull's cannons had been cast. It had recently been converted into a small factory which makes talc, and strangely enough there seemed to be a night shift at work. The twilight gave an eerie tint to the place, and the four or five cars in the parking lot were covered with a flour-like dust. A face, which seemed coated in pancake makeup like Marcel Marceau, peered briefly at us from a window. We left the car to walk around a bit, feeling edgy and apprehensive. The roadside was littered with what we at first took to be those prefabricated concrete sections of culverts you see sometimes at construction sites, but which we soon realized were imperfect castings of cannon barrels, Dr. Bull's rough drafts. It was shortly after this, as we started to drive home, that the car began to follow us, close enough to almost nudge our bumper and eventually flashing its lights. Now we were *very* edgy and apprehensive, though my friend Tony, whose yen for interesting experiences had taken him to Haiti during the fall of Aristide and to Shanghai a few weeks after Tiananmen, chose to pull over rather than to speed up. I was petrified. A tall blonde youth strode from the car and in a heavy French Canadian accent asked what we were looking for. Tony allowed that we were writers, and wanted to see something of the proving ground that had once been here. The youth instructed us to follow him, and after a bit more driving we found ourselves in front of a fairly large brick building. "This," said our guide, "is the home of the French Canadian Union of Watercolorists."

So Bull's laboratory was now, it seems, an artists' colony, run by the boy and his mother. Although the boy hinted that he'd show us some interesting Bull memorabilia, we were first made to look upon several rooms filled with watercolors, which, if they were representative of contemporary Quebecois efforts in the form, weren't exactly cutting edge or even particularly competent; they were more akin to the "sofa size" paintings you see at flea markets and roadside stands, not exactly velvet paintings, but close. We made polite grunts of appreciation, for many of the paintings had been done by the boy himself ("very lifelike stem on that flower"). It was a bad opening act to what we hoped would lead to a more impressive headliner. Eventually the boy went into a back room and came out with a huge aerial photograph of the laboratory in 1970, captions describing each of the complex's buildings. He described them in fastidious detail. "Did you know Bull?" asked Tony. "Yes," said the boy, "he was my father."

One could draw any number of glib generalizations from the end of this story. Was the boy—who spoke to us of Arab sheikhs and minions of Idi Amin emerging from limos to enter that room and enact deals with his father—laboring at his amateurish watercolors as an act of penance, turning to art because of a guilty legacy? What did his infamous father mean to him, and what did it mean that the boy's confession of his identity had first to be so closely linked to his displays of bad still lifes, studies of cardinals and robins, and Green Mountain landscapes dotted with churches and the obligatory covered bridges? Not all the offspring of the infamous show this sort of ambivalence, of course: think of the children of Josef Mengele and Klaus Barbie, who knew who their fathers were and the exact nature of their crimes but who for decades helped them to elude capture. How did the boy's sense of his father, which in his case must have invariably also been a sense of the role that history and politics play in our lives, help to turn him into a painter, yet a painter not just of only middling talent but whose work was adamantly bucolic, escapist, and clichéd? We were presented that night with a duality of a very puzzling nature, a duality almost Manichaean, in which the boy's past and his art were mutually exclusive, while at the same time symbiotically linked: the aerial photo of Bull's laboratory, captions for the foundry, the outbuildings, the firing range with its blurry image of a cannon barrel—the whole thing huge and hulking, like some epic painting from the French Academy, but propped next to an awkward study of Jay Peak in autumn, badly rendered clouds behind it.

In the past year I've thought frequently of that night and have yet to make any sense of it, save to see it as the first of a string of similarly puzzling encounters, ones which seem less about the meeting of art and politics than about their almost surrealist juxtaposition. An evening later that summer, on yet another strange odyssey with Tony, who had persuaded my wife and me to accompany him to Cuba, where he is interviewing Cuban jazz musicians. Jazz is tolerated by the Cuban government but not by any means encouraged, a sufficiently revolutionary activity only when it serves the government's somewhat inscrutable purposes. The night before, our friend Arturo, bassist for the Pucho Lopez group, had taken us to his grimy basement apartment to show us what being a working jazz musician meant for the Revolution: a snapshot of Arturo and his bandmates performing in North Korea for an audience of soldiers, who look like something from a Cold War–era B movie—shapeless Mao jackets, caps adorned with large red stars. Arturo doesn't practice as much as he once did; like every other Havana resident, he spends most of his mornings waiting in food lines for his daily bread ration. He can't use his amp during the city's daily power blackouts, and the electricity now seems to be turned off more frequently than it's on. But this evening the lights of the Malecón, Havana's seaside boulevard, are ablaze, and we're moving in Maria's Polish Fiat to visit her friend, one of Cuba's leading poets. We've been enormously lucky to have come into contact with Maria, a friend of a friend of Tony's. Maria describes herself as the Cuban Barbara Walters, and the morning TV show she used to have was immensely popular. Its popularity, however, may have had something to do with its being yanked off the air. Although she is the widow of a genuine revolutionary martyr (her husband, the general, died in Angola), she had the rather reckless habit of investigating social problems by making surprise phone calls to government officials on live TV. So now Maria's celebrity status means only that, unlike most other Cubans, she has a car (though no gas), can keep a large apartment, and as a working single mother possesses a card that entitles her to go to the head of the bread lines. The poet lives in Miramar, Havana's most prestigious neighborhood, where the embassies and mansions of diplomats and government officials hulk along wide palm-lined avenues. Here also are the almost equally sumptuous homes of various big shots in the arts, who've been given places vacated after the Revolution, when Cuba's rich chose exile over Castro. Cuba takes its artists seriously, the people because of a very genuine love for art, literature, and music, the government because of art's PR value. The government doesn't maintain its control over the arts by forcing artists into propaganda-mongering; instead, it offers stipends, perks, and permission to travel. This is the neighborhood in which the handsome jazz prodigy Gonzalo Rubocalba resides, who no doubt, like the rest of the arts community's upper crust, has a card that permits him entrance to the supermarkets and specialty stores that also dot Miramar, places well-stocked with food and consumer goods unseen by other Cubans since the days of Batista. Many of these stores, which accept dollars rather than Cuban currency, are hidden on Miramar's tree-lined streets, announced by neither signs nor parking lots, like prohibition-era speakeasies.

And what of our visit to the poet? We were met at the door by his maid:

it seems the poet and his wife have a summer place in Spain, and they weren't coming back until October. Cool Pyrenees summers are a lot more pleasant than the ones in Cuba, and besides, in Spain there are no food lines, and there is all the electricity you'd ever care to waste. How could anyone begrudge the Cuban poet whatever comforts he'd attained? Yet his feelings about his art and his country no doubt must be very conflicted. I regretted not being able to meet the poet, for I wanted to know whether the possession of privileges carried with it a bad conscience.

But maybe I'm projecting Yankee values here, the sorts of regrets which are a North American academic poet's occupational disease: you can have whatever you want as long you feel guilty about it, something else to worry about for a brief moment while you fidget in the service-department waiting room at the Saab dealer's, reading undergraduate poems for a class you've christened Dorm Love 101. This sort of guilt is a chronic condition, yet direct, overt, and extended reminders of it, which can lead to more extensive bouts of hand-wringing, are rare. But they do happen sometimes.

For example, a February evening last winter, during which my graduate students are heatedly discussing the poems of the Turkish writer Nazim Hikmet in a class called Modern Poetry in Translation. The class seems evenly divided about the merits of Hikmet. Some find his disarming emotional directness enormously appealing; others dismiss him as sentimental; and one student asks if Hikmet would be read today at all, or translated at all, had he not suffered a life of persecution and decades of imprisonment, merely because he was a communist. Do we value Hikmet because of his poems, the student asks, or because of his life? The student reads the following lines from one of Hikmet's better-known prison poems, "Since I Was Thrown Inside":

> They're ten years old now
>   the children who were born
>   the year I was thrown inside.
> And that year's foals, shaky on their spindly long legs
>   have been wide-rumped contented mares for some time.
> But the olive seedlings are still saplings,
>   children are still children.
>
> New squares have opened in my far-off city
>   since I was thrown inside
> And my family now lives
>   in a house I haven't seen
>   on a street I don't know.[2]

One student finds these lines poignant, but the student who has read them proclaims that they're maudlin. A poem such as this would be butchered in a graduate workshop, he insists. It is a naïve and rash judgment, of course, though I'm sure the student is right in saying that no self-respecting graduate workshop would let an author get away with a passage such as this. Yet the late Terence Des Pres, in an essay on Hikmet entitled "Poetry and Politics," argues that modern international poetry may be useful to American writers precisely *because* it can elicit reactions such as those of my dyspeptic student. "To speak of Hikmet's poetry," Des Pres writes, "is necessarily to consider the 'other' world of literature, a kind of art sometimes called political, sometimes called the poetry of engagement or commitment, which is strikingly different from the kind of literary product most of us have been taught to esteem."[3] Des Pres is careful in his essay to avoid oversimplification: it's not that the distinction between art and politics is denied by Hikmet but that a strict demarcation between the two has become harder and harder to determine in a century in which, as Walter Benjamin observed over fifty years ago, aesthetics and politics tend to cannibalize one another. "The logical result of Fascism," Benjamin writes in a famous passage in "Art in the Age of Mechanical Reproduction," "is the introduction of aesthetics into political life."[4] But Benjamin's subsequent point, that Fascism's corruption of aesthetics can be *reversed* by Marxism—"communism responds by politicizing art"—seems more than a bit quaint to us today, though the shortsightedness of Benjamin's claim only shows us even more intensely how difficult it is for art and ideology not to corrupt one another. We might remember that the two most historically significant ideologies of this century were dominated by a failed Austrian painter and by a failed poet from czarist Georgia. The magnificent footage of the Führer's descent from the heavens at the start of *The Triumph of the Will* ends at the gates of Auschwitz, just as the still-bedazzling photomontages of *Ten Days that Shook the World* end in gulag camps, such as the one in which Osip Mandelstam was last seen in 1939, scavenging a garbage dump for food. There is something cruelly artful, a sense of barbaric poetic justice, in the apocryphal (but still somehow quite plausible) tale of Stalin's phone call to Mandelstam after the dictator had been told about the poet's Stalin epigram. Both Hitler and Stalin regarded themselves as the principal patrons of a new and socially responsible art, though the ironies of their links to culture were generally much less intentional than that of Stalin asking the Kremlin switchboard to ring up Mandelstam for him. One of the more chilling passages in Robert Conquest's biography of Stalin is more typical: "on 12 December 1937 alone, Stalin and Molotov approved 3,167 death sentences, and then went to the cinema."[5]

Of course my students were thinking more about how to get their own lives into poems, which is a difficult enough task, than about how to make their writing engage history. And if they think about politics at all, I sometimes fear it is only to evaluate an action, a writer, or a literary work on the basis of its political correctness, an evaluation that makes the more insightful students a bit uncomfortable and that can turn the less insightful ones into boring zealots. Thus, my students felt in some vague way that they should like Hikmet's work. After all, he was a prisoner of conscience. But, as Des Pres points out, Hikmet seems both "a Marxist *and* a mystic," a combination which confounds the rules of conduct we've been handed by PC—rules more akin to Miss Manners's code of etiquette than to the results of serious aesthetic or ethical investigations. Because of dilemmas such as this, Hikmet, one of the most direct and emotionally naked poets I know of, seemed to puzzle rather than to inspire my students. Hikmet *contradicts* himself, and though these same students had earlier read Czeslaw Milosz and encountered the many varieties of his insistence that the very *essence* of the poet's role is self-contradiction, they nevertheless found Hikmet's work exasperating because of its apparent inconsistencies. How could a poet as good as Hikmet be a Stalinist, a sexist, and a sentimentalist? someone hesitantly asked. The conversation about his poems grew oddly cautious and tentative; my students wanted to be respectful toward Hikmet's work but seemed to have significant reservations about it which they were reluctant to express. This particular encounter meant that only a few big toes had been dipped into the waters of "otherness," which are more like those of Lake Erie and the Jersey Shore than like something bottled by Perrier. They are muddy, give off an acrid smell, and deposit various medical and other wastes upon the shore, along with additional dubious products such as bottles, cans, and now and then a syringe.

Who would want to swim in this? And if, as a poem by Louis Simpson would have it, "it is complicated being an American, / having the money and the bad conscience / both at the same time," then the quintessentially American way of dealing with such complication is to only very weakly acknowledge its existence or to nullify it through easy and false dualities. The former sort of response, the one my students displayed as they tiptoed around Hikmet, does not indicate that these young poets are shallow, only that it is easier to learn to talk and think like an academic than it is to become a poet. A couple of weeks into the Gulf War, my department chairman placed the following memo in our mailboxes:

> After giving the matter a fair amount of thought, it seems to me that the department might meet in order to discuss ways to make some sort

> of statement about the war. Interested faculty and students should meet on BH 342 on Tuesday, Feb. 9 for further exploration of this topic.

I'm not sure what this ringing call to action resulted in—a letter to the student newspaper perhaps, or a resolution to use the following year's lecture budget to invite a big-shot Marxist critic to talk about Gramsci's influence on Chaucer.

"Some sort of statement": the phrase is almost poignant in its fumbling equivocation, in its cautious memospeak. A similar inchoate tentativeness afflicts most American poets as they consider a poetry of social and historical engagement. The obligation to make "some sort of statement" is in many cases very genuinely felt, but daunting for a number of reasons. American poets, even in their responses to socially devastating events such as the Civil War, have never looked upon their experience in decidedly political terms. And during those rare periods in which a socially responsible poetry has been the norm—in the 1930s, for example, or at the height of the Vietnam War—most such protest poetry was unimpressive. We go back to a few of the Objectivist poets, maybe, but not to the literary sections of *New Masses.* And it was the president himself, not Robert Bly or Denise Levertov organizing read-ins against the administration's Vietnam policies, who brought about Nixon's downfall. Significant poetry about the Vietnam experience only began to appear in the 1980s, in the work of figures such as Yusef Komunyakaa and Bruce Weigl.

There is no serious tradition of social and political poetry in America in the way that there has been among this era's East European and Latin American poets, who have suffered war, revolution, the Holocaust, and other events which possess greater intrinsic dramatic value than our own conflict between greenbacks and bad conscience. And we know that these "un-American" horrors have helped to create a significant body of literature, literary responses which are remarkably various, ranging from the terse epigrammatic satire of Brecht's social poems to the haunting post-Holocaust hermeticism of Celan. It goes without saying that such historical traumas have prompted responses from continental poets which are the almost involuntary product of necessity; they do not arise from the luxury of choosing to "make some sort of statement." But in drawing such a contrast, especially in light of the American poet's lack of a strong tradition of social verse, it becomes very easy to fall prey to precisely the sorts of attitudes which cause us to approach social poetry through equivocation and oversimplification and with a decidedly unproductive (but understandable) sense of inferiority and liberal guilt. When we compare ourselves to the Mandelstams, the

Akhmatovas, and the Hikmets, how can our work seem anything but trivial? That, at least, is how the conventional wisdom would have it.

Carolyn Forché is on a mission to rescue us from these predicaments, armed with her recently published anthology, *Against Forgetting: Twentieth Century Poetry of Witness.*[6] It is in many ways a timely volume, which will no doubt receive a great deal of attention. It bears the august imprint of W. W. Norton, whose anthologies have always set the standard, at least among college and university professors, and whose textbook orders keep Norton extremely profitable. You'll find *Against Forgetting* on bookstore shelves next to the *Norton Anthology of Modern Poetry,* and by association it will probably take on the same sort of semiofficial status, one bolstered by the jacket blurbs Forché has obtained—from the likes of Arthur Miller and Nelson Mandela. Although she has only published three uneven collections of poetry, Forché has come to be regarded as her generation's principal poet of political activism, and she has a reputation as a charismatic public reader; it is not for nothing that Norton sent her on a publicity tour when the book was released. And though it may be unlikely that we'll see her chatting with Oprah and Letterman before intoning the poems exhumed with Miklos Radnóti's corpse, Norton knows a sure thing when it sees one. The beginning of John Bayley's review of the anthology in a recent *New York Review of Books* will no doubt be typical of the reception: "this is a remarkable book."[7]

Bayley is right to praise the collection, but he avoids mentioning its shortcomings. Although the volume is largely comprised of the work of European poets, problems with Forché's introduction and method of structuring the book cause it to unintentionally exemplify all of the misunderstandings American writers suffer from when confronting this century's poetry of commitment. Rather than consistently offering American readers an instructive meeting with what Des Pres terms "otherness," Forché's collection will no doubt intensify all of the dilemmas I have spoken of here. It will prod some of us to "make some kind of statement," but for all the wrong reasons.

But let me first list the volume's strengths. Forché's selection of poets is truly international, infected with none of the Anglo-American chauvinism that our twentieth-century anthologies so often display. The Auden selections are nestled between more generous selections of Alberti and Hernandez. George Oppen pops up between Cesare Pavese and the Polish poet Anna Swir; Alan Dugan's poems are followed by Ingeborg Bachman's. And Forché has subscribed neither to ideological party lines nor to ones of the imagination. The elegant meters of Anthony Hecht rub shoulders with the surrealist razzamatazz of Desnos and Éluard; Celan mourns the Holocaust through powerful hermetic neologisms, while Hikmet's prison poems have the directness of a diary. Furthermore, Forché's selection of translations is admirable; she knows that Ben Bellit can't make Neruda work in English but that Robert Bly can. She gives us the Stanley Kunitz and Max Hayward version of Akhmatova's *Requiem,* eschewing the better-known but leaden version by D. M. Thomas. Forché's selection is intelligent and generous. That's the good news.

The bad news is that Forché's method of arranging the volume is severely misguided and that her introduction is muddled and self-serving. Forché seems to have modeled her structure on Arthur Frommer guidebooks; it seems more a Baedeker than an anthology. Instead of rapid-read chapters on Italy and the Benelux, however, the chapter titles bear the names of wars, disasters, struggles, revolutions, and holocausts. Thus, we encounter Celan in "The Holocaust, the Shoah: 1940–45," Mandelstam in "Repression in the Soviet Union: 1917–91," and so on. This method of arrangement—if it's Tuesday, this must be the Armenian genocide—seems bizarre, to say the least. And the situation is not helped by Forché's preface, which seems designed as much to establish her own poetic and experiential similarities to her 145 "poets of witness" as to argue the importance of the poems that she introduces. The problem is not merely that she inaccurately claims the book to be the first anthology of its kind. (It was preceded both by Daniel Weissbort's fine Penguin collection of postwar Central and East European poets, *The Poetry of Survival,* which includes dozens of the same figures Forché presents, as well as by Kerry Flattley and Chris Wallace-Crabbe's *From the Republic of Conscience,* also designed to represent international poetry of witness. Royalties from the latter volume, says its jacket, "will be donated to Amnesty International."[8]) More irritating is Forché's insistence on establishing her activist credentials in a way which mixes some very lucid observations with some tiresome self-aggrandizement. She begins by relating the now sadly familiar story of the discovery of Hungarian poet Miklos Radnóti's powerful last poems, found when his remains, along with those of other executed prisoners of the Nazis, were discovered in a mass grave. Forché's description of this tragedy has some dramatic flair, but then, with scarcely any transition at all, she segues into this:

> This . . . volume is the result of a thirteen-year effort to understand the impress of extremity on the poetic imagination. My own journey began in 1980, upon my return from El Salvador—where I had worked as a human rights activist—and led me through the occupied West Bank, Lebanon, and South Africa. Something happened along the way to the

> introspective poet I had been. My new work seemed controversial to my American contemporaries, who argued against its "subject matter," or against the right of a North American to contemplate such issues in her work, or against any mixing of what they saw as the mutually exclusive realms of the personal and the political. . . . I realized that arguments about poetry and politics had been too narrowly defined. Regardless of subject matter, [the poems in this anthology] bear the trace of extremity within them, and they are, as such, evidence of what occurred.[9]

Later, Forché elaborates upon her reasons for rejecting such dualities:

> Poetry of witness presents the reader with an interesting interpretive problem. We are accustomed to easy categories: we distinguish between "personal" and "political" poems—the former calling to mind lyrics of love and emotional loss, the latter indicating a public partisanship that is considered divisive, even when necessary. The distinction between the personal and political gives the political realm too much and too little scope; at the same time it renders the personal too important and not important enough. If we give up the dimension of the personal, we risk relinquishing one of the most powerful sites of resistance. The celebration of the personal can indicate a myopia, an inability to see how larger structures of the economy and the state circumscribe, if not determine, the fragile realm of individuality.
>
> We need a third term, one that can describe the space between the state and the supposedly safe havens of the personal. Let us call this space "the social". . . . .[10]

Forché's claim for the need of a "third term" to describe the interaction between the personal and the political initially sounds plausible, but a closer examination reveals it to be sophistry, in part because she is unwilling to clearly define what she *means* by the "the social" and solves the problem of mixing apples and oranges by saying she will create a hybrid. This hybrid, furthermore, is mostly apple core and orange rind. Forché's wish for such genetic engineering sounds very much like a desire to obliterate ambivalence, to jettison the contradictions and ironies upon which most successful literary works depend. This is an odd goal—especially odd when we remember that many of the poets Forché represents make powerful use of the intricacies of poetic irony. And just as disturbing is Forché's implication, expressed indirectly but insistently in several places in her essay, that "the social" is achieved through "the trace of extremity." This sounds suspiciously like the old saw that the artist has to suffer to be any good.

The fact that Radnóti wrote his exquisite love poem "Letter to My

Wife" ("I believed in miracles, forgot their days / above me I see a bomber squadron cruise. /I was admiring, up there, your eyes' blue sheen / when it clouded over, and up in that machine / bombs were aching to dive. Despite them, I am alive") while on a forced march which ended with a bullet in his head is a testament both to art and to human nobility.[11] But although Radnóti's life and art were forced to become interdependent, life and art themselves are important for us to keep separate. No sane person would want to suffer Radnóti's fate for the sake of poetry, but I fear that Forché implies that a willingness—or sadly, even an eagerness—to endure such a fate will make one a better poet. She asks us to meditate on the lives of Hikmet, Radnóti, Mandelstam, and other of the century's poets who were victims of the state with the same sort of ardor that the faithful in medieval times lavished upon the lives of saints. Forché wants us to be flagellants as much as readers, a book of Akhmatova translations in one hand, a scourge to swat our backs with in the other. This *penitente* model may have worked for Forché herself in her thirteen years of activism in El Salvador, South Africa, and the West Bank, and I do not mean to question the sincerity of her quest. But however admirable her motives may be, they are also troubling. To fuse the distinctions between art and politics, to make the life and the work "codependent" rather than interdependent, creates all manner of difficulties.

Jonathan Holden does a brilliant job of debunking this attitude in his essay "Poetry and Commitment," written in reply to an earlier piece of Forché prose prompted by her visits to El Salvador during its civil war and upon which she seems to base many of the notions expressed in the introduction to *Against Forgetting*. One of Holden's passages is worth quoting at length:

> Virtually *any* act could be seen as having political significance if construed as implying all the possible political actions which the actor could have taken but did not. To buy a steak dinner (instead of eating more cheaply and instead devoting the savings in money to the cause of the oppressed) could be construed, from a radical perspective, as a de facto form of oppression. When viewed ideologically, a person's reasons for doing *anything* instead of something else can be judged. In much the same way that deconstructionist approaches to language make a mockery of the interpretation of texts, so do conventional radical denials of the distinction between "political" and "non-political" behavior make a mockery of any attempt to interpret human behavior. It is one thing to purposefully support a candidate for political office. It is another thing to eat a steak. Even to suggest that these two actions might have equal political and ideological significance is to lie. To claim, as Forché does, that "there is no such thing as a non-political

> poetry" is to redouble that lie while shrouding it within a second lie, namely the false notion that there is no distinction between "art" and "life."[12]

In the conclusion of his essay, Holden links Forché's position to the aesthetic failings of Confessional poetry and then performs a coup de grace:

> The limits of what Forché calls a "poetry of witness," like the already well-documented limits of a poetry of confession, lie in the temptations to excess, in a poetic which all too quickly can become only an iterated, mechanical cry of pain, making an ideology of guilt and outrage, a rhetoric without the authority of discovered vision.[13]

A term such as "temptation to excess" suggests that to agree with Forché's position is to open a Pandora's box, that to define "poetry of witness" as Forché does is to leave open the possibility of a moral and aesthetic relativism that can just as easily make art subservient to ideology as it can help force art to be ideologically aware. Holden implies that Forché's stance leads to the very aestheticizing of politics which Benjamin warned us against, that its end result can just as readily be Marinetti gloating over Mussolini's invasion of Ethiopia by stating that "War is beautiful because it enriches a flowering meadow with the fiery orchids of machine guns" as it can be to offer a deeper appreciation of Milosz's great lyric "Dedication."[14] Alan Shapiro has recently insisted that the role of poetry is to explore "the ethical imagination," a term which he employs in order to eschew the easy pieties of ideological party lines and the equally simplistic notions of asocial aesthetic purity that are one of Modernism's main legacies. "The ethical imagination," he writes,

> is not reducible to politics and should not be expected to have any particular (narrowly conceived) political content. Rather, it occupies a space in and beyond culture from which the institutions and discourses of political power can be held under continual review. It is turned toward the political, in other words, but views it always from a vital but significant distance, so as to see it clearly.[15]

How complicated it all is, and how complicated it must remain. A boy takes up painting because his father first tried to send up satellites, then sold cannons to Pretoria. But it's not as simple as that. A poet gets out of Havana every summer because it's hot there and he has to wait in ration lines. But there's more to it than that. A young American poet is invited to dinner. Her host, a Salvadoran officer, drops a dried peach half into a glass of water. But it's not a peach half; it fattens into a human ear. Something for your poetry, no? And indeed, the ear helps the poet write a horrifying, and magnificent, poem:

> There is no other way to say this. He took one of them in his hands, shook it in our faces, dropped it into a water glass. It came alive there. I am tired of fooling around he said. As for the rights of anyone, tell your people they can go fuck themselves. He swept the ears to the floor with his arm and held the last of his wine in the air. Something for your poetry, no? he said. Some of the ears on the floor caught this scrap of his voice. Some of the ears on the floor were pressed to the ground.[16]

But there's more to it than that. Someone will always ask whether the incident about the ear was real, and someone else will ask what the ear "symbolizes." And someone else will claim that neither ear nor symbol exists and ask if the poem is instead more accurately about "language." And all of these questions will be valid to some degree. And someone else, reading the following poem by the marvelous and fervently "political" Polish Nobel winner Wislawa Szymborska—who is represented in Forché's anthology but not by the poem which follows—will compare the ending of Forché's poem to that of Szymborska's.

Writing a Curriculum Vitae

What must you do?
You must submit an application
and enclose a Curriculum Vitae.
Regardless of how long your life is,
the Curriculum Vitae should be short.

Be concise, select facts.
Change landscapes into addresses
and vague memories into fixed dates.

Of all your loves, mention only the marital,
and of the children, only those who were born.

It's more important who knows you
then whom you know.
Travels—only if abroad.

Affiliations—to what, not why.
Awards—but not for what.

Write as if you never talked with yourself,
as if you looked at yourself from afar.

Omit dogs, cats, and birds,
mementos, friends, dreams.

State price rather than value,
title rather than content.
Shoe size, not where one is going,
the one you are supposed to be.

Enclose a photo with one ear showing.
What counts is its shape, not what it hears.

What does it hear?
The clatter of machinery that shreds paper.[17]

A real ear or a symbolic ear? And whose description of these disembodied ears is superior? After all, Szymborska's ear does not purport to document "reality" in the way that Forché does in her description of the grisly trophies of the death squads of Roberto d'Aubbison. Are we thus to regard Szymborska's ear as merely an arresting image, the product of language rather than "experience"? What can an ear made only of language hear? But there's more to it than that. Something for your poetry, no?

And there's more to it than the February evening when my students argue about Hikmet. The class is ending, and I'm wondering to myself if the snow, now falling very heavily, will make it difficult for me to get to the airport in the morning. I almost forget to tell my students that I have to cancel my office hours this week, for I'm going to be out of town, reading my poems at West Point, where fifteen hundred first-year cadets (or "plebes") have been assigned one of my books to read in a poetry course and are even writing papers about my work. The idea of the course is to travel backwards in literary history, so this year Larry Levis, Lucille Clifton, and I will read to assemblies of cadets in February. By May the plebes will arrive at Beowolf, who presumably cannot fly in for a reading. West Point's English department is fairly large, and there are in fact a substantial number of cadets who choose to major in English. Colonel Foley, who oversees the big poetry course, is voluble, enthusiastic, and passionate about literature in a way that's refreshing in an era of theory-mongering. When he spoke to me on the phone to arrange my visit he talked of how people in the military need to be trained to care for literature, a need, he said, as crucial as training for any martial discipline. He said this in a way which made me think he meant it. "If we ever have to go overseas in the way we just did in Kuwait," he added, "we want our officers to have poems in their knapsacks." And it takes more character than I have to resist that sort of ego stroke. The poems of David Wojahn, read by the light of artillery fire, in a desert foxhole, solacing some young lieutenant in the way that *A Shropshire Lad* gave comfort to Sassoon and Owen in the trenches on the eve of Paschendale.

But it's not as simple as that. Colonel Foley steps up to the podium at the center of the auditorium and introduces me to the first of two groups who will hear me, some six hundred cadets in each group. They have literally marched into the auditorium. *Mystery Train,* the book of mine they're reading, has a photo of Bob Dylan on its jacket, circa 1965, for the volume's central sequence is about the history of rock and roll (though there's more to it than that). But already I've come to see that I'm farther away from the cadet's values and frame of reference than I could have possibly imagined. I've just had lunch with some cadets—all five thousand of them eat at once, in a cavernous, baronial dining hall. One of the cadets at my table asks me how long ago my book-jacket photo was taken. I look different, she says, without my beard. I have never been mistaken for Bob Dylan before, and West Point cadets don't seem the type who would put you on. But why should I be surprised? The photo of Dylan was taken a decade before the plebes were born.

And as strange as these circumstances may be, the plebes are a most attentive audience. First-year cadets are not permitted to watch television, go to films, or even keep radios in their barracks rooms; only toward the end of the school year are they given the privilege of being addressed by name. Until that point each one is merely called "cadet." So Larry Levis, Lucille Clifton, and I are in effect the only sanctioned entertainment they'll have between the Christmas and Easter recesses. And to attain such dubious privileges the cadets have worked hard—nominated for their slots at the academy by senators and congressmen, some even admitted by presidential decree. They are eighteen years old, direct from high school, and can look forward to some twenty more years in the military. I read them poems for a half an hour and then field questions, some of them insightful, some of which take me aback: "Do you believe in God, sir?" "Sir, how would you answer the accusation that your poems are cynical and nihilistic?" Several of them request that I read individual poems from my book, and as I comply I realize that they're the ones that use "fuck" and "shit" or variants thereof. I present a different selection of poems during each session with the students, but during both readings I read a poem based on news footage I remember from the fall of Saigon: a scene of mayhem, helicopters laboring from the roof of the

American embassy, laden with soldiers, embassy officials, and Vietnamese weighed down with suitcases:

It's Only Rock and Roll But I Like It: The Fall of Saigon, 1975

The guttural stammer of the chopper blades
Raising arabesques of dust, tearing leaves
From the orange trees lining the embassy compound:
One chopper left, and a CBS cameraman leans
From inside its door, exploiting the artful
Mayhem. Somewhere a radio blares the Stones,
"I like it, like it, yes indeed. . . ." Carts full
Of files blaze in the yard. Flak-jacketed marines
Gunpoint the crowd away. The overloaded chopper strains
And blunders from the roof. An ice-cream-suited
Saigonese drops his briefcase; both hands
Now cling to the airborne skis. The camera gets
It all: the marine leaning out the copter bay,
His fists beating time. Then the hands giving way.[18]

At the end of all this Colonel Foley walks me back to my hotel. We cross the huge quadrangle where the cadets must drill each day, and snow is coming steadily down. I suddenly remember why Nazim Hikmet was first thrown into prison: he was accused of treason not simply because he was a communist but because cadets in Turkey's military academy were found to be reading his subversive poems. Colonel Foley tells me that the readings went well and that he especially liked the poem about the fall of Saigon. "But you know," he says, "most of these kids have probably never even heard about the fall of Saigon, let alone saw films of the scenes you describe. A lot of them think America *won* in Vietnam." Some kind of statement indeed, a frightening one—and no doubt a better one than I could make.

(1993)

3.

Ferality and Strange Good Fortune: Notes on Teaching and Writing

The Chair was talking, talking, talking. And we were listening. We were, in fact, "retreating"; we were "fellowshipping" and chewing our inedible bag lunches, which were themselves a sort of text, composed by caterers who must have been ABD in something, though it wasn't cookery. (In a college town, of course, even the hash slingers and mayo spreaders have done postdoctoral work). I was finishing my "health-nut sandwich" of no-fat cheese and was working on my "Rainforest Macadamia" cookie. Below its wrapper's list of ingredients I read, OUR PRODUCTS ARE NOT TESTED ON ANIMALS. And the Chair was talking on, his bald head glistening above his turtleneck. How intentional, I wondered, was the Chair's resemblance to a certain flavor-of-the-month French man of letters? I of course was being unfair to the Chair; the Chair wasn't so bad. After all, the Chair had written a book of poetry once, though now he Culture Studied. And talked. Some of the words made their way through the chewing of my rubbery cookie, and I knew I should be grateful that my arduous mastications were helping to save the Orinoco crocodile and the capybara. And I knew I should be grateful to have a job such a mine, a good job, a job I loved. And my job description, it seemed, included long spells of being made to hear the Chair talk. The Chair was using the word "Arnoldian" and looking at me and at my colleague, a somewhat explosive fiction writer of Southern European extraction. To teach "the best that has been known and said in the world," the Chair mumbled, quoting from "Culture and Anarchy" and making a kind of contemptuous clucking sound to show how nostalgic such a goal had become. No, the Chair went on, our problem was that we were "undertheorized." My colleague's eyes were narrowing, and I watched his body tense like that of a boxer in his corner before Round One. *Arnoldian?* The word was stinging my colleague like some fusillade of Sicilian slang having to do with his mother's bedpartners. But soon the Chair had monotoned off to something having to do with our department's "missioning." My colleague relaxed, I swallowed the last bit of rainforest, and the Chair talked on.

I dozed off through a couple more presentations. Then it was the turn of my colleague C., who writes fiction and must therefore, in the eyes of certain of my colleagues, also be an Arnoldian—and of a particularly egregious sort, linked as much to Benedict as to Matthew. C. is for them an apostate, a quisling, a turncoat, for she had looked forward to a promising career as a scholar and had even published a well-regarded critical study of Lawrence before abandoning that game completely in favor of her own fiction. The subjects of her presentation were the teaching of creative writing and the teaching of literature to creative writing students. It was an impassioned and eloquent talk. The statement that rang most deeply came toward the end: "teaching creative writing is what teaching literature *was*." You could see my colleagues fidget as she said this, though it's hard to say what was making them so uncomfortable. A sort of pained envy? ("The writers can still try to figure out what makes Dante great, when I have to worry about tenure and being subtheorized.") A sort of pity? ("The writers are still trying—get this!—to figure out what makes Dante great. *And I bet they've never read Lacan!*") A kind of belligerence? ("The writers are still trying to figure out what makes Dante great. I thought we'd killed that sort of stuff off. Hope it doesn't spread again.") Or a sort of wry acknowledgment that our department is now comprised of weirdly Balkanized little principalities? ("I see the Slovenes are still trying to figure out what makes Dante great. How strange their customs are to us here in Croatia.") C.'s talk was greeted with polite applause, which the Chair read as his cue to talk some more. He rose to the podium and held forth for awhile. He wished there were time for discussion, but "considering the lateness of the hour" he now had to wrap things up.

And so out of the retreat I hauled my Arnoldian ass, puzzled and ambivalent toward all of this. On the one hand, as a poet, I felt like a form of endangered species, not an exotic one like the capybara but one which at one time ranged widely but now could scarcely be found save in wildlife refuges. An Arnoldian *bison*, perhaps? The week before, while I had been giving a poetry reading at another university, I ended up having lunch with a group which included the department's other visiting lecturer, the Famous Marxist Critic, who'd garbed his portly frame in a really nice suit—Hugo Boss, I believe. It made him look for all the world like John Gotti, and his pronouncements, delivered abstractedly between bites of crab cake, sounded uncannily like the surveillance tapes that are played during mob trials: the same malevolent cackles and sentences trailing off into ellipses, though instead of talk of rubouts and busted kneecaps, we were hearing about social commodity reification and eudaemonic valorization. "I like the way you poets *bond*," he said to me. "I'm fascinated by the fervor of your cult—you see it in the trekkies and the baseball card collectors, too. It's a phenomenon worth studying, don't you think?" He was partly the Teflon Don, partly "Hugh Selwyn Mauberly"'s Mr. Nixon, and all lofty bile. He was Buffalo Bill in a white fringed leather jacket, galloping toward me on a sleek palomino, aiming his Winchester to practice trick shots on some stragglers from my dwindling herd. The Famous Marxist—who strikes me less as a Marxist than as a kind of glib Social Darwinist—seems to view the marginalization of poetry as inevitable. And on some days I think he is right.

Yet on the other hand, as I stare out my office window to the goldening autumn leaves below, watching my campus turn into a movie-set image of academia, I must admit that life in the wildlife refuge isn't so bad. For some of us things are cozy: plentiful pasturage here, even if it takes four stomachs to digest the endless reams of student poems. As a writer of poetry, I try nearly every day to practice an art that may, within a few decades, change in such a way as to be unrecognizable or, if some alarmists are to be believed, arrive at a final extinction. As a teacher of poetry, though, I am told by the various savants that I serve an *industry,* whose values may be Arnoldian but whose actual function is to replicate endlessly the same drab period-style lyric. Dana Gioia, in a well-known essay that is alternately exceedingly insightful and wrongheaded, describes the state of things in this way:

> The new poet makes a living not by publishing work but by providing specialized educational services. Most likely he or she either works for or aspires to work for a large institution—usually a state-run enterprise such as a school district, a college, or a university (or lately even a hospital or a prison)—teaching others how to write poetry or, at its highest levels, how to teach others how to write poetry.[1]

He's right, of course, at least about this point. And D. G. Myers, in a study which is, as far as I know, the only full-length *history* of creative writing in the academy, makes note of how sudden and surprising the ascendency of creative writing has been, despite an approach toward literary study which is often at odds with more traditional methods of scholarship and criticism and a general indifference among creative writers to newer theoretical approaches. Traditionally, the point of all this fiddle has been not to train ever-increasing numbers of unemployable creative writers but to apply to literary study the rules of what Myers terms "constructivism," by which he means "teaching literature from the inside, as familiar experience, rather than from the outside, as exotic phenomenon. It is intended to be an elephant's view of zoology."[2] In the industry today this possibility still exists, despite the industry's self-made corruption, despite the suspicion of or contempt for the creative writer that sometimes emerges in the very English departments with which he or she is affiliated, and despite—in the case of poetry—the increasing marginalization of poetry as an active presence in the culture. Building upon the quote above, Myers gives his study a witty and rueful title, *The Elephants Teach.* Buffalo or elephant, we can't exist but for the zoos and game preserves in which we dwell. And it is our lot as exotic pets to divide our day between the endless pacing inside our cells and the wait for our afternoon feeding. But how can we be otherwise? We are, after all, cast out of our natural habitats; like Rilke's panther, "our mighty will stands numbed." But although we are dependent we cannot be easily trained; although we greedily accept the hay bales, horsemeat, and quick-frozen mice, we like to believe that the deans and chairs think twice before they place their heads inside our jaws.

This is, to be sure, a self-flattering view, designed to make us appear as the tragic remnants of a once-noble breed. In truth the dynamic is more simple: we teach in order to have time to write, and most of us try to teach well. And it goes without saying that we are exceedingly lucky. But what does it mean to be a writer who teaches? How does this combination of callings affect our writing and our teaching? Is it accurate to claim, as Gioia does in another of his essays, that the present system can dramatically afflict the writing life by forcing the young poet to "write too much too soon, and the writing may become slick, automatic, and superfluous" thanks to the demands of "tenure, promotion, and professional prestige"?[3] Is it accurate to link, as so many critics of various stripes do, the supposed decline of poetry's audience and urgency to the rise of the creative writing industry? Are we merely the licensing bureau for a bland sort of competency in writing, as the conservative critic Joseph Epstein would have it? In this diagnosis Epstein makes a claim little different from that of the Language poets, as they rail against "Official Verse Culture," and from other critics on the left such as Charles Altieri, who likens the contemporary scene to the "highly inbred professionalism" of French Academic painting of the last century.[4] These sorts of appraisals make us look very little like barbarically yawping fauves and a whole lot like half-forgotten and unintentionally comic salon painters like Gérôme. And perhaps there is some accuracy to Altieri's analogy. But I am less interested in talking here about the teaching of writing than I am in investigating what teaching *does* to writers.

What characterizes this condition of ours is, more than anything else, a kind of intricate ambivalence, a sense that teaching both dignifies us as writers and yet also, in some inexplicable way, limits and wounds our writing. And this ambivalence is, I suspect, one felt in emotional ways rather than in intellectual ones. I am reminded of Mandelstam's characterization of his mentor, V. V. Gippius:

> He differed from other witnesses of literature precisely in [his] malign astonishment. He had a kind of feral relationship to literature, as if it

> were the only source of animal warmth. He warmed himself against literature, he rubbed against it with his fur, the ruddy bristle of his hair and his unshaven cheeks. He was a Romulus who hated his wolf mother and, hating her, taught others to love her.[5]

I suspect that there is something of Gippius's ferality in nearly all of us who teach writing, and I suspect, too, that there is something of the curious hatred of the wolf mother that is literature which must inevitably configure our own creative work. It is hard to love literature when one serves it as a writer, for literature insists to the writer that she is fickle, baffling, and apt to spurn even our most ardent testaments of devotion. We can never love her enough and can never seem to love her as much as other suitors. And yet Mandelstam would tell me that I err by characterizing this relationship in erotic terms. His feral metaphor is less consoling, more frightening. It is based upon a notion of our orphanhood; we suckle at the wolf mother's teat, subject to her inexplicable charity; perhaps we shall never know our real mothers, and surely we will never grow into wolves. Yet it is this very status, Mandelstam suggests, that may compel us to be committed teachers. How odd and exasperating is this condition of ours! And it is a condition which does not easily allow us to strictly divide our writing lives and our teaching lives in the way that I suspect many of my colleagues who teach literature and theory can. Gioia and others of course make the smug claim that this interrelationship between our writing and teaching tends to mandate mediocrity: teaching creative writing causes us to be mediocre writers, and thus even our best efforts at teaching bestow upon our students a similar mediocrity.

There are of course many reasons why Gioia is wrong. I fear that, because Gioia has made his career as a successful businessman, he tends to think that teaching poetry writing must also be conducted like a business, or at least like some sort of business seminar in which salesmen instruct others in their techniques and pitches. It is not an oversimplification to say that Gioia's analysis of our problems boils down to a notion that poetry isn't *selling* because the product is poor and its salesmen poorly trained, and I am sure that many deans, chairpeople, state legislators, and students would readily concur with Gioia's consumerist appraisal. Yet the Arnoldian in me says that as a poet I am not making and selling products but creating objects of beauty, ones that may indeed be perfectly useless. And through the making of such objects I have linked myself, however imperfectly, to an endlessly long literary tradition whose uselessness has nevertheless been an essential aspect of all human culture. (At this assertion the Chairs, Famous Marxist Critics, and my colleagues may feel free to cluck, shake their heads, and roll their eyes.)

I admit to being naïvely and stubbornly Arnoldian. I admit to having "a kind of feral relationship to literature." The writing of poetry is not a business, an activity, or a hobby, but a calling; the teaching of the writing of poetry is, similarly, a calling. And if I here cast my definition in theological terms, I do so with the full knowledge that the struggle for faith is a difficult one, requiring both personal integrity and attentiveness to the flock that must be shepherded. Such a struggle is perhaps better illustrated by testament than by argument or definition. I must try, however partially, to describe how and why I write, how and why I teach, and the nature of those occasions on which the hows and whys of both these disciplines must intertwine.

And so it is that I bring you to my study in the spring of 1995, where for the past ten months my main activity has been writing poetry. Writing has never been for me a particularly easy task, and though my work has always seemed to arise—like that of most poets—from a small number of obsessive concerns, I generally find my writing habits to be compulsive rather than obsessive, filled with stops and starts and various self-lacerating doubts. For the past several months, however, the work has arrived differently; every day I have written, and on some days I have finished a poem in the morning only to start another in the afternoon. This is not to say that I feel inspired as much as that I feel driven, as though the writing were the only thing able to help me make sense of my life, a life which, in the year since my wife's sudden death in an auto accident, seems composed largely of grieving. And the poems, dark and bitter, seem the purest and most solacing expression of this grieving. It is as though nothing makes sense to me but the work. Consequently, the work makes me feel confident and giddy on the one hand, sorrowful and anguished on the other. The poems are the singing from the wound from which the blues derive; they are kaddishes and dirges and addresses to the whirlwind. Still, their catharsis arrives not exclusively from their spirit of elegy but from a new delight I have taken in the shapes of the poems, in form, in finding a way in which I can weld traditional prosodies to my own expressive idiosyncrasies and style—and to the urgency I feel now about my writing. I feel as if the unresolved and relentless grief I have experienced can only be expressed in poems unlike those I have ever written before, in a kind of antimatter version of Crane's "new thresholds, new anatomies." Of course, this total attention to my writing has been a gift, partly of the muse, but more specifically of the NEA—a writing grant has permitted me to take a year off from teaching. I have been able to focus on the work in a way that I never would have, had I been teaching. The questions one asks oneself about writing's relationship to teaching at times like this are complex and perplexing. MLA interviewers routinely ask creative writing candidates if they would quit teaching if they had the financial means to do so and expect, I'm sure, that the candidate will reply as Jarrell did when he said that if he had to he'd *pay* to be able to teach. But I think most serious writers would sooner *not* teach, and I have seen too many examples of writing teachers treating their classroom responsibilities as a duty as painful as Victorian sex and their students as unteachable dolts. In almost twenty years of teaching I've not always been immune to such cynicism myself, much as I am aware of my good fortune at having a good job, a good teaching load, and tenure in an age when such things are likely to be heading the way of the passenger pigeon. But the fact remains that when I am teaching I reach a point during every semester when I think I'd give anything to stop talking about others' poems and simply write my own. And during those times when I am not teaching and have the luxury to devote myself exclusively to writing, I find myself eventually missing the classroom (though I must admit that at such times the yearning to teach is always considerably less pronounced than the yearning to be done with teaching that can assail me during a busy semester). On top of all this hand-wringing comes the inevitable question of whether I would be a better writer if I had not had to devote myself to teaching the same discipline that I practice. Is a teaching life more costly to the writing life than, say, a factory job, a profession, or an editorial position? Dana Gioia and others of course feel that they know the answers to these questions. But I am here talking not about the sort of glibly prescriptive appraisals of literary culture that social critics can trumpet but about the ruthless sorts of doubts and self-questionings that can keep you sleepless at four A.M. Ambivalence? Always.

And in the spring of 1995 my stance toward myself and toward poetry is also complicated by the project of seeing through its publication a posthumous collection of poetry by Lynda Hull—my wife. The book was not completed at the time of her death, though Lynda had talked to me often about possible titles and arrangements for the collection, her third volume of poetry. In the months after her death, I had arranged the poems into a structure that seemed to me as close as possible to the one which Lynda had envisioned, and through the good graces of Robert Jones, a senior editor at HarperCollins who had earlier expressed enthusiasm about Lynda's work, Harper arranged to bring the collection out in 1995, with a brief introduction which I had written and a lengthier afterword by Mark Doty, whose friendship with Lynda had been long and deep. Working on the book has of course been a bittersweet process. I find myself grateful that Lynda's legacy as a writer will now be preserved, grateful that my efforts at getting her collection published have been very easy in an era when commercial publishers have all but abandoned poetry. But it is hard to separate the self that edits the book from the self that grieves Lynda and is filled with relentlessly complicated feelings toward her memory: and this grieving self is, I know, the same self which has written my new poems.

On some days I find myself enormously solaced by the task of overseeing the book's release—the proofs on my desk, the blurbs and jacket copy that arrive from the publisher. On other days the process confounds and depresses me. Has my work on the book been close enough to Lynda's wishes? Would someone who had known Lynda less intimately have been a better choice to edit the volume? Although I was always the first reader of her poems, and although we shared the particular intensities of our writing lives for eleven years, I sometimes feel I am not the best choice. My grief at her loss and my fear that I may be producing this book as much for my own self-interest as for the sake of Lynda and her work often make me feel as though my judgment in the process has been clouded or imperfect. My worst moment of crisis comes only weeks before the book is published, when it is already at the bindery; I've had two chances to look over proofs, and suddenly, as I again read my preface, I see that in it I have egregiously—and tellingly—misquoted a poem. The passage I have misquoted comes at the end of "Red Velvet Jacket," which is, like so many of Lynda's poems, a jittery mixture of memory and elegy. The poem is triggered by the speaker's drive through an "almost Biblical" scene of slum and ruin in the South Bronx. This in turn causes the speaker to remember the velvet jacket "that hangs even now in the mind flaring its slow veronicas" and prompts a long Whitmanesque tale of reverie and horror about the speaker's youth. A narrative of drug use and desolation ensues, counterpointed by an oddly and unsettlingly parallel set of memories of the speaker's visit, during a trip to Eastern Europe, to a museum commemorating the Warsaw ghetto. The key event in the narrative describes the young speaker, "some hopped-up 16 year old with police colored skin," performing almost unwillingly an act of great moral courage—she prevents a battling junkie couple from throwing their crying baby from a window. And, as the poem concludes, its several motifs coalesce into a passage of extraordinary rhetorical power:

God I was innocent then, clean as a beast in the streets.
At the fringes of Warsaw's ghetto
stands a prison where they sorted Jews from politicals,
politicals from homosexuals,

where masses dispersed to nameless erasure. There's a tree there,
lopped and blackened, yet it shines,
enshrined in prayer scrolls, nailed icons. Oh, lucky life,
I didn't understand until tonight,

called back from the ruins in that jacket, dark stain blooming
through the sleeve, the child squalling
in my useless arms. I don't know what happened to the jacket
& all those people are lost to a Diaspora
the borough incinerated around them, nowhere in this night
I drive through. Silk velvet and its rich hiss
the shade of flames offering its drapery, its charm,
against the world burning ruthless, crucial & exacting.[6]

Like George Herbert's "The Collar" and James Wright's "St. Judas," "Red Velvet Jacket" is about redemption, and its agonizingly circuitous arrival. The speaker—involuntarily, it seems—glimpses what the poem calls an "accidental grace." It is a poem, then, which addresses the mysteries of faith. And thus my misquotation from the poem in the preface is an especially significant one, illustrating, perhaps, my own bad faith. "The world burning ruthless, crucial & exacting" becomes "The world burning ruthless, cruel & exacting." My misquotation tells me that, on its most fundamental level, I have misunderstood the poem and that perhaps I cannot understand it. And it is now too late to correct my error: the book will be out in a matter of weeks.

"Oh the many lives that have fountained through my own," writes Lynda in "The Window," which I know she had intended to place as the final poem in *The Only World.* One must read this line as a continuation of Whitman's avowal that the poet must "contain multitudes," yet Lynda's sense of this containment is always ambivalent, laden with ironies that must be obliterated before transcendence can be glimpsed. "I have been so fractured, so multiple & dazzling," she writes, in another of "The Window"'s stanzas. To embrace the world, as all mystics know and as Whitman so surely did, is also to embrace its pain and contradiction. And Lynda's poetry never shirks its understanding of the sheer annihilating savagery of such an embrace. Nor its belief in the grace that can be its progeny.

But need I add that these beliefs—in the multiplicity of the self and in the self as conjoined somehow with the world—are neither fashionable nor exceedingly "American"? The consumerist society of late capitalism runs in part because it makes compartmentalization, both economic and spiritual, a kind of necessity. Such compartmentalization allows us to explain away the inequality upon which our society is built, to acknowledge such things as poverty, homelessness, and human suffering while at the same time channel surfing over their stations. We can relegate such problems to the periphery; they can dwell in their special neglected netherworlds, like late-night infomercials, telepreachers, and psychic hotlines. Poems of course can do little to solve this neglect, let alone the injustice which it ignores. And perhaps for most of us the act of writing poetry is often merely an enactment of the very compartmentalization against which I am railing. But Lynda's poems were never written in such a manner.

Yet where, after these digressions and jeremiads, does all this leave me? In the spring of 1995 it leaves me still confused, still both exhilarated and desolate. I am writing and writing, but still know next to nothing about grace, let alone about what "The Window" calls "that harsh economy, the world." And although I already in some way understand that the relentless momentum of my writing will, by the middle of the summer, slow to a trickle and then to nothing, the confusion does not end. And perhaps, if anything, I have learned that the confusion *cannot* end. Yet in my more lucid and self-forgiving moments I wonder if this is another way of saying that I am learning to let the various selves which dwell within me interact more pointedly. As a writer and teacher of writing, I have always professed such a linkage. But my year of grief and poetry has taught me, I think, that these interactions had been more limited and fruitless than I had led myself to believe. And now? My boundaries at last are more fluid; the selves are engaged in their uneasy dialogue. Or so I hope, and whether this new stance is one of wisdom, simple helplessness, or mere illusion is not yet for me to say.

But by the start of the fall I am back in the classroom—or more specifically the lecture hall. The faces of some 175 undergraduates are staring at me as I present my weekly lecture for Introduction to Creative Writing. The various lecture halls in which I have taught this course are spread out all over the campus. One semester the lectures took place in the building that houses the Kinsey Institute of Sexual Research, another semester in the physics building, next to a door with a large black-and-yellow warning sign that read "DANGER: RADIATION." The current lecture hall happens to be in the optometry building, and each week I find myself erasing blackboard sketches showing cross-sections of corneas and optic nerves. The classroom is preposterously constructed, the tiers of chairs rising at what seems to be a forty-five-degree angle. The acoustics, too, are bad: I have to hook myself up to an indifferently working microphone before I can speak. I suppose I could claim that these preparations create a certain suspense or drama before I start the lectures, but this would assume that the students are paying attention to me, and that is not always the case—much as I try to make the lectures entertaining. Furthermore, there isn't much *reason* for the students to listen. They're largely freshmen and sophomores who are taking the course to meet distribution requirements, and their grades are given to them by the ten graduate assistants who work with me in the course and teach small groups of individual students in writing workshops. My lecture is given on Mondays, and the workshops with the teaching assistants take place later in the week. The class is a godsend for the teaching assistants, who are given a chance to teach something they care about. This class is their respite from the tedium of freshman English—and their teaching tends to be enthusiastic and attentive. But despite my insistence to the students that the lectures are closely linked to the writing workshops, and despite the midterm and final exams I give on the lecture material, students quickly come to see the lectures as the part of the course which is easiest to miss or doze through. It's a flawed structure, but the class serves a purpose. Most students come to it with little or no exposure to serious fiction or poetry. And yet the course asks that they spend a semester reading both genres seriously and doing creative writing themselves. Hope springs eternal, I suppose.

So I find myself in week three or so of the semester, in the "poetry unit," and I'm going over a handout with poems geared to the students' second writing assignment, "a poem about a family member." Admittedly, it's a terribly pedestrian choice for an exercise, but there is some truth to the saw that people should write about what they know, and with careful guidance the students can make the assignment avoid the expected pitfalls of sentimentality and vague abstractions. The poems I'm talking about as models for the assignment range from Ben Jonson to Philip Levine, and I end with a discussion of a scathing and emotionally complicated poem by Yusef Komunyakaa entitled "My Father's Love Letters"—and a poem by Lynda, "Shore Leave."

In preparing my handouts for the lecture, I thought I'd be immune to the emotional consequences of teaching Lynda's poem. Or perhaps I was trying to prove to myself that I now had attained some small degree of perspective or mastery over my grieving. I could teach the poem for its own merits, maybe, and not see it exclusively as a reminder of my loss of Lynda's. Is this what it means to teach with "an elephant's view of zoology"? I am discussing, before 175 mostly bored and blank faces, a poem by my dead wife, an exquisitely rich narrative. I am not sure that, were the students to know of my relationship to its author, they would pay much more attention to the lecture. But as I teach it my mind goes back to a rented house in London in 1988, a sprawling place with a large and elegantly appointed study downstairs, where Lynda worked that year, and a smaller one upstairs, where I would write. But as the year went on Lynda finally abandoned the study, with its brocade curtains and its plaster life mask of Keats, and ended up writing on the third floor, in the tiny empty room that had been designed for the maid. She preferred the light there, the harsh spareness of bare boards and the wobbly table. And it was from there she called me, and I climbed the stairs to hear her read from the poem she'd been working on. The brightness of the room comes back, the ugly little Canon typewriter she worked on that year, the notebook open on her desk, the pile of drafts. She'd been thinking about her father, who'd once been a merchant seaman, and about his charm and shadiness. As so often happens to writers in response to travel, the foggy London spring did not inspire her so much as throw her back into the past, into the squalor and wrong-side-of-the-Hudson landscape of the New Jersey Meadowlands where she grew up. From a typescript festooned with the spidery cursive of her notes and corrections, she read to me in the haunted and incantatory voice she reserved for her poems:

> She wears the sailor suit—a blouse with anchors
> skirt puffed to stiff tiers above her thin
> knees, those spit-shined party shoes. Behind her
> a Cadillac's fabulous fins gleam and reflected
> in the showroom window her father's a mirage.
> The camera blocks her face as he frames
> a shot that freezes her serious grin,
> the splendid awkwardness of almost-adolescence.
> He's all charm with the car dealer and fast talks
> them a test drive in a convertible like the one on
> display, a two-tone Coupe de Ville. But once
> around the corner he lowers the top and soon
> they're fishtailing down dump-truck paths,
> the Jersey Meadows smoldering with trash fires.
> He's shouting *Maybelline, why can't you be true,*
> and seagulls lift in a tattered curtain across
> Manhattan's hazy skyline. Dust-yellow clouds
> behind him. He's handsome as a matinee idol,
> wavy hair blown straight by sheer velocity.
> Tall marsh weeds bend, radiant as her heart's
> relentless tide. They rip past gaping Frigidaires,
> ragged hulks of cranes abandoned to the weather.
> Her father teases her she's getting so pretty

he'll have to jump ship sometime and take her
on a real whirl, maybe paint the whole town red.
For her *merchant marine* conjures names like
condiments—Malabar, Marseilles—places where
the laws of gravity don't hold. She can't believe
her father's breakneck luck will ever run out.[7]

As I stand at the podium reading the poem, my amplified voice ringing out above my throng—some of them fidgeting, some of them snoring—I am aware of being in three places at once: here beside the blackboard with its hastily sketched corneas; in London as Lynda intones the elegant hexameters, spring rain beating against the pane; and in the vista of "gaping Frigidaires" and weeds that the borrowed Caddy weaves through, the sailor father yelping Chuck Berry along with the radio. Yet part of me is also talking shop—the imagery and alliteration of "skirt puffed in stiff tiers," the giddy zigzagging diction of "wavy hair blown straight by sheer velocity." Part of me is talking characterization, "initiation story," and the cultural significance of the author of "Johnny B. Goode." And part of me is trying to explain to a gaggle of eighteen-year-olds who have probably never been east of Fort Wayne the curious mixture of astonishment and horror that accompanies the view from the Pulaski Skyway. And when I reach the passage about how the father's "breakneck luck will never run out," I wonder aloud about foreshadowing. I want them to see the sorrowful majesty of the poem's final scene and to see it with the same cathartic intensity with which I beheld it so many years before, as Lynda shuffled pages, jotted a note to herself, inhaled, and read to the end. The pair are in a roadhouse, the father drunkenly jitterbugging with a "barmaid sinuous in red taffeta":

The girl thinks someday she'll cover her skin
with roses, then spins, dizzy on the barstool.
She doesn't hear the woman call her foolish
mortal father a two-bit trick because she's whirling
until the room's a band of light continuous
with the light the city's glittering showrooms throw
all night long over the sleek, impossible cars.

And now the rear-wall clock has moved within a minute of the period's end, and already some of my charges are folding their notebooks up, reaching for their jackets, and carefully placing baseball caps backwards on their closely cropped heads. "Any questions?" I ask. Only one raised hand: "How much of this will be covered in the midterm?" Then, before I can answer, the bell sounds and they all rise up in unison, herding out the doors like white water, with a quickness almost violent. I lift the mike from my neck, and I'm down the street before the weeping starts. I tell myself these are tears begotten not from sorrow or frustration but from a skewed, mysterious gratitude. It is autumn; the trees along the campus avenues are suddenly ablaze, and my mind turns to another of Lynda's poems, a harrowing elegy for a high school friend who died of AIDS. It's the end of the poem I'm recalling. "Listen," it says,

> how all along the avenue trees
> are shaken with rumor of this strange good fortune.

(1996)

4.

The State You Are Entering: Depression and Contemporary Poetry

The notion that there may be therapeutic value in sending a series of electrical shocks through one's brain sounds primitive and quaint to us today, like something out of the Hammer Studio horror films. But shock therapy has made a small comeback in the past decade, and the moniker that the treatment now goes by, ECT (electroconvulsive therapy), is no doubt meant in part to diminish the horror we associate with the process: in quintessentially American fashion, we have tried to make it innocent by making it abstract. Furthermore, most states now have legal safeguards against indiscriminate application of the treatment. When my father was given ECT in the mid-1980s, both my mother and I were made to sign forms citing our agreement as next of kin, duly witnessed by my wife and an attending physician. Signing such a document makes you realize why seriously ill patients and their families, when all the conventional treatments have failed, are often willing to resort to experimental and even bizarre therapies. No one knows why ECT works, save that, in some individuals, it can change the chemical composition of the brain—the doctor likened it to a bottle of half-flat seltzer water being shaken back to a state of carbonation. She offered this metaphor with a somewhat bored shrug, as though she may as well have been suggesting medicinal leeches.

I can't say that ECT helped to alleviate my father's depression, though in time his doctors felt that his condition had stabilized enough to permit his release from the hospital, where he ended up again for the same reasons a few months later, after a halfhearted suicide attempt, and underwent more ECT. A deeply inarticulate man, my father could not talk much about his melancholy, though in retrospect I can see that he was clinically depressed for most of his seventy years. For a long time I ascribed his utter inability to talk about his feelings to his upbringing. He came from a large and particularly taciturn South Dakota German farm family, grew up during the Depression, and was forced to end his schooling after the eighth grade. A decorated army medic in World War II, he saw the worst sort of battlefield carnage, events which no doubt scarred him emotionally but about which he never spoke. Because my father was a man of few words, I concluded, his depression could not readily be verbalized.

With a son's invariable sort of hubris about his father, I spent my twenties and thirties thinking that because I made my living with words, I could resist the sort of mind-numbing depressions which had so long plagued him. I could *talk* about what ailed me, could even express my feelings in poems. And yet, on a day not long ago, as yet another psychiatrist—the fourth I'd consulted in as many years for my ongoing depression—took down my medical history, I became my father. Or perhaps I should say that I came to somewhat better understand my father's inability to talk about his feelings and especially to talk about his depression. Yes, I could list for the doctor my "symptoms"—the sleeplessness and night panics; the bouts of lethargy and sudden weeping; the utter lack of interest in my work, my writing, or even such things as food—but to try to describe my condition in any way but the most barely verbal fashion seemed wholly beyond my resources. It was not simply a question of "words failing me," for it was not a *question* of finding the right words; like everything else at this moment, talking itself seemed irrelevant, academic, for my feelings were neither so complex that they could be charted with labyrinthine, Jamesian complexity nor so simple that they could be distilled to some useful epigram or instructive slogan.

Neither simple nor complex; instead, so oppressive and confusing that they could not be talked about. The doctor's response to my dilemma was to utter some well-meaning but well-rehearsed platitudes: many depressive patients experience a similar "malaise"; the talking cure seems not as effective against depression as against other emotional disorders; many other writers and artists have also been victims of depression; and of course there are pharmaceutical treatments, and other therapies if they fail. In my state of panic and confusion I was already envisioning my new doctor in a white robe, accompanied by some burly nurses, bending down to administer the ECT. But of course the real result of my visit was less dire. I left armed with a prescription for a Prozac cousin called Zoloft, feeling a bit dubious about a drug whose name sounded like a Red Army general's. It would be pleasant to say that in the past months Field Marshal Zoloft has scored a series of immense victories. Yet I am not sure if the antidepressant has worked, exactly, only that its effects have, at least, caused no damage. Depression is, for many patients, a chronic condition. I can now discuss my difficulties with a bit less of a sense of dread, and I can now at least find something intriguing about the moment in the doctor's office during which I felt that my depression absolutely defied verbalization. Recalling that moment has made me understand somewhat better how depression works for and against creative expression and specifically how it might affect poetry, both as a theme and as a subject, both as an aesthetic issue and as an expression of the poet's psychological state.

Before proceeding, I should make a disclaimer: I am not interested here in providing elaborate definitions of depression or in making hairsplitting distinctions between depressive ailments and other emotional malaises. The disease concept has, fortunately, replaced the mystification and social stigmas which so often accompanied past definitions of the disorder. Depression is now seen as an organic state rather than as a "character flaw," and post-Freudian thinking rejects the notion that it is exclusively the result of childhood or subsequent traumas. Current definitions tend to be plain and surprisingly straightforward. "A depressive disorder," reads a recent National Institute of Mental Health publication, "is a 'whole body' illness involving . . . body, mood, and thoughts. It affects the way you eat and sleep, the way you feel about yourself, and the way you think about things."[1] There are various types of depression, of course: the disabling condition that my father suffered from, which carries the bald label of "major depression"; chronic but less severe depression, known as dysthmia; and bipolar disorder, a susceptibility to extreme mood swings—what used to be known as manic depression. The disease afflicts a staggering number of Americans; recent estimates put the figure at about nine million. It is probably safe to say that poets and other creative artists have been affected by depression in significantly larger proportions than has the general population. Swift and Dr. Johnson surely had to contend with the disease. "The Wasteland" was composed, remember, during Eliot's stay in a Swiss sanitarium, where he had sought treatment for mental exhaustion. The roll call of "mad" British poets who spent good portions of their lives in asylums is as extensive as it is familiar: Smart, Cowper, Clare, Ivor Guerney. It should be noted that the tendency to valorize such figures, to turn them into hyper-romantic geniuses whose madness inspired great poetry, is to ignore the facts. All were relatively minor poets, and all would no doubt today be diagnosed as depressive rather than schizoid—and none would be seen as inspired by some ennobling lunatic life force. Between their bouts of religious mania, both Smart and Cowper suffered acute and relentless periods of melancholy. As Roy Porter puts it in his *Social History of Madness,* "Never does Cowper entertain the slightest fantasy that madness confers upon him great poetic powers. He wrote to keep madness away . . . madness and the muse were essentially at odds."[2] The opposition between mental dysfunction and the muse is similarly present in Clare's poetry and in Guerney's.

Significantly, some of the most memorable lines by both writers can be read as descriptions of writer's block brought on by depression or as outright rejections of the belief that poetry had therapeutic value in helping them to cope with their ailment. Poetry was even seen by them as a pernicious force. "Literature destroyed my head and brought me here," the aged Clare told a visitor to Northampton Asylum.[3] Like the badger in his famous poem, Clare fights a losing battle against the forces which he sees as tormenting him, but unlike the badger's, Clare's adversaries are internal:

> My mind is dark and fathomless and wears
> The hues of hopeless agony and hell;
> No plummet ever sounds the soul's affairs.
> There death eternal never sounds the knell.[4]

These lines are far removed from the bucolic evocations of nature which had informed Clare's early poetry. And Guerney, whose rhapsodic descriptions of rural life a century after Clare are in his early career little different from his predecessor's, eventually comes to write a similarly tortured expression of mental defeat. Here is "Moments" in its entirety:

> I think the loathed minutes one by one
> That tear and then go past are little worth
> Save nearer to the blindness to the sun
> They bring me, and the farewell to all earth
>
> Save to that six-foot-length I must lie in
> Sodden with mud, and not to grieve again
> Because high autumn goes beyond my pen
> And snow lies inexprest in the deep lane.[5]

Lurking behind Guerney's plangent Georgianisms is a sense of the most abject existential despair. Even death, he insists, is preferable to enduring the "loathed minutes," and the world around us is one we cannot even adequately describe, let alone one from which we can draw solace.

And of course the tradition of mad British versifiers has its parallel in America's so-called middle-generation poets, a label I here use in order to avoid the more common—and creepy—tags of "confessional," "extremist," or "tragic." Lowell, Jarrell, Berryman, Sexton, Plath, and Roethke all shared more than friendship or acquaintance. All suffered bouts of acute mental anguish resulting in extended hospitalization. Berryman, Sexton, Plath, and possibly Jarrell all took their own lives. It is impossible to know how much the sorry ends of these writers were a result of willful, quintessentially romantic flirtation with madness and derangement and how much they were a result of a plainer and more helpless succumbing to mental disease. However, the example of Roethke may be instructive. Roethke, a victim of particularly acute bipolar disorder, had major breakdowns in 1935, 1945, 1953, and 1957.[6] A 1946 letter from Roethke to Kenneth Burke speaks admiringly of Rimbaud's archetypally romantic vow to "become a visionary through a complete disordering of the senses," but by the time of Roethke's fourth breakdown the aesthetic charm of madness has clearly worn off, having exacted a considerable emotional—and financial—cost.[7] Roethke's letters are by no means very interesting literary documents, for they are filled mostly with gossip and tedious displays of his rampant careerism. But one of his letters to James Wright, his former student and fellow manic-depressive, is uncharacteristically poignant:

> But the chief point now, as I see it, is you. I've been through all this before, through the wringer, bud, so please respect my advice. Once you become too hyperactive and lose too much sleep, you'll cross a threshold where chaos (and terror) ensue. And believe me, chum, it's always a chancy thing whether you get back or not. When I was 27 I thought I was made of rubber; I skipped, habitually, a night of sleep a week. I held three or four jobs, etc. etc. I was, probably, in better physical shape than you (the tennis, etc.). . . . And yet I just gave out, at last.
>
> To come to my point: it would set my mind at rest if you would go to see some professional (yes a psychiatrist) and tell him what's been going on in the past two weeks. If you aren't sleeping, there are drugs. Sure, it's expensive—20 bucks, anyway, but it might save you five or ten thousand—his advice at the right time. Here's one last point: those closest to you don't usually recognize the "signs" of a manic, or any other phase. Please do this, Jim, just as a kind of insurance. . . .[8]

Roethke's weary and genuine concern for Wright debunks the notion, expressed by Jeffrey Meyers and other critics, that Roethke regarded his manic depression as a kind of blessed Dionysian frenzy. Even as early as the mid-1930s, in a poem entitled "Lines upon Leaving a Sanitarium," Roethke clearly regrets rather than revels in his illness: one of the poem's couplets reads, "The mirror may tell some truth, but not / Enough to merit constant thought."[9]

This is about as close as Roethke gets to an autobiographical exploration of his condition. But it goes without saying that several of his fellow middle-generation poets explore the consequences of their mental breakdowns more directly. Throughout the 1960s poems about psychiatric hospitalizations were about as ubiquitous as bell-bottoms and lava lamps—and the genre today seems almost as dated. Poems such as Sexton's "Flee on Your Donkey" and Berryman's "The Hell Poem" are among their authors' least compelling efforts and are by any standards terrible. With a few notable exceptions, such as Lowell's "Waking in the Blue" and "Home After Three Months Away," or Hayden Carruth's stark and affecting "The Bloomingdale Papers," the most remarkable thing about this subgenre is that the majority of its poems are utterly lacking in insight about both their speakers' own situations and about their surroundings. Berryman's "Hell Poem" opts for mere vagaries:

> Everybody is jolly, patients, nurses,
> orderlies, some psychiatrists. Anguishes,
> gnawings. Protractions of return
> to the now desired but frightful outer world.[10]

Sexton's "Flee on Your Donkey" alternates between clumsy efforts at introspection ("I spent most of my time, / a stranger, damned and in trance") and catalogues of stereotypes:

> Now it's din din din
> while the ladies upstairs argue
> and pick their teeth.
> Upstairs a girl curls like a snail;
> in another room someone tries to eat a shoe. . . .[11]

It's hard to say whether these efforts are simply bad poems by good poets or whether they are mostly the mental disorders talking. Fortunately, the really pathological writing from the middle generations' breakdowns, tantalizingly reported in biographical studies—the hundred-odd poems the manic Jarrell wrote during one of his final hospitalizations, the psych-ward jottings of Lowell during the phase when he seems to have harbored the notion that he was Adolf Hitler—will, let us hope, never see the light of day.[12] It has often been observed that the problem with Confessional verse is that its function is almost exclusively therapeutic: Sexton, for example, began writing poetry at the suggestion of her psychiatrist, Dr. Martin Orne (who was later the subject of much controversy within the medical community for making available recordings of some of Sexton's therapy sessions to biographer Diane Wood Middlebrook). But therapeutic actions are not always intended to directly address one's disorder. To be given a shot of Demerol won't help heal your broken leg, but it will certainly have the therapeutic value of making you feel better. Confessional poetry may indeed have been therapeutic, but we can be sure that the middle generation was not "inspired" by mental anguish any more than Cowper or Clare had been.

The reasons why psychological disorders in general and depression in particular have not been much conducive to significant creative expression are, needless to say, enormously complex. But two of the main reasons may be easy to identify: to distort Larkin a bit, unhappiness writes white, and even when it does write does so with no particular readership in mind. Perhaps the most commonly reported symptom of clinical depression is not mere lethargy or a blue mood but a mind-numbing lack of engagement with the world. How do you write poetry at a time when even tying your shoes seems a Herculean labor? And how do you talk to someone about such a frightening predicament? One's whole physical being is affected by a paradoxical condition of relentless and obsessive thinking on the one hand and physical lethargy on the other. One is turned inward, but in a bedevilling rather than nurturing fashion. This exasperating state is frequently remarked upon, but nowhere more eloquently than by William Styron in his moving memoir of a depressive breakdown, *Darkness Visible.* Commenting on the essentially antisocial nature of depression and its links to depression's physical manifestations, Styron notes that,

> With their minds turned agonizingly inward, people with depression are usually dangerous only to themselves. The madness of depression is, generally speaking, the antithesis of violence. It is a storm indeed, but a storm of murk. Soon evident are the slowed-down responses, near paralysis, psychic energy throttled close to zero. Ultimately, the body feels sapped, drained.[13]

To write from within this "storm of murk" is of course possible, but unlikely. Even a cursory reading of the middle generation's poems about psychiatric hospitalizations reveals an interesting pattern: the poems tend to be not so much about the nature of their writers' diseases as about the poems' *settings.* "Waking in the Blue" tells us more about Lowell's wardrobe ("turtle-necked French sailor's jersey") and weight ("two hundred pounds") than about his mental condition.[14] Lowell's descriptions of his fellow patients at McLean's are designed to reveal the decadence of New England's aristocracy—the "Mayflower screwballs" and "thoroughbred mental cases"—and succeed brilliantly at that goal. Lowell surely understands that there is something considerably more dramatically engaging about the "victorious figures of bravado" who "ossified young" than about the fundamentally undramatic nature of his own disorder's murky drizzles and rain puddles. "Our obsessions," Richard Hugo was fond of saying, "ignore relative dramatic values"—and depression is nothing if not obsessive. To write directly of depression is to forego many of the structural and thematic symmetries upon which literature thrives. And yet anyone who has suffered a major depression knows that the desire to reestablish some sense of focus and order is a depressive's almost desperate goal. The depressive wants coherence, not a Rimbaudian disordering of the senses; the endless circularities of obsessive thinking utterly disregard the niceties of rising action, falling action, cause and effect. And we should bear in mind that this gap between thought and expression, between the phenomenological chaos of perception and the orderliness of art, is not seen by depressives as a mere philosophical or aesthetic problem but as a conundrum that afflicts one's very soul. To write convincingly about such a problem may be beyond the resources of even a poet as formidable as Lowell.

So my subject presents an interesting dilemma. Contrary to the comments made by friends and colleagues when I told them about the topic of this discussion—all a variant of "Well, you'll have a lot of poems to choose from"—the number of poets and poems that actually confront my issue is rather small. But there are two poets I want to examine in greater detail. One is a well-known contemporary poet, Richard Hugo; the other, Frederick Seidel, is highly regarded but, unfortunately, little read. The pair would appear to have nothing in common. Hugo was his era's arch-regionalist, drawing resonantly (detractors would say limitingly) upon his native rural Northwest. Seidel is the most urbane of urban poets—a Harvard man who talks of lunches at Elaine's and 1960s weekends at the Chelsea Hotel; who draws elaborate metaphorical connections between, say, the Holocaust and the 1987 fire in London's Charing Cross tube station. Hugo's poems are characterized by an intensely vital persona—intimate and charming (sometimes cloyingly so), with a comic's sense of timing, an irony borrowed from the hard-boiled detective novels he so admired and attempted himself, and a stunning capacity to reveal pathos. Seidel's voice, in contrast, is caustic; his observations on self and history are stoic, even misanthropic. He can, for example, admiringly allude to Cicero in a title—"Not To Be Born Is Obviously Best of All." If one of Hugo's main faults is his St. Bernard–like tic of demanding that we love him, Seidel's problem is that he is utterly (but often fascinatingly) unlikeable. Hugo is the most slobbering example of Auden's definition of a dog poet, Seidel the most Siamese of cat poets. Yet the two share a number of prosodic and thematic qualities. Both are essentially formalist and narrative in their approaches, yet both manipulate and distort these effects—at times their work seems almost expressionistic. Hugo spawned a number of imitators during the 1970s, but none of these karaoke Montanans could convincingly replicate the oddball elegance of his voice. And though Seidel's approach clearly derives from Lowell, his style is more radical and strange than his mentor's. Both Hugo and Seidel are idiosyncratic stylists with unmistakable voices whose methods are characterized by the obsessive circuitous brooding which is so symptomatic of clinical depression.

But of course what is significant about this is not merely that the pair seem quite familiar with depression as a *subject* but that they have made this condition reflect their prosody and syntax, resulting in some singularly affecting and original writing. Hugo's "Goodbye, Iowa" and Seidel's "The Blue-Eyed Doe" are perhaps more confessional than most of the pair's other work. But both poems are otherwise typical of their authors' methods, and in them we see the inner workings of mental depression in detail far more revealing than in the hospital poems of writers such as Berryman and Sexton.

Hugo is commonly regarded as a landscape poet, and a look at the table of contents of his collected poems would certainly cause one to agree with this claim. The poems' titles read like town names reeled off at random from a Montana roadmap—"Graves at Elkhorn," "The Milltown Union Bar," "Pishkun," "Silver Star," "Helena, Where Houses Go Mad." Yet Hugo is more typically a romantic than he is a realist, seeing in landscape metaphors for the self and its relations to friends and loved ones. This process is rarely enacted with much subtlety, and perhaps it is the very relentlessness and earnestness of Hugo's method that gives the poems their rough majesty. Hugo's best-known poem, "Degrees of Gray at Philipsburg," is a good example of this technique. At first, the speaker's sense of personal failure and the dying mining town are depicted as suffering a kind of parallel decline:

> You might come here Sunday on a whim.
> Say your life broke down. The last good kiss
> you had was years ago. You walk these streets
> laid out by the insane, past hotels
> that didn't last, bars that did, the tortured try
> of local drivers to accelerate their lives. . . .[15]

The opening is standard conceit-making, but as the poem continues it goes beyond familiar elaborations of metaphor to a sort of white-hot fusion of tenor and vehicle, as in the penultimate stanza:

> Isn't this your life? That ancient kiss
> still burning out your eyes. Isn't this defeat
> so accurate the church bell simply seems
> a pure announcement: ring and no one comes?

Perhaps one reason why this poem has so deservedly entered the anthologies is its quality of what Jarrell called "helplessness"—although the poem is masterful, there's nothing neat or plotted about its conceit. Hugo attempts to obsessively, almost involuntarily draw his parallel between the moribund silver town and the protagonist's sense of his own life breaking down, and Hugo's gruff pentameter, laden with spondees and trochaic inversions, intensifies the effect. To say the poem is about low self-esteem is to patina it in the blandishments of psychobabble, for it is more properly a description of the self in throes of agony, and neither Hugo's Chandleresque black humor nor the poem's deus ex machina conclusion (and least convincing gesture), with its transcendent image of the waitress whose "red hair lights the wall," offer the protagonist any credible epiphany. In a fitting irony, the poem's sense of defeat is "so accurate" that its grasp for redemption is its weakest aspect.

"Goodbye, Iowa" is instructive to examine after reading "Degrees of Gray at Philipsburg," for the two poems' methods are quite similar. Written several years after "Degrees of Gray," "Goodbye" appears in Hugo's 1975 volume, *What Thou Lovest Well Remains American,* and both echoes and replies to the earlier poem. Although it is finally less successful than its predecessor, the poem possesses a greater emotional range and avoids the tonal blunder of "Degrees of Gray"'s puzzlingly upbeat ending. It is a more psychologically complex effort, revealing the intricacies of depression in a fashion which few contemporary poems can claim.

Like "Degrees of Gray," the poem begins with an in medias res bluntness. Here is the opening stanza:

> Once more you've degraded yourself on the road.
> The freeway turned you back in on yourself
> and you found nothing, not even a good false name.
> The waitress mocked you and you paid your bill
> sweating in her glare. You tried to tell her
> how many lovers you've had. Only a croak came out.
> Your hand shook when she put hot coins in it.
> Your face was hot and you ran face down to the car.[16]

Self-excoriating gestures are common in Hugo's poems, but this opening is particularly painful. It is worth noting that the poem dates from shortly after Hugo's teaching stint at the University of Iowa, a time during which, to judge from references in some of his other poems, Hugo suffered a mental breakdown. The stanza creates tensions on several levels. Most obviously, we see the protagonist's self-image lacerated by his encounter with the waitress, a very different figure from the waitress described at the conclusion of "Degrees of Gray." But just as revealing is his apparent inability to cope with his anxiety by attempting a "geographical cure." The title and opening line imply that escape from Iowa—here seen as a condition as much as a flat Midwestern state—will somehow relieve the speaker of his turmoil. Hugo's protagonist is hitting the road in classic Huck Finn/*Easy Rider* style, but the solitude of interstate travel has an effect opposite from the one intended: "The freeway turned you back in on yourself / and you found nothing, not even a good false name." These lines are revealing not only for the way they reveal the "you"'s helpless and oppressive introspection but also for the way they show us how inadequate his gestures of self-forgetfulness have become for him. He can't even find "a good false name," and while Hugo's characteristic use of "you" can be argued to be a gesture meant to avoid the cloying effect of casting such bald speculations in the first person, it is also revealed at the same time to be an enactment of Hugo's inability to find a credible alias, a mask of confidence to conceal the protagonist's sense of inadequacy. The mask appears no longer able to hide the "you"'s true nature.

The second stanza turns the protaganist back in on himself in an even more aggrieved fashion, and attempts at gaining perspective amount to nothing more than obsessive, circular thinking:

> Miles you hated her. Then you remembered what
> the doctor said: really a hatred of self. Where
> in flashes of past, the gravestone
> you looked for years and never found, was there
> a dignified time? Only when alone,
> those solitary times with sky gray as a freeway.

Perhaps even more significant than the protaganist's lack of desired perspective is a paradoxical condition which is familiar to many suffering from depression. He detests his introspection, feels he cannot comprehend his condition, yet at the same time draws a near-masochistic comfort from these anxiety-riddled meditations, like a horse going back to its stall during a barnfire. It is the oxymoronic condition that Julia Kristeva describes as "the sad voluptuousness [and] despondent intoxication" of melancholia.[17] The final stanza continues in this fashion and introduces some fragmentary references to a memory of an earlier humiliation:

> And now you are alone. The waitress
> will never see you again. You often pretend
> you don't remember people you do. You joke back
> spasms of shame from a night long ago.
> Splintered glass. Bewildering blue swirl
> of police. Light in your eyes. Hard questions.
> Your car is cruising. You cross with ease
> at eighty the state line and the state
> you are entering always treated you well.

Nothing new happens here, save that the poem's motifs crescendo to a greater self-lacerating intensity: the ending's pun on "state" possesses the sort of grim humor characteristic of Hugo at his best. As the car speeds up, so too does the protagonist's obsessive state of depression. And if we assume that the car is most likely traveling west, then the state which "always treated you well" is . . . *Nebraska.* Wry, psychologically intricate, performing the difficult task of addressing abjection while evading self-pity, "Goodbye, Iowa" should be figured among Hugo's more notable poems. And, as a study of the bedevilling nature of depression, it is unsettlingly acute.

Frederick Seidel's "The Blue-Eyed Doe" is even more frightening in this respect. Although more traditionally Freudian than Hugo's poem in its insistence upon locating the source of the speaker's depression in a particular Oedipal trauma, the poem shares with Hugo's a sense of the circular, resolutionless nature of this particular mental anguish. The poem's opening moves slowly to its disclosure of the speaker's mother's illness, and Seidel, who is in other poems a master of formal prosody, seems here to deliberately employ a staccato pentameter and a decidedly inelegant use of the elegiac stanza, traditionally the most stately of verse forms. It's as though the quatrains are helping to convey the very *willfulness* of what Seidel is attempting to articulate:

> I look at Broadway in the bitter cold,
> The center strip benches empty like today,
> And see St. Louis. Often I am old
> Enough to leave my childhood, but I stay.
>
> A winter sky as total as repression
> Above a street the color of the sky;
> A sky the same gray as a deep depression;
> A boulevard the color of a sigh:
>
> Where Waterman and Union meet the
> Apartment building I'm regressing to.
> My key is in the door; I am the key;
> I'm opening the door. I think it's true
>
> Childhood is your mother even if
> Your mother is in hospitals for years
> And then lobotomized, like mine. A whiff
> of her perfume; behind her veil, her tears.[18]

It's no wonder that the speaker is so reluctant to convey the information contained in the fourth stanza. The opening functions as a kind of self-hypnosis, regressing the speaker back to childhood, first to a dream-like vision of the apartment where he lived and then to a fugue of other memories:

She wasn't crying any more. Oh try.
No afterward she wasn't anymore.
But yes she will, she is. Oh try to cry.
I'm here—right now I'm walking through the door.

The pond was quite wide, but the happy dog
Swam back and forth called by the boy, then by
His sister on the other side, a log
Of love putt-putting back and forth from fry

To freeze, from freeze to fry, a normal pair
Of the extremes of normal, on and on.
The dog was getting tired; the children stare—
Their childhood's over. Everyone is gone.

Forest Park's deserted; still they call.
It's very cold. Soprano puffs of breath,
Small voices calling in the dusk is all
We ever are, pale speech balloons. One death,

Two ghosts. . . .

The pace of the poem has now quickened, the repetitions growing more incantatory, allowing the poem to make jagged jump cuts from recollection to recollection, from apartment to bucolic summer pond to desolate winter park. If one of the most frequently cited aspects of depression is the mind's inability to control its zigzag from memories of pleasure to memories of torment, then Seidel has found a convincing form for replicating this process. A few stanzas later a new motif is introduced, which in turn brings us back to descriptions of the mother:

The statue of St. Louis on Art Hill
In front of the museum, turns into
A blue-eyed doe. Next it will breathe. Soon will
Be sighing, dripping tears as thick as glue.

Stags do that when the hunt has cornered them.
The horn is blown. Bah-ooo. Her mind a doe
Which will be crying soon at bay. The stem
Between the autumn leaf and branch lets go.

My mother suddenly began to sob.
If only she could do that now. Oh try.

I feel the lock unlock. Now try the knob.
Sobbed uncontrollably. Oh try to cry.

How easily I can erase an error,
The typos my recalling this will cause,
But no correcting key eases terror.
One ambulance attendant flashed his claws,

The other plunged the needle in. They squeeze
The plunger down, the brainwash out. Bah-ooo.
Calm deepened in her slowly. There, they ease
Her to her feet. White goddess, blond, eyes blue—

Even from two rooms away I see
The blue, if that is possible! Bright white
Of the attendants; and the mystery
And calm of the madonna; and my fright.

I flee, but to a mirror. In it, they
Are rooms behind me in our entrance hall
About to leave—the image that will stay
With me. My future was behind me. All

The future is a mirror in which they
Are still behind me in the entrance hall. . . .

As with the Hugo poem, Seidel's goal is not to resolve the trauma of this horrible set of events, but only to confront their obsessive power over him. In the stanzas that follow, the speaker again makes an attempt to stanch his recollection of the mother's departure by invoking a bucolic memory, in this case of a park in autumn. But once again the gesture proves futile:

Once upon a time, a fall

So long ago they were burning leaves,
Which wasn't yet against the law, I looked
Away. I watched the slowly flowing sleeves
Of smoke, the blood-raw leaf piles being cooked,

Sweet smelling scenes of mellow preparation
Around a blood-stained altar, but instead
Of human sacrifice, a separation.
My blue-eyed doe! The severed blue head!

The windows were wide-open through which I
Could flee to nowhere—nowhere meaning how
The past is portable, and therefore why
The future of the past was always now

A treeless Art Hill gleaming on the snow. . . .

The sacrificial imagery veers to the histrionic, but Seidel recovers control of the poem in the psychological speculation which immediately follows. But if, as Hugo contends, the nature of obsession is to ignore relative dramatic values, then the histrionic must sometimes be confronted if we are to convincingly replicate obsession. Seidel does not wholly avoid the imitative fallacy in this passage, however, yet in the poem's concluding stanzas he regains the opening's commanding acuity:

Warm sun, blue sky; blond hair, blue eyes; of course
They'll shave her head for the lobotomy,
They'll cut her brain, they'll kill her at the source.
When she's wheeled out, blue eyes are all I see.

The bandages—down to her eyes—give her
A turbaned Twenties look, but I'm confused.
There were no bandages. I saw a blur.
They didn't touch a hair—but I'm confused.

I breathe mist in the mirror. . . . I am here—
Blonde hair that will darken till it does,
Blue eyes that will need glasses in a year—
I'm here and disappear, the boy I was . . .

The son who lifts his sword above Art Hill
Who holds it almost like a dagger but
In blessing, handle up, and not to kill;
Who holds it by the blade that cannot cut.

The most remarkable aspect of the ending is how it wrests a powerful and convincing rhetorical trope from a passage which seems in danger of breaking down into incoherence. The obsessive reliving of the aftermath of the mother's lobotomy turns into a helpless confusion, an "air of lost connections" in which even the poem's grammar breaks down to a telegraphic jumble of fragments, dashes, and ellipses. The final stanza, however, is masterful: the child Seidel raises his sword in a gesture of sanctification, yet the image also implies an uneasy stasis, one which does not harbor the illusion of resolving the speaker's depressive fugue of recollection, but which nevertheless transforms it into a fitting memorial. Like the best elegies, "The Blue-Eyed Doe" understands the intricacies of mourning and both does honor to its subject and offers solace—albeit of a very tentative sort—to the living.

I have here reached the place where form demands that I perform what has to be a similarly transcendent bit of magic, pulling the rabbit of perspective from the hat of these dour speculations. But as I stare out my study window, onto the frost-starred roofs of Chicago's coldest Christmas Eve day on record, I fear that my ability to perform this task is no better than my uncertain capacity for metaphor. I know, at least, that the state I have entered does not appear to be treating me well. I have just been to the hospital, where my wife is recuperating from a car wreck that has caused her to undergo two extensive surgeries in scarcely a week. She peers out from a photo on my desk, beside a snapshot of my late mother, circa 1940, and one of my father, dead two years ago this week, and in the sepia barely twenty, baby-faced in his corporal's stripes. I think of Rilke's ode to his own father photographed in military garb, one of the more frequently translated Rilke poems, generally entitled "Cadet Portrait of My Father." Like many of the "thing poems" from Rilke's *New Poems* volumes, it is an act of the most concentrated, numinous sort of looking, of a mysteriously interactive gazing, in which the object of meditation seems to gaze back upon the poet with an equally fervent fixity. It is description of rapt intensity. But more importantly, "Cadet Portrait of My Father" is about legacies, how the dead live on in us in a way that is the source both of burden and of wonder. The poem's final lines are perhaps the most telling. "Oh quickly disappearing photograph," Rilke exclaims, "in my more slowly disappearing hand."

(1992)

5.

A Cavalier and Doomed Lot: James L. White, a Memoir

The poet James. L. White has now been dead for nineteen years, killed in his sleep—by a heart attack—in Minneapolis in the summer of 1981. He was the author of four collections of poetry, and his work has suffered the fate one might expect for a good but finally minor poet: a few people still read him, and certain poets of my own generation can be said to have been influenced by him, though none of his books remain in print. *Good but minor:* it is a description I employ with caution, for I do not mean it to be pejorative. Weldon Kees is good but minor, and several of his poems I know by heart. Good but minor is a category which includes many poets whose work I love: Thomas Traherne, John Clare, Ivor Guerney, Lorine Neidecker, and John Logan come to mind. But my purpose here is not to evaluate the poetry of James L. White, though I plan to discuss certain of his poems in detail. Nor is it to draw some hairsplitting distinction between major and minor (is Kees a minor-major poet or a major-minor poet?), especially when I fear that my own poetic career may not even qualify me for a place in one of the farm clubs of Parnassus. What I instead intend to discuss is something more perplexing and intricate, for James L. White was my poetic mentor, and it is to him I owe many of my notions about the practice and teaching of poetry. In talking about Jim, I want also to discuss the issue of mentoring, a subject which has recently been of some interest to me, if only because the dynamics of mentoring are curious ones, subject to few strict rules. And mentoring is also a tale likely to produce an unhappy ending: it is a story which begins in nurture but which tends to end in rejection or loss. Yet good stories rarely possess happy endings. And if the relationship of a mentor to his/her disciple can be likened to that of a parent to a child, it should come as no surprise that the end of mentoring is that we become our mentors, in the same way that it is my late father's face which stares at me from the mirror each morning. Yet I am not my father. And when I set a poem down in my notebook or on the screen of my laptop, I sometimes feel that it is the presence of James L. White that helps guide my pen or fingertips. Yet I am not Jim White, although I now am nearly as old as Jim White at the time of his own death. When, then, does mentoring end? And when it ends, what then are we left with? Jim White, like so many of those who have meant the most to me, now dwells among the shades, and it is said that the shades seek for themselves only the balm of forgetfulness; they are indifferent to our eulogies, indifferent to our problems. That I conjure him for selfish reasons should come as no surprise.

I first met Jim White twenty-five years ago, on a snowy November night in Minnesota. Two friends and I were coordinating a series of poetry readings by local writers at a neighborhood community center, which, after a couple of years of existence, had been funded by the State Arts Board with a princely grant of five hundred dollars; with this, donations, and money from our own pockets, we could pay our readers a fifty-dollar honorarium. James L. White, whose work I knew from the local poetry scene and his two small-press books, had agreed to read on the night in question, but it did not seem likely that the reading, which he was to give with another local poet, James Moore, was going to take place. Nearly a foot of snow had fallen, and so the first time I ever spoke with Jim was during my phone call to suggest we cancel the reading. Jim, however, would have none of it, so the reading took place that night with six or seven people in attendance, the wind and snow battering the windows behind the podium, though the scene was far from dramatic. There's always something embarrassing about a poetry reading before an audience as tiny as the one that had gathered that night; readers tend to respond to the intimacy of such situations by retreating into shyness and quietude. Not so with Jim White, who read a group of his newer poems in a highly intense and mellifluous fashion; his wasn't the booming sort of declamatory reading I'd come to expect from Midwestern writers of that era, such as the then-ubiquitous Robert Bly. The performance was far more controlled and far less rhetorical and stagy than that. More importantly, though, the poems were powerful and emotionally gripping, like nothing I had heard before from a local poet. The prevailing style, locally, aimed for a bland and mildly surrealist miniature: little epiphanies in cornfields were the norm.

How different such poems were from the first poem Jim read that night, which was later included in his posthumous collection, *The Salt Ecstacies:*

Summer News

Transients loiter in downtown parks with
the stillness of foxes.
One smiles as if I knew him near a fountain
in his center of light,
wearing a faded shirt like summer news.

His body invites conversation.
They threaten tornadoes through the city as
hunters and prey agree on common shelter.
The storm enters our skin gathering
as we begin the familiar gestures.

In his room I speak of death, its promise of ending.
He undresses me, telling me how tired I am,
that friends have brought me their truths all day.
He seems as beautiful as I wish my life was
in the boiling light of our slight sweating.

Now the old blues
before the bad gin and storm.
We vow total selfishness
and we begin to touch

and we begin to rain. . . .[1]

What's immediately striking about this poem, both twenty-five years ago and as I read it today, is the honesty and directness of its content. No hermeticism and vaguely Jungian musings here. The poem is direct in its narrative and unabashedly "out"—and to write openly of gay sexuality in those days, even in a supposed bastion of liberality such as Minnesota, was to violate a number of aesthetic taboos. Yet the valor of the poem derives from other factors as well. Its diction achieves a delicate equipoise between simplicity and adamant lyrical flourish: the plaintive and almost embarrassingly bald "He seems as beautiful as I wish my life was" is followed by the exquisitely modulated consonance of "in the boiling light of our slight sweating." And this, in turn, is followed by the clipped and weary "Now the old blues / before the bad gin and storm." Huge shifts in diction abound in the poem, but their effect is seamless. Furthermore, the poem's narrative evolves with a strict and evocative delicacy: there's the erotic charge of the initial encounter in the park, followed by the tender (yet furtive and almost desperate) scene of the two men in the apartment. The poem's imagery—the repeated references to water and storm as both erotic life force and a kind of terrifying deluge—is insistent but inobtrusive. The poem's language and motifs combine to create what is often the most memorable aspect of Jim's best poems, a speaking voice astonishingly vulnerable, strikingly idiosyncratic, and for the most part shorn of self-pity. The models for this style seem to me two poets also admired for this sort of speaking voice, Cavafy and James Wright. It's not merely the homoerotic subject matter of the poem which recalls Cavafy but also a language that rapidly shifts between an incantatory formality and an idiomatic flatness. The echoes of Wright can be heard in the poem's imagery and in a kind of deadpan exposition. (Compare the opening of "Summer News" to certain middle-period Wright poems such as "The Poor Washed Up by Chicago Winter" or "Inscription for the Tank.") The choice of models of course says a lot about a writer, and Cavafy and Wright are difficult masters, precisely because of the deceptive simplicity of their manners.

The other poems which Jim read that night shared these qualities, and some of the poems later appeared (in different form, for Jim was a painstaking reviser) in *The Salt Ecstacies*. The most notable of them was a long fugue-like poem, reminiscent of Lorca's bullfighter elegy, entitled "The Clay Dancer." The poem mixes the psalmic and liturgical surrealism of Lorca's poem with a series of autobiographical vignettes centered on sexual awakening and coming out. The method is audacious, and more so even than in "Summer News," the poem successfully mixes a galvanic and fluent music with a plainspoken vulnerability. Yet the most startling aspect of the poem is that we are asked to read it as Jim's self-elegy: the protagonist seems, in a bizarre mixture of *Sunset Boulevard* and any number of Hardy poems, to be addressing us and himself from the grave. And its self-elegizing ranges from tenderness to the most brutal sort of chastisement. It is a frightening and morbidly prophetic piece of work, snarling in its self-interrogation but scored with the stately solemnities of requiem. Perhaps every good poet must eventually write a version of the "Ode to a Nightingale," and "The Clay Dancer" was Jim's. It was the last thing Jim read that night, and our little group, huddled around the podium as snow beat against the windowpanes, received the close of the poem with a kind of entranced collective silence. Minutes seemed to pass before the applause began.

My friendship with Jim White began on that evening. I was twenty-three, and Jim was just shy of forty. My life had thus far been an uneventful and sheltered product of Midwestern suburbia, and though Jim and I shared Midwestern backgrounds—he'd grown up in Indianapolis—his life had been anything but uneventful. He'd in fact lived several lives. Jim's first passion was dance, and shortly after his sixteenth birthday he won a scholarship to study in New York at the American Ballet Theater. He danced professionally with several troupes, both here and in Europe, served briefly in the navy, received English degrees from Indiana University and Colorado State, and then, toward the end of the 1960s, headed for the Southwest, where he lived for several years among the Navajo and Hopi, first as a teacher and later as the artistic director of a Native American theater group based in New Mexico. By the time I met him, he had been in Minnesota for several years, teaching in the Writers in the Schools program, mostly in reservation schools. It was the sort of itinerant existence, traveling from school to school around the state for very little money, to which Jim had by this point in his life grown accustomed. I doubt that he regarded this chronicle of wanderings and rootlessness as a romantic one, however. He was, no doubt, a good dancer, but not talented enough to turn dancing into a lifelong career. And his involvement with Native Americans, long-standing as it was, could never change his status as an outsider among those cultures. Even as a poet, he dwelled outside the pale, never willing to sell himself for the purpose of landing an easy academic position and never fitting very comfortably into a provincial literary community whose values and ambitions were quite different from his own. And finally, as a gay writer from a generation born too early to reap the benefits of the post-Stonewall era, he felt acutely the cost of coming out. The epigraph to *The Salt Ecstacies* is an ominous quotation from Leviticus: "Whosever liveth with these scars / shall dwell outside the tribe." For the vulnerable and shy Jim White, obsessed as he clearly was with the desire for a community—whether of artists, tribal peoples, or fellow gays—there was no clan in which to truly dwell, and his deeply contingent honorary memberships in the communities he sought only served to remind him of his difference. His life of wandering had also, Jim thought, been one of the reasons for his frail health. He believed that the physical punishments of the dancer's life had helped to cause the angina that would prove fatal to him—though Jim's history of sporadic substance abuse might also have been a factor.

My friendship with Jim began at a point of important transition in his life. He had entered middle age with a vague but emphatic sense that he did not have long to live. His existence had been full but rootless, and he was coming to suspect, after a series of unhappy love affairs, that it was also a life in which solitude would be his destiny. I think he was also troubled by the suspicion that in his various lives he had displayed talent in many disciplines but had achieved mastery of none. He had now been publishing his poems for the better part of a decade, but the voice of his first two collections—they appeared in 1972 and '74—is neither his own nor very interesting, and Jim must have known this. Although some of the poems display a precise and deftly lyric engagement with the landscape of the Southwest and with Native American cultures, their speaker is self-effaced to the point of concealment, and the poems, finally, never begin to get off the ground. Jim White, at forty, was not undergoing a midlife crisis, but was instead experiencing the throes of something far more intense: I suppose the best term for it is a crisis of the soul, a *noche oscura.* He confronted this condition in some of the era's expected ways, of course: he stopped his drinking and drug use and engaged in an intense study of Zen Buddhism; he started visiting a therapist. But the greatest change took place in Jim's poetry. Suddenly the poems mattered. Like "Summer News," Jim's new poems were starkly self-confrontational, sure in their music, and stamped with an urgency that his work had never before possessed. The poems were keeping Jim alive: I make this statement with full awareness of its hyperbolic implications, yet in Jim's case no other characterization will suffice. I have known a handful of other writers who were sustained by poetry in this way, for whom the craft went beyond self-expression or self-therapy and became instead a kind of life-support system. They are figures to whom we must respond with a mixture of awe and sorrow, for I doubt if theirs is a condition we would wish upon those we love. But such was to be Jim White's fate.

This is not to say that I knew any of this as I began, in the months after I met Jim, to foist my poems upon him. Like most young poets, I craved attention, and like most young poets I had no idea whether my work was good. This was a blissful ignorance, surely, because if I had suspected just how ghastly my work really was I probably would have given up on it. But I was wholly intoxicated by poetry, reading every collection of contemporary verse I could find and trying my hand at every conceivable period style: I was Olson on one day, Merwin on the next, and never patient enough to let my poems go beyond my borrowed styles' surface mannerisms. I had taken some writing classes at the University of Minnesota with the expatriate British poet Michael Dennis Browne, who was a charismatic and generous teacher. But I felt more like an autodidact than a student and possessed an autodidact's mixture of arrogance and confusion. I had the good fortune to have taken a night watchman's job, working four nights a week alone in a large medical building. It gave me plenty of time to read and write, so the Lowery Medical Arts building became my classroom, where I'd churn out poems and, perhaps even more importantly, weekly book reviews for the university student paper, *The Minnesota Daily.* Fiction, biography, criticism, and especially poetry: the editors let me write about anything I chose, and in the pages of the *Daily* I worked out my opinions about many writers who would grow essential for me: Ashbery, Wright, Cavafy, Ritsos, Pavese, as well as younger writers such as Norman Dubie and Heather McHugh. I doubt if these pieces were very perceptive, but I quickly mastered the reviewer's art of making myself look smart, and I reveled in my newfound sense of power. I was an opinion maker! Writers of the books I reviewed even wrote notes of thanks and (sometimes) condemnation to me. "Dear David Wojahn," wrote Heather McHugh on the occasion of my review of her first book, "if all the pans are as bright as yours, I will be well-fried." My appenticeship to this point was an odd one: I was laboring in solitude, as I thought a poet should. But my ambitions were decidedly po-biz.

Over the next two years, until I left Minnesota for graduate school, Jim White became my tutor, though I doubt if we would have described our relationship in such formal terms. Every few weeks I'd meet with him, in coffee shops or in his apartment, and show him my poems. His place was small and sparely furnished, just a pair of living room chairs, a kitchen table, and on the floor his antique Navajo rug, the only one of his possessions which he claimed to be proud of. I remember little of our conversations, save that he listened with care as I read him my work and that he annotated the poems very carefully, in a spidery cursive. From time to time he'd offer a few suggestions for revising the poems, yet Jim was not the sort of teacher who was given to pronouncements. I remember nothing specific about his comments, and I'm sure that even the most pointed of suggestions wouldn't have helped to salvage my wretched scribblings. What counted for more, although I only dimly perceived it then, was Jim's gracious *attentiveness* to the poems. He read them as if they were worthy of respectful attention. I have no idea why Jim chose to honor my poems in this way. Perhaps his newfound seriousness about his own work had given him a similar stance toward the work of others, even a tyro such as myself. Perhaps he recognized some talent in me, or at least some requisite ambition that could be different from mere careerism. And perhaps, too, it was gratifying for him to know that a young poet respected his work and opinions in the way that I so clearly did. At any rate, I had found a mentor. A mentor, not a teacher. Not someone paid to offer advice, but someone who, in the awkward and mysteriously reciprocal fashion in which mentoring seems to be enacted, helped to bring me to a clearer awareness of what it meant to write poems. Jim gave me instruction and advice, of course, but also, and perhaps more importantly, he showed me kindness, a quality which does not exist these days in much abundance. Yet it is kindness such as Jim displayed, this scrupulous philanthropy of expertise, which counted the most in our relationship, more so, I think, than the actual usefulness of his advice.

And it goes without saying that mentors needn't give the best advice in order to be of crucial value. Literary history provides countless cases of well-intentioned mentors who offer useless or even damaging counsel to their charges: maudlin Leigh Hunts, trigger-happy Verlaines, and bone-headed Thomas Higginsons abound. And, as the example of Verlaine so pathetically illustrates, mentors can often change into lovers, Svengalis, or ego-trippers, to the detriment of both mentor and disciple. Surely there are some literary mentorings which can survive such complications. The tryst between Louise

Bogan and her much younger admirer, Theodore Roethke, is bracingly described by Bogan's biographer Elizabeth Frank as a liaison which "evolved, through distance, tact, and a recognition of the circumstances of each other's lives, into one of those bonds which closely resembles a love affair, namely, an intense mutual attachment between student and teacher."[2] This sounds like a much more fruitful pattern than the more typical scenario of middle-aged professors hitting on their students. Perhaps just as drably typical is the tendency of mentors to break with disciples when the disciples come into their own as artists and in doing so appear to reject their mentors' counsel and example. Allen Tate, for whom autobiographical poems were anathema, was profoundly distressed by the Confessional verse of his one-time student Robert Lowell: "But Cal," wrote Tate to Lowell upon the publication of *Life Studies,* "it's not *poetry.*" And in *Becoming a Poet,* David Kalstone's brilliant analysis of Elizabeth Bishop's literary friendships with Marianne Moore and Lowell, we see the erosion of mentoring in sadly vivid detail. Moore's championing of Bishop's work ended, for the most part, after Bishop refused to adopt the revisions which Moore had suggested for Bishop's "Roosters," and a good thing it was that Bishop would not be swayed. Moore offered Bishop a bizarrely revised version of the poem, one which mangled the delicacy of its triple-rhyme stanzas and bowdlerized vocabulary that Moore deemed indelicate: "water closet" seems to have offended Moore, though, ironically, she naïvely suggested that Bishop might change her title to "The Cock." She sought to turn a subtle psychological allegory of sexual outsiderhood and survival into a merely descriptive word machine: a Modernist poem such as one of Moore's, in other words. After the "Roosters" fiasco, nothing was ever the same between the two. "The rift," writes Kalstone, "was more startling than its comic origins suggest. Recalling the farrago years later, Bishop said she never again sent Moore any of her poems for suggestions or approval."[3]

So artistic mentors may give bad advice, may in fact give dangerous advice. And how, furthermore, does a disciple distinguish between the mentor's message and the example of the mentor's own life? Kappus was fortunate to have known Rilke only through his *Letters to a Young Poet* and thus was not presented with the insufferable high-class gigolo who was in fact the letters' author. Or is it instead *regrettable* that Kappus did not encounter Rilke in his Eurotrash aspect, Rilke as sycophant and deadbeat dad? Perhaps it is better to see the chinks in our mentors' armor and to see them early. Mentoring is a complicated business because it is conducted always in a state of unease. The disciple wants to be changed by the mentor, changed utterly. And yet the self is more likely to resist such change than to welcome it.

Michael Heller, in a canny memoir about his mentor George Oppen, puts it this way: "The uneasiness of poetic interrelation, of 'influence' (as Harold Bloom might inflect the word) lies buried in the factorials of poetic learning. Every transmission from 'mentor' to student abrades the self's inertial desires to maintain the fiction of its own 'gracefulness,' its own completeness."[4] I imagine that I first sought Jim White's advice because I wanted someone to listen to me, to praise me, to coddle my bumbling and misshapen poetic aspirations. But what I was given by Jim was instead an education in the emotional and spiritual costliness of poetic endeavor. Success, happiness, and security all proved elusive for Jim. And through Jim I came to see how likely such a fate can be for a serious poet in our era. Not the inevitable fate, surely, but a fate shared by others like Jim whom I have since known and known well. Yet it need not be considered a cruel and unjust fate. I am reminded of the painter Donald Evans, who wrote that his life was about "the *why* of art, and the *I give up* of finding love or happiness." Jim White, more than anyone else I have known, showed me the *why* of art.

I first dimly perceived this as Jim's essential message one afternoon when I was visiting him in his apartment. He read me a draft of the poem destined to open *The Salt Ecstacies.* Like several of Jim's best poems, it is an ars poetica of an urgently expressive sort:

An Ordinary Composure

I question what poetry will tremble the wall into hearing or tilt the stone angel's slight wings at words of the past like a memory caught in elms. We see nothing ahead. My people and I lean against great medical buildings with news of our predicted death, and give up mostly between one and three in the morning, never finding space large enough for a true departure, so our eyes gaze earthward, wanting to say something simple as *the meal's too small: I want more.* Then we empty from a room on intensive care into the sea, releasing our being to the slap of waves.

Poems break down here at the thought of arms never coupling into full moons by holding those we love again, and so we resort to the romantic: a white horse, set quivering like a slab of marble into dancing flesh.

Why remember being around a picnic table over at Brookside Park? We played softball that afternoon. My mother wore her sweater in the summer because of the diabetes. Night blackened the lake like a caught breath. We packed things up. I think I was going to school that fall or

> a job somewhere. Michael'd go to Korea. Before we left I hit the torn softball into the lake and Michael said, "You can't do that for shit James Lee."
>
> Going back, I realized the picnic was for us. It started raining in a totally different way, knowing we'd grow up right on into wars and trains and deaths and loving people and leaving them and being left and being alone.
>
> That's the way of my life, the ordinary composure of loving, loneliness, and death, and too these prayers at the waves, the white horse shimmering, bringing it toward us out of coldest marble.[5]

As with "Summer News," what we first notice about the poem is its mixing of dictions. The high rhetoric of the opening clause is followed by the quirky surrealism of the sentence's conclusion, which is in turn followed by the gruff flatness of "We see nothing ahead." And then comes the eerie meditation on mortality which concludes the opening paragraph. (By this time Jim's doctors had diagnosed his heart condition as inoperable and likely to be fatal.) The contrast drawn between the certainty of mortality and the blandishments of art is amplified in the second paragraph, but suddenly the poem departs from these motifs entirely. The memory of the picnic is described reportorially, almost casually. This in turn prepares us for the even flatter vocabulary of the fourth paragraph, yet in the context of the poem's quirky musicality the disarmingly plain language of a passage such as "we'd grow up right on into wars and trains and death and loving people and leaving them" has the effect of revelation. And when the poem returns in its final sentence to its speculations on the art of poetry, the dichotomy between art and life which with the poem has struggled is now obliterated—not resolved, exactly, but transformed into a haunted stasis. And I needn't add that such a poem is difficult to bring off: Jim struggled through many drafts to get the tone right, to find the proper mixture of lyric and demotic. A version of the poem published in an obscure quarterly called *The Chowder Review* is considerably different from the one which eventually appeared in *The Salt Ecstacies.*

I remember my feelings of astonishment when Jim read me this poem. I was flattered that Jim had decided to ask me for advice about his work, and it signaled, I think, a turning point in our relationship. From that day on, it seemed that Jim regarded me as his peer and confidante as much as his student, and in perceiving my new role I felt honored, admitted to the writerly company at last. This is not to say that our new relationship was uncomplicated. Jim's vulnerability and hypersensitive devotion to the art could sometimes turn to mere peevishness and even to a kind of paranoia. The burden of his life of wanderings and his deep loneliness was now wearing heavily upon him. His devotion to his writing seemed not to translate into any sort of public recognition: he continued to feel that he labored in obscurity within a backwater literary community that could not appreciate his new work. And Jim also believed that many of his straight friends had cooled to him when he chose to come out. And he, in turn, severed his ties with them. As one of the poems of *The Salt Ecstacies* laments, "I have left so many this year / who felt too comfortable with my old design." Also, like so many gay men of his generation, he chose to hide his gayness from his family. He was deeply devoted to his sister and his aging mother, who knew that Jim was a poet, but Jim never told them about the publication of *The Del Rio Hotel,* his third book and the first of his collections to overtly treat gay themes. About *The Salt Ecstacies,* the collection which meant so much to him, they seem also to have known nothing, at least while Jim was alive. Although he ostensibly remained as gentle-tempered and gracious as he had ever been, Jim became increasingly isolated and dejected in his "new design." Meanwhile, Jim's poems grew even more urgent and risky. Darkly retrospective and increasingly imbued with Jim's awareness of his mortality, the poems seem at once both personal and prophetic. And, for whatever reasons, Jim felt that I could serve as a first reader and audience for many of these poems; sometimes it seemed as though Jim feared that his audience would never grow beyond myself and a handful of his other friends. Jim's last years became an ever- increasing struggle against the fear that he would die with his mission as a poet incomplete and with his work unread. Increasingly, Jim's small inner circle of friends was composed of those who seemed to him to comprehend his absolute devotion to this struggle and to accept its mixture of integrity, asceticism, and desperation. To be Jim's friend at this point was often a bit of a challenge. As one of Jim's few straight male friends, I was asked to lend a disinterested ear to Jim's tales of his infatuations and troubled love affairs, which tended to end badly. And I of course was too young and inept to offer any useful counsel. Several times Jim felt he was on the verge of forming a lasting partnership with one of his lovers, but in every case these liaisons faltered. By the end of his life, Jim's sexual encounters were limited to anonymous couplings in a Hennepin Avenue bathhouse—this was several years before the emergence of AIDS—a place where I'd often drop him off, for Jim never learned to drive, after our dinners or meetings to discuss our poems. As Jim resigned himself to the *I give up* of finding love, however, his obsession with the *why* of art grew more pervasive, in both good ways and bad. On the one hand, his poems grew more stark, Cavafian, and heartbreaking.

"Making Love to Myself," both rhapsodic in its eroticism and a work of the deepest resignation, is Jim's version of Cavafy poems such as "Days of 1908" and "The Bandaged Shoulder":

Making Love to Myself

When I do it I remember how it was with us.
Then my hands remember too,
and you're with me again, just the way it was.

After work you'd come in and turn the TV off and sit on the edge of the bed,
filling the room with gasoline smell from your overalls,
trying not to wake me which you always did.
I'd breathe out long and say,
'His Jess, you tired, baby?'
You'd say not so bad and rub my belly,
not after me, really, just being sweet,
and I always thought I'd die a little
because you smelt like burnt leaves or woodsmoke.

We were poor as Job's turkey but we lived well—
the food, a few good movies, good dope, lots of talk,
lots of you and me trying on each other's skin.

What a sweet gift this is,
done with my memory, my cock and hands.

Sometimes I'd wake up wondering if I should fix
coffee for us before work,
almost thinking you're here again, almost seeing
your work jacket on the chair.

I wonder if you remember what
we promised when you took that job in Laramie?
Our way of staying with each other.
We promised there'd always be times
when the sky was perfectly lucid,
that we could remember each other through that.
You could remember me at my worktable
or in the all-night diners,
though we'd never call or write.

I have to stop here Jess.
I just have to stop.[6]

As with Cavafy's erotic poems, the portraiture here is spare but acutely cast, and the poem's narrative framework—the masturbatory fantasy as the catalyst for the story of the couple's relationship—helps to create the plain-spoken but very surprising and affecting turn in the poem's final stanza. In its combination of minimalism and madrigal-like grace notes, it is perhaps the most characteristic of Jim's later poems. But it is also the sort of poem that had no place in the mainstream of American poetry in the late 1970s.

Jim finished *The Salt Ecstacies* around 1978, thanks largely to a writing grant from the Bush Foundation. He had great hopes for the book, but his efforts at finding a publisher for it looked as though they would come to nothing. Jim was obsessed with the hope that the book would be brought out by a major publisher. The small presses that released Jim's previous work could never offer Jim the sort of distribution and readership he craved for *The Salt Ecstacies.* And he feared that even if he were to offer the book to one of these presses, the editors would blanch at the newfound sexual frankness of a poet who had previously been identified with a mere picturesque regionalism. He felt equally uneasy with the possibility of sending the book to a house which specialized in gay poetry—there were very few of them in those days, and he felt that to publish with such a press would ghettoize his work. So Jim engaged in a quixotic mission to have the book appear from a trade house, despite a fear that trade publishers would be even more apt to find his work too specialized, too gay. The commercial presses were for the most part uninterested, of course. But in two or three instances it seemed that Jim was close to being offered a contract. The rejections, coming after Jim had allowed his hopes to soar, were especially painful, and he railed against a pair of editors who he felt had lead him on and against the work of poets these editors had taken on instead of Jim. Such a chronicle of rejection is typical for even the best of contemporary poets, but it went on at the same time as Jim's health continued its precipitous decline. His heart attacks grew more frequent, and on more than one occasion he found himself opening his rejection slips after his mail had been brought to him in intensive care. *The Salt Ecstacies* had become Jim's sole legacy.

By this time I had moved away from Minneapolis to attend graduate school in Arizona, and because one of my teachers there, Tess Gallagher, had been a judge for the Bush Foundation grant that Jim had received, he enlisted me in the struggle with *Salt.* He'd had another heart attack, and called me one day shortly after he'd been released from the hospital. Would I make a copy of *The Salt Ecstacies* and give it to Tess? Perhaps she could use her connections to help Jim find a publisher for the book. So that week I went to Tess's office with the manuscript, explaining something of Jim's situation and asking if she'd read the collection and write Jim with her appraisal. Remembering Jim's work from the Bush competition, she eagerly agreed to look at the manuscript and, over the next few years, became a tireless champion of Jim's work. She not only read the book but also offered Jim a flurry of editorial advice: not just regarding the arrangement of the poems but also line-by-line criticism of almost all of the manuscript's efforts. In some cases she suggested fairly radical alterations for the poems, most of which Jim adopted. Although certain of her suggestions now seem to me a bit ill-advised—Jim's early versions of some of the poems strike me as more elegant and musical than those which emerged after Tess's blue-pencilings—the best of her advice was superb, especially in regard to matters of style: her edits helped Jim's tonal and dictional shifts, one of his greatest strengths, to seem even more abrupt and surprising. Just as importantly, I think, Tess became a supportive correspondent; the two began a regular and affectionate exchange of letters that continued until Jim's death. Thanks to Tess's encouragement and promises to help him find a publisher for *The Salt Ecstacies,* Jim went back to his poems with a renewed vigor, dropping a number of less successful pieces from the manuscript and adding a small number of new poems.

One of these new poems Jim read to me when we met during one of my visits home; it was inspired by a conversation Jim had recently had with his cardiologist, a former navy doctor, who had in his youth worked in a military hospital for tertiary syphilitics. Given that so many of Jim's recent poems had alluded to illness, the title of the poem, "Syphilis Prior to Penicillin" came as no surprise. But that the poem, like "An Ordinary Composure," asked to be read as an ars poetica came as a considerable surprise:

Syphilis Prior to Penicillin

The United States Coast Guard had a
hospital for it in New York until 1952.
My doctor said if you knew syphilis
you knew medicine because it
perfectly imitated other diseases.
That in the last stages when it went rampant,
(besides their minds)
sailors would lose a nose or ear,
the disease mimicking leprosy.

And it was never cured or stabilized
so the sailors carried themselves as
loaded weapons into every port.

The whores could never really tell either
for they were eaten with it too.
Those who knew their condition
often banded together
trying not to infect others with
a "taste for the mud" as the French say.

They were a cavalier and doomed lot,
trying to hold back the dawn
in their foreign hotels,
where the night porters filled rooms
with verbena and gardenias
to hide the cooking smell of sulfur ointments.

At the last there were signs they couldn't hide.
The motor nerves giving way so they walked with
odd flickering steps. That's why Amelia and Rose Montana
would sit the evening through playing mah-jong,
and the old sailors, Paul and James,
rarely asked the whores to dance.[7]

The offhand but precise descriptions, and the mixture of wry portraiture and grotesquerie, are characteristic of Jim's best work. So too is the poem's empathy for those who "dwell outside the tribe." Whether they be syphilitics, queers, poets, or queer-poets, the poem builds its allegory with a rueful tenderness. "I think," said Jim when he'd read me the poem, "that you and I must be Paul and James." The cavalier and doomed lot: although the label undoubtedly seeks to valorize these roles, it is also slyly ironic. As Jim once put it in a conversation about a mutual friend, "P—— is too *dumb* to be anything but a poet."

Cavalier, doomed, and dumb: in *The Salt Ecstacies* the poem is dedicated to me.

Yet for Jim, *doomed* seemed already the sole way to describe his future. His letters and phone conversations with me showed him even closer to despair about his work. His book continued to be rejected, despite Tess's efforts on Jim's part, despite his recent revisions of the collection. More importantly, Jim's heart condition had worsened, and he knew the end was near. He'd made out a will, and though he still continued to sit at zazen, he had also started attending services, renewing his childhood connection to the Episcopal church. His most serious heart attack yet had occurred in early 1981, and while he was in intensive care another attack took place, during which Jim died: in the minute or two before he was brought back, he had an especially intense near-death experience. He saw himself walking down a long corridor, a huge Anglican cathedral on his left, a long candle-lit row of Buddhas on his right. I was living on Cape Cod at that point, and my calls to Jim as he languished on ICU were dispiriting. The drugs he was being given made him sound confused and groggy; he seemed already resigned to what one of his poems describes as giving "silently all and everything into dying."

But a day or two later I heard from Jim again. He had just received a call—put through to him in intensive care—from Scott Walker, publisher of Graywolf Press. *The Salt Ecstacies* had finally found a publisher, thanks in large part to Tess's lobbying on the book's behalf. I honestly think that this phone call permitted Jim the four more months he had to live; without it, he would have died on the hospital ward. But now he was permitted what he called "a brief remission" and the knowledge that his book could assure him a posthumous life.

A few weeks later I was back in Minneapolis, living there until I could find something to do with my own life. I'd gotten by for the past year on a writing fellowship from the Fine Arts Work Center in Provincetown, but now the fellowship was over and my prospects were nill: no book of my own—though I'd been circulating my manuscript—and no possibility of finding the teaching jobs I'd been applying for. I saw Jim often during this period, and his spirits were for once very high; his health had temporarily stabilized, and he was ecstatic about the pending publication of his book. My own spirits, however, were in the cellar. Yet suddenly, within the space of two days, I'd found a teaching job at the University of New Orleans—it would begin the following autumn—and then was informed by Richard Hugo that my book was his selection for that year's Yale Younger Poets Prize. One of the best things about my delight at this good news was to see how pleased it made Jim, who had gone over my manuscript with his usual gentle acuity, and he spoke about my luck with a kind of avuncular glee. We now shared some good fortune, some cause for celebration: the cavalier lot more than the doomed. And in June of 1981 it turned out that Jim would finally have a chance to meet Tess Gallagher in person. She was spending the summer in Wisconsin, acting in a friend's independent film project, and had arranged to fly to Minneapolis for a weekend.

I did not suspect it at the time, but this was also to be Jim's weekend of farewells. We drove to the airport to meet Tess's plane, and at Jim's apartment I watched the two of them spend several hours chattering like long-lost friends. Two incidents from that afternoon stand out. First, Jim suddenly rinsed out the cups and teapot of the antique Japanese tea set we were drinking from and presented the pot and two of the cups to Tess. "When you drink from this," he told her, "I want you to fill both cups—and to think of me." It was the sort of sudden sentimental gesture—not to mention liturgical one—that I had seen Jim make before, but this time it was accompanied by a kind of solemn gravity that took both Tess and me by surprise. The conversation stalled for a minute. But then Jim's doorbell rang—it was a FedEx courier, bearing the proofs of *The Salt Ecstacies.* We sat around Jim's kitchen table for awhile and admired them.

Later the three of us, joined by an ex-student of Tess's who would play host to her for the rest of the weekend, had dinner in a Japanese restaurant, and I dropped Jim off at his apartment. I was probably the last person to see him alive. Two days later, Jim's body was discovered by his friend George Roberts, who had a key to the apartment and was worried when Jim did not answer his phone. He'd died in his sleep. On his bedside table were the proofs of *The Salt Ecstacies,* his glasses folded on top of them. One year after Jim's death, *The Salt Ecstacies* appeared, in a simple and elegant edition. I wish that I could say that the book received attention, but of course even the best books of contemporary poetry are for the most part ignored, and posthumous collections tend to suffer from an even greater neglect. Still, the name of James L. White remains alive. There is, in fact, a tiny but fervent cult. Patricia Hampl has published a wonderfully unmournful and ebullient elegy for him. And in 1983, while we were browsing in a Vermont bookstore, I convinced my friend Mark Doty to purchase a copy of *The Salt Ecstacies,* and I am sure that Jim would have been pleased to know that he has influenced the work of one of the principal poets of my generation. Mark's 1991 collection, *Bethlehem in Broad Daylight,* contains a masterful elegy for Jim. It is an ambitious sort of threnody, mixing an autobiographical narrative about the speaker's own coming out with an ardent and celebratory meditation on the meaning of desire. The poem ends with an almost prayerful address to Jim: "And so I want you to wake again / in longing, like the rest of us." And Jim would surely have been thrilled to know that one of the better known gay literary magazines is called *The James White Review.* But given the tenor of literary politics in our era and the financial realities of poetry publishing, Jim's cult will, I fear, always remain a small one. At one point several years ago Kate Green, Jim's literary executor, gave me access to all of Jim's manuscripts and notebooks. We had the notion that there might be enough strong unpublished work to warrant the publication of a collected poems. But only a handful of unpublished and uncollected poems exist, and Jim had for the most part rejected the work which appeared before *The Salt Ecstacies.* Jim wanted *Salt* to be his sole legacy, and so it will continue to be.

Jim's mother, Marie White, whom Jim had written about with such tenderness, lies buried beside him, sharing with Jim a rose-colored granite stone in a vile Indianapolis cemetery. "Together Forever," the stone reads. The place is huge, and abuts an even larger sprawl of suburban shopping centers and strip malls. From the gravesite you can look up beyond the fence to a noisy boulevard of fast-food joints and tanning parlors. And in this it recalls the graves of my parents, who wanted to lie in a military cemetery in St. Paul, their gravesite only yards from a cyclone fence which scrapes against the runway lights of Twin Cities International Airport. Look in the opposite direction, and you can see the parking lot of Minnesota's premier tourist attraction, "The World's Largest Shopping Mall." In the Midwest, tawdriness is destiny. And in February, in the Washington Park East Cemetery of Indianapolis, the brown disheveled grass and the equally brown Christmas garlands that still pock so many of the graves endow the landscape with a starker sort of barrenness, with the "plain sense of things" described in the Stevens poem, a place where it is "difficult even to choose the adjective / for this blank cold." That Jim, after his career of such unceasing wandering, should now lie here, in this bleakest parody of home, seems a final brutal irony. But home, for poets, is the cadence of the written word and not a place. And I would like to believe that Jim White's monument is not only the small but graceful mausoleum of *The Salt Ecstacies* but also his voice as it echoes—faintly and distantly perhaps, but always hauntedly—in the work of those poets who have read him well. It is to Jim White—who urged me to become a poet—and to Lynda Hull—whose finest book also appeared a year after her death, and who showed me during the decade of our marriage what it meant to live as a poet—that I owe my identity as a writer. These shades are my truest and only mentors. That I am the one who can write this, the letters unscrolling blue on the computer screen, seems today a blessing, and I am instructed again to form these words with lapidary care, to be mindful that these characters I shape shall always be written to honor these my teachers, my difficult masters—as legacy, as elegy, as homage. For it is of them, my masters and my masters' words, that I am now composed.

(1996)

II.

6.

"Mad Means Something": Anger, Invective, and the Period Style

The subject of the following epigram by Catullus, the "putresecent Victius," merits only the most brusque of footnotes in Charles Martin's recent versions of Catullus. "Victius," we're told, "is unidentifiable." Here, two thousand years later, is what remains of Victius's memory, Catullus's ninety-eighth epigram:

> What everyone says of pretentious, babbling asses,
> fits you, if anyone, putresecent Victius:
> that tongue of yours is perfectly suited for scouring
> the rudest rustic's leathery boots and asshole.
> If you should ever decide to wipe us out utterly, Victius,
> open your mouth: just utter your wish and it's granted.[1]

Readers familiar with Catullus might observe that Rome's most vitriolic poet is being uncharacteristically gentle in his invective here. Yes, Victius eats shit, but shit-eating is a relatively minor and common offense when compared to the failings and exotic perversions which Catullus associates with many of Victius's peers. Romans of the late Republic and early Imperial period seem to have happily indulged in behaviors which contemporary readers would label, at the very least, as "antisocial." Rome's other great curmudgeon, Martial, for example, makes note of an acquaintance's penchant for bestiality ("People have the weirdest kinks / My friend Flaccus fancies, ears and all, a lynx").[2] Although we may remember Catullus best for his agonized, ambivalent obsession with his beloved (and bedevilling) Lesbia, Catullus's skill with invective is nearly as memorable. It was a dangerous skill of course: his epigrams addressed to Julius Caesar's mistress Mamarra made Catullus something of a pariah, and the supposed indecency of many of Catullus's poems caused his reputation to be eclipsed for nearly twenty centuries in favor of the work of more stolid and moralizing figures, such as Horace. We now say that Catullus's sensibility was more "modern" than that of Horace, and thus his rediscovery had to wait until the twentieth century. And although we might see a Catullan skill with rant and insult emerging in certain key Modernist and contemporary texts—*The Cantos,* for example, or the Gatling-gun assaults on "Moloch" in *Howl*—the fact remains that mainstream contemporary poetry finds it difficult to admit any degree of anger and invective and, even when it does, seems unable to employ them with much success.

This is a bit surprising when one considers that contemporary American poets have a good many things which they can rightly claim to be angry about—abusive childhoods, sexual and racial bigotry, bad love, and the stupidity of politicians. Yet such subjects are dealt with badly, when they are dealt with at all. Has a single good poem emerged as a result of the Gulf War? Have the turgid poems of Sharon Olds cornered the market on the issue of parental abuse of children? Are elegy and, more rarely, a kind of unfocused anger the sole pair of responses poets can have to the AIDS epidemic? Contemporary poetry, its detractors say, has grown insular and marginal. And when I ask the above questions, I fear that the detractors' criticism may have some validity, for the absence of invective in our poetry, its general lack of a truly empowering variety of anger, may suggest that we have chosen stances which actively invite marginality. Put simply, most contemporary poems aim for a particular sort of emotional and tonal decorum that will not admit emotions as messy and unwieldy as anger or, for that matter, the wide array of complicated and ambivalent emotional responses to our lives which people truly feel. One sees such emotional and tonal range in much of the poetry of recent African American writers and in that of other people of color, who have consistently raised their voices in often outraged opposition to society's injustices. But the vast majority of American poets have, unfortunately, not heard their cries. To admit any degree of emotional range into our poems is emphatically not a part of our agendas: the curse of the contemporary poet is that he or she is supposed to be nice.

What do I mean by tonal and emotional decorum, by niceness? It is interestingly alluded to in a recent interview Celia Farber conducted with our most indecorous of literary critics, Camille Paglia. Although Paglia is of course more interested in speaking vitriolically about pet peeves such as feminism and the contemporary academic, she also adds, rather blithely, that "no one reads poetry anymore." In the course of the pages which follow, Farber attempts, among other things, to find some reasons for poetry's lack of audience:

> I asked a friend of mine who is a poet about this, and he said, "Now that you mention it, I would never sit down to write a poem if I was feeling very emotional and intense. I guard my poetry, in a way, against passion, because I'm afraid of seeming trite."[3]

A statement like this allows us to deduce an unusually large percentage of the tics and knee-jerk responses found in the contemporary poem. As the anonymous poet says, our tendency is to explicate rather than to evoke or seem to reexperience the emotions which prompt the poem. And for all the ascendency of a supposedly self-oriented poetry that occurred in the poetry of the 1960s and 1970s in Confessional and Deep Image writing, the self in its frustratingly anarchic complexity has a relatively minor place in the contemporary poem. Mainstream poets tend to efface the self through an elegiac stance—hence the numbingly large number of poems pining about childhood or mourning dead family, friends, and public figures—or to mask the self in persona poems. Language poets ascribe to the aesthetic cop-out of dismissing the self entirely, claiming it is merely one of many dubious linguistic constructs. With a wholly effaced self acting as narrator of the poem, it is no wonder that the poet must "guard . . . against passion." The following poem (the poet will remain nameless) seems to me typical of the period style:

Starlings

As if the tree itself
were straining to fly off,
peppering the branches,
the hiss of shuffled cards,
until they're more than she
can bear. Earthbound, shouting
in her nightgown she stumbles
out with a spoon, a lobster pot

to fend them off, though always
they return, until by sundown
nothing disturbs their sleep.
Derision so absolute
she's weeping in the porch light's
yellow arc, the evening
choked with them. I wake
to spy her from my room,

the noise like tin-roof rain.
Probably she's drunk
again. It's probably a night
my father is two thousand
miles away, unloading

on some Indian reservation
    mailsacks from a baggage car.
I know she'll stay awake

    all night. I'll rise again
at five—the clock face's radium
    shimmer—then creep into
the livingroom, where finally
    she's bowed her head,
her romance fallen open
    on the carpet, the pages
trembling in the morning breeze.

    Outside, they're waking too,
their *sh sh sh* a sound
    at first I think is meant
to quiet us. I want to slither
    into her lap. I want to be
the book she reads, before the noise
    begins to deafen us, before
she wakes and never sleeps again.[4]

The poet possesses a certain skill with current poetic vernacular. There's a hushed, incantatory quality in the writing. The loose iambic tetrameter seems an appropriate meter for the poem, helping to imbue it with a dream-like, almost visionary tone that seems appropriate for an effort which seeks to recapture an event from childhood. The dramatic situation is fairly engaging, too. The scene of the mother banging on the pan to frighten away the starlings has some vigor, and the presence of the swarm of birds, described through both visual and auditory imagery, gives an eerie symbolic undertone to the relationship between the mother and the son (the author of the poem is male). The tone is melancholy, elegiac, and seems modeled on the recently-quite-fashionable poems about childhood of Elizabeth Bishop. Yet where Bishop's reticence about her difficult childhood gives her poems of recollection their majestic authority, in "Starlings" we see a writer seeking to skirt the most compelling issues at stake in the poem. Although the poem rather coyly alludes to some very loaded topics—the mother's apparent alcoholism, the father's absence, the son's perception of the mother's emotional distance from him, and the son's Oedipal feelings toward the mother—it seems to me that the poem's refusal to confront these issues in any way but through a passive and elegiac acknowledgment of them causes the poem to fail. In some degree the poem effectively replicates the child's perceptions as he tentatively tries to understand his feelings toward his mother. But is it not fair to ask that this poem—and the hundreds of poems one could name that resemble it—more complexly explore the emotional and psychological issues which it has implied? Yes, we know how the speaker felt as a child, but is it not fair to ask how he feels now, as an adult? Reticence, as we know from Bishop's greatest poems, can be empowering. But it can also be confining and dishonest—dishonest because reticence can seek to simplify emotions that are obsessive, strongly felt, or ambivalent. Writing with Bishopian reserve lets the poet of "Starlings" smooth out the rumpled bed of his emotions. Yet the feelings which seem to prompt the poem are more messy than this. And they are more contradictory. Contradiction, however, is not permitted within the confines of the stylistic parameters of "Starlings": the speaker seems to be both compelled and guilt-ridden by his Oedipal feelings, both tender and angry at the mother, and he seems not to have resolved these conflicts. Instead of opting to present the conflicts *as conflicts* the poet opts for the kind of easy wish fulfillment that characterizes so many competently written but finally mediocre poems. The poet has presented the "nice" side that seems his best profile, but the real issues at stake in the poem demand that he confront feelings that are "not so nice."

I want to contrast the above effort with a much more interesting poem by James Wright. It comes from his 1972 volume, *Two Citizens,* a collection much derided, even by Wright's strongest advocates, and in effect disowned by the poet himself.[5] Yet to my mind *Two Citizens,* for all its unevenness, is perhaps Wright's most interesting individual volume, for in many of its poems Wright divests himself of a habit of covering with a patina of lyricality even his most scathing portraits and descriptions. Wright's anthology pieces, such as "Autumn Begins in Martins Ferry, Ohio," seem finally to sugarcoat those forces which Wright so strongly seeks to condemn. Not so "Ars Poetica: Some Recent Criticism," which opens *Two Citizens.* The poem unfolds slowly, but Wright has stated that its ultimate goal is to elaborate a curse.[6] Here is section 1:

> I loved my country
> When I was a little boy.
> Agnes is my aunt
> And she doesn't even know
> If I love anything
> On this God's
> Green little apple.

I have no idea why Uncle Sherman
Who is dead
Fell in with her.
He wasn't all that drunk.
He longed all life long
To open a package store,
And he never did anything.
But he fell in with Agnes.
She is no more to me
Than my mind is,
Which I bless. She was a homely woman
In the snow, alone.

Sherman sang bad
But he could sing.
I too have fallen in
With a luminous woman.

There must be something.

The only bright thing
Agnes ever did
That I know of
Was to get hurt and angry.
When Sherman met my other uncle
Emerson Buchanan, who thinks he is not dead,
At the wedding of Agnes
Uncle Emerson smirked:
"What's the use buying a cow,
When you can get the milk free?"

She didn't weep.
She got mad.
Mad means something.
"You guys are making
Fun out of me."[7]

Rambling, by turns garrulous and terse, the poem appears to go off in several directions at once. We have a thesis-like opening pair of lines, but the decidedly awkward passage completing the first stanza seems to bear no relation to the opening. The movement of the section is made even more choppy by the flat diction, lack of enjambment, predictable stanza breaks, and seemingly pointless tangents ("I too have fallen in / with a luminous woman").

There's an intimacy to the tone, yet we have no clear idea who is being addressed. The manner is too rhetorical to seem a private, hermetic meditation, yet the identity of the audience is by no means certain. And the portraits of Aunt Agnes and the two uncles are so gruffly sardonic that we almost long for the passive sorts of portrayal found in "Starlings." No one is idealized, but Wright tellingly insists that "The only bright thing / Agnes ever did . . . / Was to get hurt and angry," that "Mad means something."

Section 2 continues in this scathing fashion. "She stank / Her house stank." Uncle Sherman is characterized as "One of the heroes of love, because he lay down / With my Aunt Agnes / Twice at least." This fact strikes the speaker as so sadly remarkable that he must insist upon it: "Listen, lay down with her / Even when she went crazy." It is through an aside such as this, and through an even more pointed one in section 3—"I could tell you, / If you have read this far / That the nut house in Cambridge / Where Agnes is dying / Is no more Harvard than you will ever be"—that we at last start to suspect that we ourselves are the object of Wright's curse. The poem's moment of highest drama, if one could call it that, describes Agnes saving a circus goat from the cruelty of a group of young boys:

> 4.
> Why do I care for her,
> That slob,
> So fat and stupid?
> One afternoon
> At Aetnaville, Ohio,
> A broken goat escaped
> From a carnival,
> From one of those hooch dances
> They used to hold
> Down by the river.
> Scrawny the goat panicked
> Down Agnes' alley,
> Which is my country,
> If you haven't noticed,
> America,
> Which I loved when I was young.
>
> 5.
> The goat ran down the alley
> And many boys giggled
> While they tried to stone our fellow
> Goat to death.

And my Aunt Agnes
Who stank and lied,
Threw stones back at the boys
And gathered the goat,
Nuts as she was,
Into her sloppy arms.

Despite the deliberately awkward style, these sections show a highly complex and sly design. Without idealizing Agnes, Wright makes the reader understand that her minor heroic act is one of genuine tenderness and purity. Similarly, another seemingly random aside about the speaker's boyhood love for his country has forced the reader to almost involuntarily identify him/herself with the cruel gang of boys and, by extension, with "America." We are now aware of how painstakingly Wright strived to create these links. In the section which follows Wright tightens the noose, performing the familiar rhetorician's trick of denying one's actual intentions at the very moment when they are being most explicitly stressed:

6.
Reader,
We had a lovely language.
We would not listen.
I don't believe in your God.
I don't believe my Aunt Agnes is a Saint.
I don't believe the little boys
Who stoned the poor
Son of a bitch goat
Are charming
Tom Sawyers.

I don't believe in the goat either.

"Mad means something," remember, and now Wright has found the moment when the poem's anger has found its most focused power. The poem's final section:

7.
When I was a boy
I loved my country.

Ense petit placidam
Sub libertate quietam.

Hell, I ain't got nothing.
Ah, you bastards,

How I hate you.

This is a most unsettling conclusion, a curse upon us and a curse upon America. (One of *Two Citizens*'s later poems uses as its title the well-known line from *The Man Without a Country*—"I Wish That I May Never Hear of the United States Again.") The plainspoken viciousness of the final three lines, ironically set against the sentence in Latin (from Horace: "With the sword he seeks a calm repose under liberty"), bring the poem to a powerful closure, one arguably as memorable as those of Wright's more flashy and adamantly lyrical poems. Like Wright's famous "Lying in a Hammock at William Dufy's Farm in Pine Island, Minnesota," "Ars Poetica" follows a highly deliberate structure designed to achieve its effect by continually subverting the reader's expectations. Although its raw and aggressive texture will no doubt keep it out of the *Norton Anthology*, one might argue that "Ars Poetica" is one of Wright's most urgent and complex poems.

Of course, I by no means seek to imply that simply by acknowledging feelings of anger can writers point the way to memorable poetry. A poem which successfully brings forth anger and invective realizes, as Wright's "Ars Poetica" does, that these emotions are as highly volatile in poems as they are in public life. Mindless rage is an ineffective poetic tool, and impressive poems of invective tend to focus their rage through any of a number of structural and formal devices that channel and focus the tenor of the speaker's invective. The epigram immediately comes to mind; in the work of Catullus and Martial, and even at times in that of twentieth-century figures such as J. V. Cunningham, the strictness of meter and rhyme distills the writer's message to a highly compact snarl. In "Ars Poetica: Some Recent Criticism," Wright employs a more subtle but no less focused set of devices—in this case rhetorical devices rather than metrical ones—to achieve a similar effect. For a poem of invective to work as it should, a writer must in most cases be especially careful to counterbalance the development of his/her argument with structural or formal devices which sharpen and underscore the writer's conviction and rage. Richard Wilbur's well-known adage about the advantage of meter and rhyme over free verse might apply to the poem of invective: "the genie is always more powerful when imprisoned in the bottle." The Genie of Invective seems to work his most powerful magic when he asks the poet to speak in form, or via an insistent device such as anaphora (consider "Howl" again), or within the confines of a carefully constructed conceit.

When such counterbalancing elements are absent or poorly executed, the poem of invective will probably fail at its goal. Consider the following effort by Sharon Olds, "History: 13":

> When I found my father that night, the blood
> smeared on his head and face, I did not
> know who had done it. I had loved his body
> whole, his head, his face, untouched
> and now he floated on the couch, his arms
> up, like Mussolini hanging
> upside down in the air, his head
> dangling where they could reach him with boards and their
> fingernails, those who had lived
> under his tyranny.
> I saw how the inside of the body could be
> brought to the surface, to cover the skin,
> his heart standing on his face, the weight of his
> body pressing down on his head,
> his life slung in the bag of his scalp,
> and who had done it? Had I, had my mother,
> my brother, my sister, we who had been silent
> under him, under him for years? He lay in his
> gore all night, as the body hung all
> day in the gas station in
> Milan, and when they helped him up and
> washed him and he left, I did not see it—
> I was not there for the ashes, I had been there
> only for the fire, I had seen my father
> strung and mottled, mauled as if taken and
> raked by a crowd, and I of the crowd
> over his body, and how could the day be
> good after that, how could anything be good
> in such a world, I turned my back
> on happiness, at 13 I entered
> a life of mourning, of mourning for the Fascist.[8]

Those who are familiar with her poems know that, like Pound, Plath, and Lowell, Olds has a thing about dictators. In another of her poems Olds elaborately likens the speaker's sister to Hitler triumphantly riding into Paris. And, to be charitable to "History: 13," one could argue that Olds does at least as competent a job with dead-Mussolini imagery as Pound brings off in *The Pisan Cantos,* which obsessively return to the image of the corpses of "The Boss" and his mistress, Clara Petacci, hoisted upside-down above a Milan gas station. But of course Pound is referring to the real Mussolini, not to Mussolini as a symbol of the repressiveness of the speaker's father. Clearly, "History: 13" is an angry poem, meant to curse the father for the insidious legacy he has willed to his daughter. But the poem has little of the clarity and strong sense of purpose of an effective curse and fails to emerge as anything more than a rather miasmic rant.

What goes wrong? Two crucial problems immediately come to mind. First, the poem gives us no clear dramatic context upon which Olds can build her conceit. The memory which prompts the poem—the adolescent speaker seeing her father lying on a couch, bleeding from a head wound—is a highly charged one. Yet Olds never even begins to answer our most obvious question: what caused him to appear to her like this? A domestic squabble? Some fight he has been involved with on the street or in some bar? Although the speaker tells us that when she first witnessed this event she did not know why the father had been wounded, her refusal to tell us what happened remains a continual source of exasperation for the reader, for to know why the father had been wounded will help us to understand why the speaker must compare him to Mussolini. Admittedly, children in abusive and alcoholic families are prone to blame themselves for the family's woes, a dynamic Olds hints at in line 16 ("and who had done it? Had I, had my mother"). But in this case we must understand why the father was wounded if the risky Mussolini conceit is to be effective. (Even later in the poem, when a mysterious "they"—the mother and sisters? ambulance attendants?—come to look after the father, the enigma remains.) Olds builds her metaphorical house upon sand.

But an absence of a context for the conceit only partially explains why the poem is ineffective. Part of Olds's problem is that she insists upon the urgency of comparing the bleeding father to the dead Mussolini while at the same time failing to satisfyingly elaborate upon the comparison. The conceit first emerges in line 6 of the poem, and just when we suspect that Olds will embark upon a point-by-point comparison of the father to the dead dictator and of the family to the dictator's subjects, she veers off upon a less promising tangent. We are suddenly subjected to a badly done meditation upon blood, replete with mixed metaphors and nonsequiturs:

> I saw how the inside of the body could be
> brought to the surface, to cover the skin,
> his heart standing on his face, the weight of his
> body pressing down on his head,
> his life slung in the bag of his scalp. . . .

Although Olds later tries to link this motif with the Mussolini motif ("He lay in his / gore all night, as the body hung all / day in the gas station in / Milan"), the effort seems clumsy at best.

The misuse of metaphor intensifies in the final passages of the poem: the puzzling "I was not there for the ashes, I had been there / only for the fire . . . ."; the ambiguity of Olds's application of tenor and vehicle in "I had seen my father / strung and mottled, mauled as if taken and / raked by a crowd, and I og the crowd / over his body. . . ." The comma splices and seemingly random enjambments don't help matters, of course. One might excuse this wild inconsistency of metaphor if this were an exercise in the deliberate irrationality of surrealism, but Olds clearly has sought to make the poem a more systematic effort at conceit-making. Yet once the conceit emerges it grows confused and contradictory. A taut and strictly elaborated use of the Mussolini conceit may have given Olds the ability to effectively structure and empower the resentment which so obviously charges her poem. But, as it stands, both Il Duce and the father get the better of the writer. (As one of the not-very-vocal minority who find Plath's "Daddy" one of her least successful poems, I wonder if this has something to do with the problematic nature, both politically and aesthetically, of almost all Nazi and Fascist references and imagery in poetry: Celan's "Fugue of Death," arguably the greatest poem about the Holocaust, confronts the spectre of Nazism in a decidedly elliptical fashion. Similarly, the century's most biting poet of invective, Bertolt Brecht, who suffered directly the consequences of Nazism, only rarely refers to Hitler by name in his political poems. Brecht achieves a greater sardonic effect by instead repeatedly referring to Der Führer as "The Housepainter.")

I would like to contrast the misdirected stridency of Olds's poem with a more complex and successful effort, "Tiara," by Mark Doty. Ostensibly an elegy set during the funeral service for a man who has died of AIDS, yet soon veering from this setting into a lengthy lyrical reverie, the poem's fundamental purpose is nevertheless as much one of invective as that of "Ars Poetica: Some Recent Criticism." The poem's anger emerges slowly and at first appears in a seemingly offhand fashion. Yet we eventually see that the poem's narrative and lyrical elements are designed to be at the service of impassioned argument against a particularly puritanical (and particularly American) form of moralizing. The poem begins in a leisurely but unsettling fashion, cataloguing the forced jocularity we so often encounter at wakes:

> Peter died in a paper tiara
> cut from a book of princess paper dolls;
> he loved royalty, sashes,

and jewels. *I don't know,*
he said, when he woke in the hospice,
I was watching the Bette Davis film festival

on Channel 57 and then—
At the wake, the tension broke
when someone guessed

the casket closed because
he was *in there in a big wig*
and heels, and someone said,

You know he's always late,
he probably isn't there yet—
he's still fixing his makeup.

And someone said he asked for it.[9]

One can almost sense the silence that surely entered the room as this last statement was made. In terms of the poem's immediate dramatic context it's a remark of such overt insensitivity that it brings the poem to an abrupt halt. And we should bear in mind that the remark comes not from a homophobic fundamentalist preacher or Republican congressman, but from one of the deceased's own mourners. One would imagine that after reporting a gaffe such as this the poet would now have the opportunity to counter the statement's glibness with an outraged reply. Yet Doty's response is more intricate than this. He instead repeats the remark and uses it as the catalyst for a passage of erotic lyricality designed at first, in the classic manner of elegy, to justify and beautify Peter's life:

Asked for it—
when all he did was go down

into the salt tide
of wanting as much as he wanted,
giving himself over so drunk

it didn't matter who,
though they were beautiful,
stampeding into him in the simple,

ravishing music of their hurry.

Doty does not stop here, however, and shifts the patterns of imagery once again. In the fashion of mystical literature ranging from *The Song of Songs* to the visions of St. Teresa of Avila, Doty now insists that the erotic and the spiritual are deeply entwined. Doty sees Peter's longings as an intrinsically human yearning for paradise, be it earthly or heavenly:

> I think heaven is perfect stasis
> poised over the realms of desire
>
> where dreaming and waking men lie
> on the grass while wet horses
> roam among them, huge fragments
>
> of the music we die into
> in the body's paradise.
> Sometimes we wake not knowing
>
> how we came to lie here,
> and who has crowned us with these temporary
> precious stones.

Behind this lyrical reverie is a highly deliberate rhetorical design. Perhaps even more significant than the imagery itself is Doty's shift from the seemingly reportorial style of the opening passage to the highly subjective, even declamatory, vision of "heaven" as "perfect stasis." This gesture is almost immediately followed by another shift in point of view, to the first-person plural. We are asked to identify with Peter as we wake "crowned with these temporary / precious stones." This is a tried and true rhetorician's tool of course: begin the argument anecdotally, sharpen it with a statement of personal conviction, and end with an exhortation which the audience will now wholeheartedly accept. Once this has been achieved, one can also, as Doty now does, devastate the opposition.

> And given
>
> the world's perfectly turned shoulders,
> the deep hollows blued by longing,
> given the irreplaceable silk
>
> of horses rippling in orchards,
> fruit thundering and chiming down,
> given the ordinary marvels of form

and gravity, what could he do,
what could any of us ever do
but ask for it?

In these final stanzas we are again reminded that the poem's underlying purpose is not simply to elegize Peter but also to silence his detractors, all those who would take the intricate dramas of human sexuality and even spiritual aspiration and reduce them to cautionary tales about character failings and the advisability of safe sex. This crude reductiveness, so chillingly exemplified by "he asked for it," is masterfully subverted by Doty as he turns this very statement into the poem's sorrowful but triumphant conclusion. Like the work of many other contemporary gay poets, Doty's cannot cavalierly separate personal issues such as the death of a friend or acquaintance from public issues such as the AIDS epidemic and society's insensitivities to it. The world Doty dwells in is too complex and troubling to allow for easy and simplistic stances.

And yet it is an unfortunate fact that most of us long for easy and simplistic stances, as people and—especially—as poets. The doomsayers who write the invariable semiannual reports of contemporary poetry's collapse—Dana Gioia in *The Atlantic* last year and Joseph Epstein a bit less recently in *The American Scholar*—to a large degree pine for a poetry of simplistic homily, although such longings are disguised as calls for a poetry of "memorability," a poetry which speaks to the man on the street. Poets themselves, despite their general derision of such jeremiads, are in danger of simplistic writing of a different sort, succumbing to hermeticism and a narrow emotional range which all of the technical virtuosity in the world cannot compensate for. One symptom of this narrowing is that we rarely permit ourselves to get mad. One cannot of course say that anger is the key to American poetry's salvation, but our distrust of anger is something American poets, especially mainstream poets, should more closely investigate. We need many things in our poetry today, not the least of which may be the bile of Catullus, the outrage of the best of Brecht, the nervy shamelessness of Wright during his *Two Citizens* phase, and the dyspectic snarl of underrated but essential contemporaries such as Alan Dugan and Louis Simpson. One cannot achieve the authority we admire in the work of the poets on this list by being nice and by playing it safe, qualities which arise from a mistrust of the complicated and often contradictory emotions that prompt a good poem.

(1991)

7.

Without a Deep Delight: Neo-Narrative Poetry and Its Problems

"Tell me a story of deep delight."
—Robert Penn Warren, Audubon: A Vision

To rephrase a line from a well-known recent poem by Robert Hass, "all the new thinking is about narrative," or at least it seems that way when one examines the poetry of the 1980s and the critical treatments to which our poetry has recently been subjected. *Narrative* has become the decade's buzzword, just as *image* was the prevailing buzzword in discussions of poetry in the 1960s and 1970s. Of course, we all know that such labels are ultimately useless. At best they may describe a period style, and perhaps they are essential to us during an age when changes in period style seem to occur from decade to decade rather than at the comfortably slow pace of earlier literary eras. When we note that a poem is reminiscent of eighteenth-century poetry, we can fairly safely assume that it employs the heroic couplet as its form and an essayistic mode as its approach. Recently, however, poetic fashion, for those who care to pay attention to it, shifts with dizzying speed. The poets of the Confessional school and the Deep Image group are now, it seems, relegated to the poetic bargain basement, their writings about as fashionable as the polyester leisure suit or the Nehru jacket. To be sure, the best poems of these movements will continue to insist upon their importance, and no good poet who claims to be writing "narrative" poetry can fail to be influenced by the major works of these two schools. Isn't Robert Lowell's "Skunk Hour" a narrative poem? Isn't there an explicitly rendered narrative structure in James Wright's "A Blessing"? Our decade's interest in the narrative will wane, probably in the not-too-distant future. Some other movement will be waiting in the wings to replace it—and let us hope the new dynasty will not be comprised of the more reactionary elements of the New Formalism or of those who champion the least successful Language writing.

I consider myself a narrative poet, little interested in the short lyric but much interested in poems that can perform according to the rules we would normally require of a short story—plot, character, conflict. Yet I've grown increasingly frustrated in recent years with my desire to follow such rules and by the sometimes slavish adherence to these standards that I see in my contemporaries. Let me identify some of the shortcomings of recent narrative verse and see how they may be corrected without fundamentally changing the storytelling impulse, the concern for characters in conflict that lies at the heart of the best recent narrative poetry. Such a project may not help to give the new narrative verse any more staying power as it struggles to extend its fifteen minutes of poetry fame into twenty or twenty-five, but it may help us to enliven our approach to narrative and to question some of its more shaky assumptions. We want the sort of contemporary poem which we can rightly call, in Robert Penn Warren's words, "a story of deep delight."

It's hard to say when "narrative" became one of the decade's most talked about issues in poetry, though the most fearless champions of the narrative movement have surely been Mark Jarman and Robert McDowell, the editors of the quarterly *The Reaper,* which began publication in 1980. *The Reaper* is one of the best contemporary examples of the curmudgeonly little magazine, the successor to such projects as William Carlos Williams's *Contact* in the 1920s; George Hitchcock's polemically neosurrealist *Kayak* in the more recent past; and, of course, Robert Bly's cantankerous *The Sixties.* Like their forerunners, the editors of *The Reaper* believe they are on a mission from God. They've surveyed the contemporary literary scene, and they don't much like what they see. They propose some solutions to contemporary literature's shortcomings, and—as with Bly's influential essays published in *The Sixties*—their prescriptions for American verse's salvation are somewhat dire and narrow-minded. But Jarman and McDowell do at times utter some uncomfortably sensible statements, and many of them focus strongly on issues of narrative. Here, from a 1981 issue of the journal, are *The Reaper*'s "non-negotiable demands," ten guidelines for changes that must take place in American poetry:

1. Take prosody off the hit list.
2. Stop calling formless writing poetry.
3. Accuracy, at all costs.
4. No emotion without narrative.
5. No more meditating on the meditation.
6. No more poems about poetry.
7. No more irresponsibility of expression.
8. Raze the house of fashion.
9. Dismantle the office of translation.
10. Spring open the jail of the self.[1]

I need not devote much discussion to explaining *The Reaper*'s demands. The problems the editors identify, however telegraphically, are ones self-evident to any serious reader of contemporary poetry. Of course, some of the problems *The Reaper* poses its scythe above are ones that will always be with poetry, elements of bad writing at any point in literary history. Who would not want poetry to strive for accuracy, or not want it to be indifferent to the whims of literary fashion? Who would seek to advocate "irresponsibility of expression"? But of the remaining seven conditions that *The Reaper* demands, a good many have, in the years that have followed Jarman and McDowell's pronouncement, begun to come to pass. Certainly more poets are paying attention to the value of narrative as a way of conveying emotion and are doing so to the point that the meditative and Confessional poems so frequent during the past few decades are disappearing from first books and little magazines. The long narrative poem has made a comeback, as evidenced by efforts such as Alfred Corn's *Notes from a Child of Paradise,* Anthony Hecht's *The Venetian Vespers,* and Frederick Turner's *New World.* The translation boom seems to have subsided a bit. Graduate writing students are now more likely to be ploughing through Thomas Hardy's *Collected Poems* than to be puzzling over bad translations of Neruda. And finally, if any topic aside from narrative is being discussed with fervor at the moment, then that topic is surely prosody. For better or for worse, we now have among us the group of younger poets known as the New Formalists—writers such as Dana Gioia, Brad Leithauser, and Gjertrud Schnackenberg, all of whom write almost exclusively in traditional forms and meters and, in the case of such members of the group as Leithauser, have even written polemics that defend the New Formalism with reactionary zeal.

In 1989, then, it's possible to say that generalissimos Jarman and McDowell have perhaps not won their war against contemporary poetry, but they have certainly won a number of important battles. Yet the ascendancy of the sort of poetry that *The Reaper* has advocated, which has come to be known as Neo-Narrative verse, has brought with it problems of its own, problems that are in many ways as exasperating as those that the movement has sought to correct.

What constitutes Neo-Narrative poetry? As with most literary and artistic movements, the Neo-Narrative school has developed to a large degree as a reaction to fashionable earlier modes. The Neo-Narrative poets reject the primacy of metaphor and simile that was so insisted upon by the American Surrealist and Deep Image writers. Similarly, they question the engagement with nonlinear meditative poetry as practiced by the Language writers and the many poets who are followers of Ashbery. And finally, unlike the writers we associate with the Deep Image and Confessional schools, the writer of the Neo-Narrative does indeed seek to "spring open the jail of the self." The

Confessional poet's need for the appearance of autobiographical authenticity and the Deep Imagist's introspective intensity are generally abandoned in pursuit of a pristine faithfulness to the narrative impulse. The need to disclose the author's subjective feelings is secondary to the need to simply *tell the story.* As a consequence of their reaction to earlier modes in contemporary poetry, the poets of the Neo-Narrative seek to modify our now-comfortable notions of the poet's role as author of the poem, of the poem's method of disclosure, and finally, of the poem's sense of form and the line.

Because in the Neo-Narrative poem the storytelling or anecdotal impulse supercedes the writer's need for bald confession—even when the poem's narrator is a principal participant in the poem's events—the speaker of the Neo-Narrative tends to seek devices that will place him at a certain aesthetic distance from the poem's main action. As Jonathan Holden has pointed out, Louis Simpson's poems consciously strive to put their speaker in the role of the omniscient narrator we find in many nineteenth-century novels.[2] True to this role, Simpson's speakers rarely themselves participate in the poem's action, though they frequently exercise their right to control or comment upon the poem's events. Similarly, the speaker of the unsettling trilogy of poems that ends Stephen Dobyns's *Black Dog, Red Dog,* who is recalling his days as a Detroit crime reporter, employs a carefully objective tone as he recreates the events surrounding three particularly gruesome murders. In the poems, ironically titled "Art," "Truth," and "Beauty," the journalistic mode of disclosure serves both to intensify the horror of the events described and to subtly indict the speaker for his jaded response to the deaths he has witnessed. Furthermore, since many of the poems of the Neo-Narrative school seek to investigate the meaning of memory and the writer's individual past, even those poems that are ostensibly "personal" tend to be reflective, narrated with a coolness that seeks perspective rather than with an immediacy that seeks simple disclosure. The poems of writers such as Herbert Morris and David St. John tend to be Wordsworthian, using autobiography to navigate a mythic landscape of the poet's past: autobiography becomes a means to an end rather than an end in itself.

Of course, by removing from the poet the primacy of self which lies at the heart of most Deep Image and Confessional poetry—and almost all lyric poetry, for that matter—it is reasonable to assume that the poet might turn, if not to abstract meditation, then to narrative as a means of giving focus to his concerns. Since the speaker of the Neo-Narrative refuses the solipsism that must always announce itself in the Deep Image or Confessional poem, he must more readily take on the role of objective narrator of the poem's events or that of a character who plays a relatively minor part within a larger framework of action. The poets of the Neo-Narrative are interested less in sensibility than in exploring point of view. To explore point of view demands plot, character development, complication, and conflict—in short, all the elements of fiction which we associate with the realist short story.

While it is an extremely compressed piece of writing, David St. John's "Meridian" has all the rich complexity of a short story and is a good example of Neo-Narrative verse at its best. In the opening scene, we are introduced quite vividly to the poem's setting and its characters:

> The day seemed suddenly to give to black & white
> The falcon tearing at the glove
> Clare yanking down the hood over its banked eyes
> & handing the bird
> Its body still rippling & shuddering & flecked
> Here or there with blood
>   to her son Louis
> & as we walked back up the overgrown stone trail
> To the castle now in the public trust
> For tax reasons she admitted
> Supposing one more turn in the grave couldn't harm
> Her father the Count much at this point anyway[3]

There is no easy exoticism to the description of this European setting. The Countess Clare, an aging beauty, may indeed be practicing the preposterously effete sport of falconry, but St. John clearly emphasizes the violence of her pastime, just as he makes sure that we see the countess and her domain as decadent. In the poem's second scene, the speaker's involvement in the action becomes more direct, and the decadent gives way to the tragic. Segueing into the conclusion of the lengthy unpunctuated sentence which began much earlier in the poem, St. John offers this:

> I could think only of her body still muscled like a
> Snake's & how she lay sprawled last night
> Naked on the blue tiles of the bathroom floor
> & as I stepped into the doorway
> I could see the bathroom speckled with vomit
> The syringe still hanging limply from a vein in her
> Thigh & she was swearing
> As she grasped for the glass vial
> That had rolled out of reach behind the toilet
> Then she had it
> Drawing herself up slowly as she
> Turned her body slightly to look up at me

& she said nothing
Simply waiting until I turned & walked away
The door closing with its soft collapse
Behind me

The graphic disclosure of the countess's secret drug addiction has greatly complicated the speaker's relationship with her. Although we are not told the details of their relationship—are they lovers or just acquaintances?—we need not know anything else about the pair, since the speaker's new revelation about the countess's character will now color every thought he has of her, creating for them both a kind of sorrowful and helpless intimacy. Appropriately, the imagery of the final passage evokes an uneasy stasis:

now over lunch on the terrace
I pin a small sprig of parsley to her jacket lapel
A kind of truce a soldier's decoration
& above us the sun drags the day toward its meridian
Of heat & red wine & circumstance from which
We can neither look back nor step ever
Visibly beyond yet as we
Look at each other in the brash eclipsing glare
We know what bridging silence to respect
Now that neither of us has the heart to care

Though in "Meridian" St. John has not felt constrained slavishly to follow all the rules of Fiction Writing 101, he has given us the tonal *impact* of a short story or novella and has in streamlined fashion incorporated many of the elements we expect from a good work of short fiction. Yet the poem's high degree of lyric compression and its stark unpunctuated form insist always upon its identity as a poem following some of fiction's patterns—it is not merely a story set into verse. In fact, the tension between the poem's highly stylized form and its sometimes tersely reportorial method of description is the main reason for the poem's prosodic success. No one can accuse "Meridian" of simply being prose chopped up into lines, for the demands of narrative within a distinctly poetic (if not traditionally metrical) framework have caused St. John to seek a method in which form and content must intertwine. The poets of the Neo-Narrative tend to be much more concerned with questions of form than were their Deep Image and Confessional forebears, for the Neo-Narrative poets reject the notion that content is of greater significance than form. For Bly and other Deep Image poets, the powerful emotions that they regarded as arising from the unconscious were to be explored in their freshest and most unedited form; to tether such emotions to any formal program but the most anything-goes free verse was seen as a betrayal of the poem's motivating force. And in the later work of the Confessional poets, especially the last books of Anne Sexton, the urgency of the utterance—the desperate need simply to *get the statement down* under the duress of personal crisis—militates against anything but the most rudimentary form of free verse or, as in the case of Berryman's final *Dream Songs,* spasmodically repeats a formal pattern that has exhausted its effectiveness. When we look back at the last three decades of American poetry, it's easy to see that Creeley's famous dictum that "form is never more than an extension of content" has been programmatically ignored by most of the prevailing schools. But for the Neo-Narrative poets content and form are meant to exist in a true symbiosis. It goes without saying that to employ a narrative strategy is to employ a form—disclosure must follow or depart from a particular sequential pattern. And, as opposed to most short lyric poetry, in which the sensibility of the speaker—in other words, the content of the speaker's message—is of primary concern, in a poetry that emphasizes narrative it is the unfolding pattern of the story that is most crucially emphasized. But of course, since the narrative poem's primary information comes from the unfolding of its story, the story must serve to a large degree as both the poem's content and its form.

And yet, how does a poet insist upon a narrative's identity as a poem while at the same time employing many of the conventions we associate with fiction and drama? As we've seen from St. John's poem, structural compression is a partial solution to this problem. Regarding the use of the line itself, poets of the Neo-Narrative have taken a number of approaches. Some figures—Herbert Morris and Maura Stanton, for example—have explored blank verse as the best method for giving form to their often very lengthy narrative meditations. Others, such as C. K. Williams, Rodney Jones, and Stephen Dobyns, have adopted extremely long lines which bear an ostensible resemblance to prose, though their poems' frequent use of spondees, anaphora, and syntactical inversion nevertheless insists upon their identity as verse and nothing else. Other figures, most notably St. John and Tess Gallagher, have pursued a highly idiosyncratic free verse of abrupt enjambments and surprising stanza breaks and have dropped punctuation entirely from certain poems. The alienating effect of such structures, their militant unpredictability, also helps to insist upon the narratives' distinction from prose. Whatever form or metrical scheme they adopt, the poets of the Neo-Narrative must think of form as it applies to a large framework, to a structure more unwieldy and more leisurely in its unfolding than that of the short lyric.

I have now come to the second part of my discussion. The narrative's popularity is producing many bad poems, whose shortcomings, predictably enough, are quite different from the shortcomings of the poems in fashion ten or twenty years ago. If we are truly to gauge the importance of the Neo-Narrative movement, we must also clearly define the dangers lurking within the narrative approach. Many would-be Neo-Narrativists approach the blank page with the notion that a narrative is rather easy to write. After all, one needs simply to tell a story. But soon the complications arise. How does one sustain a story which may demand several pages of development? What sort of form will the poem require? What if, after several stanzas or pages of the poem, our budding narrativist realizes that the story that must be told should actually be a quite different one?

Perhaps the most common shortcoming of our narrative poems results from what might be called the mimetic fallacy. We're told, by *The Reaper* and by other partisans of the Neo-Narrative, that our poems should adhere to the rules we associate with the realist short story or even the novel. In some ways, this advice makes perfect sense. But it is quite easy to carry the analogy to fiction too far. There are many elements of fiction which have no place in poetry. The careful exposition and precise scene-setting that one finds in the stories of *Dubliners,* or even the careful listing of brand names and pop-culture kitsch that opens many of the stories by writers of the Minimalist school, will probably merely stultify the opening of a poem. Analogies can be useful when they point out the similarities that exist between two essentially dissimilar modes of expression, but some advocates of Neo-Narrative use narrative poetry's similarities to fiction as a way of saying that the distinction between narrative verse and prose fiction has now become insignificant. Thus Bruce Bawer, in a fawning *New Criterion* review of Vikram Seth's ludicrous novel-in-verse about San Francisco yuppiedom, *The Golden Gate,* can admit that if we judge Seth's book according to our standards of fiction, it is a failure. Regarding the work as a hybrid of the two genres, however, Bawer sees it as an unqualified success. Why carp about genre, Bawer asks, when the end product works so well? But the problem is that Seth's production doesn't work, and is in fact a kind of monstrosity. Although Seth can sometimes be an engaging technician, handling his tetrameter sonnets with a virtuosic flair, the book's real shortcoming results from its desire to pose as a novel. This is not to complain about the book's plot or characters. The BMW set is just as valid a milieu as any other that Seth might have chosen. (Detractors of *The Golden Gate* err when they charge that the book is bad because its characters are vapid; the characters are no more vapid than those of *Madame Bovary.*) The problem is that we have to spend so much *time* with Seth's yuppies, for Seth must introduce and develop their characters as a novelist would, yet he must do so within the cumbersome constraints of his stanzaic form. The result is narrative poetry, certainly, but funereally paced. By following the rules of fiction as closely as he does, Seth has allowed his prosodic framework to become merely an obstacle. The verse does not enhance our appreciation of the story; it serves only as an irritant. Look, for example, at how a new character is introduced in the third chapter. Turning from the budding romance of Lawyer Liz and Computer Wiz John, the poet now presents Phil and his young son:

A tow-haired boy sits with his father
Upon a rock that caps a hill.
The son (Paul) says that he would rather
Catch centipedes. The father (Phil,
John's school chum, whom we mentioned earlier)
Looks on amused as Paul grows surlier.
Paul's six, his father's twenty-eight;
And as they sit and altercate,
Phil rests his hand on his son's shoulder.
"When I was his age," Phil recalls,
"My moods were as unfixed as Paul's.
I wonder why, as we grow older. . . ."
Paul cuts in, "Dad, you're going bald."
"I know," replies Phil, enthralled.[4]

Yes, the scene between father and son on the hillside is one that in a novel might be a most appropriate device for giving us our first glimpse of Phil and Paul. But notice how laboriously the pair must be described for us. The rhyming may be witty (*earlier* and *surlier,* for example), but it just as frequently pulls the characters out of focus, and though Seth's main goal is to give a clear portrayal of his creations, much of the narrative action must be triggered by the strictures of the rhyme. Sometimes the rhyme may propel the narrative forward in a pleasantly serendipitous fashion, but more often than not it causes Seth to shoot himself in the foot. Since Seth has earlier selected "Phil" as the father's name, he has little choice but to introduce the pair while they are sitting on "a rock that caps a hill. " The choice of locale is functional, but only marginally so: the two might just as well be "communing by the windowsill" or, alas, "tossing out the evening's swill. "

A much better example of narrative poetry is the following short piece by Robert Hass, "A Story About the Body." Though it is written as a prose sketch and—as Hass's title implies—it is adamant about its function as a narrative, the effort is surely more interestingly *poetic* than any of Seth's stilted imitations of Pushkin's *Eugene Onegin* stanza. Here is Hass's poem in its entirety:

> The young composer, working that summer at an artist's colony, had watched her for a week. She was Japanese, a painter, almost sixty, and he thought he was in love with her. He loved her work, and her work was like the way she moved her body, used her hands, looked at him directly when she made amused and considered answers to his questions. One night, walking back from a concert, they came to her door and she turned to him and said, "I think you would like to have me. I would like that too, but I must tell you that I have had a double mastectomy," and when he didn't understand, "I've lost both my breasts." The radiance that he had carried around in his belly and chest cavity—like music—withered, very quickly, and he made himself look at her when he said, "I'm sorry. I don't think I could." He walked back to his own cabin through the pines, and in the morning he found a small blue bowl on the porch outside his door. It looked to be full of rose petals but he found when he picked it up the rose petals were on top; the rest of the bowl—she must have swept them from the corners of her studio—was full of dead bees.[5]

There are many reasons why this chilling poem impresses us. Although the characters of the young composer and the Japanese painter are presented to us so tersely that they could almost be construed as allegorical figures, we have no trouble seeing them as individuals; they never degenerate into types, despite Hass's title, which suggests that we must read the poem for its abstract and symbolic implications—as a variety of parable. That the poem is meant to be an examination of the mind/body duality is made even more clear to us as we read of the painter's gift to the composer—the rose petals in a cup that cover the dead bees. Still, this image has a sharp visual impact, and the painter's decision to present this unusual gift to the composer is very much in keeping with what we know about her character. The poem's final two sentences do not simply serve as a neat symbolic closure, for they also resonantly complete the narrative action, as we can see from Hass's masterfully chosen aside—"she must have swept them up from the corners of her studio. . . ."

Yet it is not this poem's deft handling of character and image that is finally the secret of its success as a narrative. Unlike Seth, Hass does not feel compelled to introduce and resolve the actions he describes according to the rules of prose fiction; Hass instead seeks to invest his narrative with the immediacy of anecdote. The poem has the curious authority, the in media res streamlining of detail and event, that we associate with the most lively dinner conversation and late-night bar talk. We sense—rightly or not—that this must be a true story, heard at one time by the poet and now reported to his audience of intimates. The poem's structure is clearly a narrative one, but its method is that which Jonathan Holden has termed "the contemporary conversation poem." Such conversational poetry adheres to a set of formal prerequisites at least as rigorous as those of Seth's tetrameter sonnets, for as Holden points out, the conversation poem must "satisfy two paradoxical requirements: it must provide sufficient journalistic detail so as to render a vivid historical sense of the speaker's past experiences; simultaneously, however, it must transcend the narrowly personal, so that the speaker's story acquires, like a saint's life, a mythic rather than merely a journalistic significance."[6] It is the effectiveness of Hass's testimony within a conversational context that makes his story vivid for us. Were Hass to render the poem according to the format of a *New Yorker* short story or within the formal straitjacket of Seth's ersatz Pushkin, we can easily imagine how deadening the effect would be.

If the mimetic fallacy results from a poem's too-rigorous application of the structural rules of the realist short story, the expositional fallacy arises in poems which misguidedly follow certain aesthetic principles of the realist short story. One of the exasperating legacies of nineteenth-century literary realism is what might be termed the "Detective Joe Friday Approach." Television's *Dragnet* protagonist would routinely respond to the complicated and highly subjective testimony of witnesses to crimes with glibly Hemingwayesque instructions: "Just the facts, please, Ma'am." If a story is worth its salt, says the Friday Approach, it's presented purely, with no intervention by the storyteller that will prevent readers from drawing their own conclusions about the narrative. Such striving for presentational objectivity has its place in fiction, but it often has a less useful role in poetry. Some recent narrative poems highlight narrative action to the point of entirely eliminating the poem's opportunities for abstract discourse and lyricism. A good narrative poem thinks, sings, and tells a story. Sadly, a poem such as Richard Tillinghast's "Fossils, Metal, and the Blue Limit," despite its intriguing title, adheres so relentlessly to its anecdotal impulse that the poem feels practically no need to imply much of anything within its twelve pages, and though Tillinghast is a superb technician, his poem's language is at best merely arch—it rarely rises to the level of intensity that we would describe as lyrical. The poem is mostly a description of a fishing trip. The speaker, a friend, and two of their children set out from San Francisco for the mountains. The poem is quite busy with detail, as the following passage illustrates:

> Three fiberglass poles, and a nine-foot, willowy fly rod
> of the lightest material made
> bounce easily to the even pace of the engine
> as my customized classic

1966 VW microbus, forest green
with white trim,
or as I might call it
in moments of gloom,
"decrepit old wreck"—[7]

What happens beyond this in the poem? Not much. The van breaks down, is repaired, and the speaker and his companions resume their journey. There are places where the poem appears to seek to enlarge itself beyond static description, but they seem merely asides and digressions, as in this passage, elicited when the microbus begins to burn oil:

OIL! the engine-opening black
As the underground streams
of Arabia, black
as the fingernails and secret dreams
of the Ayatollah.

We glut it with an extra quart, then another,
and point it toward the exit
though it smokes
like pointillist paintings of London weather
and early Marxist pollution-stacks.

Like those long first paragraphs of *Bleak House,*
creeping, deliberate, ominous,
we nose the cloud into the town of Weed. . . .

The reference to *Bleak House* and the ironic fandango of imagery alluding to Middle Eastern oil may attempt to give the poem a kind of social consciousness, but motifs such as these, though they recur rather pointedly in the poem, always seem to be parenthetical, knee-jerk commentaries on the poem's action that never fuse with the story line. Later, the poem's most important revelation occurs, the disclosure that the speaker's companion will

two weeks from now

. . . take a knife in the gut
and be in all the papers
as he and the passenger in his cab
go after a man who is trying to further
the evolution of the human race

by raping a nurse as she goes home from work,
for God's sake,
on Nob Hill at four in the morning.

He's one of the lucky ones, however:
only his flesh is wounded.
He'll soon recover.

But the effect of this aside is simply to stall the poem's forward movement. The poem may coyly hint that it is something larger than a piece of travelogue journalism, but Tillinghast—who in many of his other efforts displays significant talent—here flounders in the transparent.

A poem more willing to work meditation into an essentially narrative framework is William Matthews's "Whiplash." It begins in a straightforward anecdotal manner, and Matthews, like Tillinghast, is eager to draw a series of generalizations from the narrative action. Unlike Tillinghast's poem, however, "Whiplash" places these generalizations in the foreground of the action. Matthews is careful to see that the poem's narrative movement and discursive elements are firmly enmeshed. Here is the poem's long first stanza:

That month he was broke,
so when the brakes to his car
went sloshy, he let them go.
Next month his mother came
to visit, and out they went
to gawk, to shop, to have something
to do while they talked besides
sitting down like a seminar
to talk. One day soon he'd fix
the brakes, or—as he joked
after nearly bashing a cab
and skidding widdershins
through the intersection
of Viewcrest and Edgecliff—
they'd fix him, one of these
oncoming days. We like
to explain our lives to ourselves,
so many of our fictions
are about causality—chess
problems (where the ?! after
White's 16th move marks
the beginning of disaster),
insurance policies, box scores,

psychotherapy ("Were your
needs being met in this
relationship?"), readers' guides
to pity and terror—, and about
the possibility that because
ageing is relentless, logic too
runs straight and one way only.[8]

While a narrative about bad brakes and a visit from the protagonist's mother dominates the first half of the stanza, the first person plural "we"—certainly the most rhetorically effective choice for abstract discourse—comes to dominate the stanza's second half. Of course, by the end of the stanza the poem seems to have grown wholly discursive. Matthews corrects this problem in the second stanza, shifting from his meditation on "bad breaks" to a return to our hero and his car's bad brakes (here we see Matthews's characteristic delight in horrendous puns):

our disaster almost shatters us,
it would make sense to say
the accident he drove into
the day after his mother left
began the month he was broke.
Though why was he broke?
Because of decisions he'd made
the month before to balance
decisions the month before that,
and so on all the way back
to birth and beyond, for his
mother and father brought
to his life the luck of theirs.

The poem's discursive and narrative elements most truly fuse in the final stanza, in which the sassy metaphors that have given the poem its meditative urgency come together with the resolution of the poem's narrative movement. The effect of this union is to make us see causality in its most sinister and tragic aspect, as a force we willfully embrace but which only serves, finally, to victimize us:

And so when his car one slick day
oversped its dwindling ability
to stop itself and smacked two
parked cars and lightly kissed
another, like a satisfying
billiard shot, and all this action

(so slow in compression and
preparation) exploded so quickly,
it seemed not that his whole life
swam or skidded before him,
but that his whole life was behind
him, like a physical force,
the way a dinosaur's body
was behind its brain and the news
surged up and down its vast
and clumsy spine like an early
version of the blues; indeed,
indeed, what might he do
but sing, as if to remind himself
by the power of anthem that the body's
disparate and selfish provinces
are connected. And that's how
the police found him, full-throated,
dried blood on his white suit
as if he'd been caught in a rust-
storm, song running back and forth
along his hurt body like the action
of a wave, which is not water,
strictly speaking, but a force
which water welcomes and displays.

"Whiplash" is a strong narrative effort because it does not let the narrative itself dominate the poem's action. Like many of the most memorable narratives, it insists on placing itself within the venerable tradition of the cautionary tale, and in doing so it establishes a moral and discursive authority that "Fossils, Metal, and the Blue Limit" cannot attain. At times Neo-Narrative poetry takes Pound's advice to "tread in fear of abstraction" to an absurd extreme. As "Whiplash" so ably shows, there's nothing innately wrong with didacticism.

I'm sure, however, that the Neo-Narrative purist would counter the above remarks by stating that "Whiplash" should not be construed as a narrative, for its purposes are too discursive. The editors of *The Reaper* would probably argue that Matthews's many digressions within the poem betray any narrative impulse, since *The Reaper* tends to cast a very cold eye on poems which depart in any way from strict linear disclosure. Tangents and asides, or the episodic narrative structure that Jack Myers and Michael Simms in *The Longman Dictionary and Handbook of Poetry* refer to as the "fractured narrative," appear to have no place within *The Reaper*'s definition of storytelling poetry.[9] Thus, in a 1984 *Reaper* essay which, among other things, examines a Larry Levis poem, "My Story in a Late Style of a Fire," the editors present the poem in its published form and then offer a drastically edited version which purports to improve upon the original by allowing *only* the poem's narrative framework to remain. The editing is a travesty, turning a poem about memory, perspective, and the essential self-destructiveness of American culture into a skeletal account of the speaker's botched love affair with a disturbed woman.[10] *The Reaper*'s "party line" in this essay advocates what seems to me the third common pitfall of the Neo-Narrative—a kind of narrative single-mindedness. *The Reaper*'s rigid definition of narrative not only diminishes the importance of discursive approaches within the poem but also suggests that the strong narrative poem must tell only one story and must do so in a pointedly linear fashion. Fractured narratives, or poems that incorporate several narrative strands, seem to have no place within *The Reaper*'s narrative pantheon.

It goes without saying that *The Reaper*'s stance is one that severely limits the narrative's expressive possibilities. And even the editors of *The Reaper* do not themselves always practice what they preach, for Jarman and McDowell have become two of our most interesting narrative poets, largely through poems which depart from *The Reaper*'s strident narrative program. Their least successful poems, however, fail because they doctrinairily apply *The Reaper*'s rules of narrative unity. McDowell's "Coed Day at the Spa" is a good illustration of the problems inherent in narrative single-mindedness. Here are the opening lines:

> Sunday. He ought to be in church.
> But he's here instead to sweat with women.
> Bicycle wheels hum, treadmills grind
> Like equations in a teacher's faulty lesson plan.
> One smart-ass reads a novel on his bike;
> Another, humping language, gulps air
> Between each word about the local news—
> The fortunes of the AAA ball team,
> Who shot the mayor, the widening of Division Street. . . .[11]

The forty-four-line poem continues in this minimalist vein. The moment of greatest narrative complexity occurs in the final two stanzas:

> He stretches in a corner, shy and misunderstood.
> He knows The Women group him with the others,
> One more Jupiter with microscopic prick
> Who lifts to show his strength—

One big push and he's done . . .
"You ought to give up smoking," Ms. Tri-State says.
"Do you always shave before a workout?"
"Do you?" he counters. She smiles like a spasm.
"Let's pump some iron," she says.

So it's him she wants. She knows
The subtle art of shrinking men.
On the curl machine she is tireless,
On the bench press she cranks out twenty reps at 225.
Nobody presses like her, least of all himself.
Though he's added half a size to his neck,
Though his arms, once thin and flaky
As chicken legs in a crock pot, bulge with terror,
He lies down like a victim, overmatched.
Looking up he asks, "Do you think this might be love?"
She sets the weight. Laughter swells like a bicep.

The poem has chosen to limit itself to broad social satire. The man and woman both cut ridiculous figures, in part because the pair is so shallowly portrayed. McDowell pays lip service to exploring issues of sexism and feminism, issues which invariably arise from the situation he describes, but the poem's final effect is to be simplistic and easy, both in its implicit message of social criticism and—more importantly—in its portrayal of the two characters. And yet, how can we glean anything beyond the baldly satirical when we are not allowed to see the characters in any setting but on the gym floor, where the action takes place, and only through the point of view of the man? McDowell seems to have chosen to structure his poem within the classical unities of time, place, and action; such strictures may have been fruitful choices for Racine, but in "Coed Day at the Spa" they cause the poem to wither. We end up yearning for some emotional complexity beyond dyspeptic satire, yet the poem's barren deployment of scene and setting cannot provide the characters with opportunities to rise above the level of caricature. How much more satisfying the poem would be if it were to begin with satire and end with a more intricate revelation of human frailty, as do the best of Hardy's poems or so many of the stories of Chekhov. But because he does not bring us beyond the gym floor, McDowell has only a single narrative action to relate, in which his characters are severely limited in their choices and responses. Compared to Hass's "A Story About the Body," a poem which transcends its similarly limited means, "Coed Day at the Spa" is merely clever. Narrative single-mindedness does not create for McDowell the vivid sort of parable we find in the Hass poem; instead, McDowell's narrative strategy causes his characters to be little more than objects of ridicule.

A more ambitious and exciting effort is Susan Mitchell's "A Story," a poem rather ironically titled, for it is less a story than it is a narrative which, in fugue-like fashion, incorporates several *layers* of a story, no single one of which dominates the poem. It is a good example of what Myers and Simms would call a fractured narrative, since it is less interested in establishing the linear coherence of the realist short story than in mapping consciousness; therefore the poem understands that it must permit within its structure the circularity and distortions that imbue the process of memory, the stories we tell ourselves about our pasts in order to come to some tentative perspective on our lives. Mitchell does not relate these stories with the static dispassionateness that limits the effectiveness of the Tillinghast and McDowell poems, for her project is one of urgent self-discovery. Furthermore, her poem's structure is such that the speaker finds within the process of self-discovery a need to enlarge her meditation from one of solipsism to one of communion. Such a noble set of goals is difficult to attain in any poem, let alone one of only seventy-six lines. But Mitchell succeeds admirably. Here is the poem's opening:

> There is a bar I go to when I'm in Chicago
> which is like a bar I used to go to when I lived in New York.
> There are the same men racing toy cars
> at a back table, the money passing so fast
> from hand to hand, I never know who's winning, who's losing,
> only in the New York bar the racers sport Hawaiian shirts
> while in the Chicago bar they wear Confederate caps
> with crossed gold rifles pinned to their bands.
> Both have bars with oversized TV's and bathrooms
> you wouldn't want to be caught dead in,
> though some have. Once in the New York bar I watched a film
> on psychic surgery, and I swear to you
> the surgeon waved a plumb hand—
> the hand hovered like a dove over the patient's back,
> and where wings grow out of an angel's shoulders
> a liquid jetted, a clear water, as if pain
> were something you could see into like a window.[12]

There are some familiar narrative flourishes here. The bars are described with a novelist's precision. But by juxtaposing descriptions of the Chicago bar and of its New York City counterpart and by providing these jump cuts even within the same sentence, Mitchell insists that it is memory that provides the setting for the poem; events will take place within a psychological context rather than according to the premise that the bars are the stage for the poem's activity. Unlike McDowell's poem, here events are linked not because of the setting alone but because the two bars have fused associatively within the speaker's panorama of recollection. Thus, the poem's field of action can be a very large one, permitting not only the simultaneity of the descriptions of the two bars but also—even within this brief opening passage—a number of shifts in diction and rhetorical effect.

As the poem continues, the speaker walks home from the New York bar with a friend and, in another gesture of unexpected humor that seems very much in keeping with an inebriated midnight ramble, "practices psychic surgery" on her apartment building, expecting that a "pure roach anguish" will burst forth from it. This description triggers another recollection, of walking to the Chicago bar. Almost offhandedly, this description in turn brings us to yet another motif, one that will eventually become every bit as significant as the descriptions of the two bars and that will also bring us to the point of the poem's greatest dramatic intensity:

> In the Chicago bar there were men who never watched TV
> or played the video games, mainly from the plains tribes they
> sat in silence over their whiskey, and looking at them,
> I could even hear the IRT as it roared through
> the long tunnel between Borough Hall and Wall Street,
> the screech of darkness on steel.
> And it happened one night that a man,
> his hair loose to his shoulders, stood up and pulled
> a knife from his boot and another man
> who must have been waiting all his life for this
> stood up in silence too, and in seconds
> one of them curled around the knife in his chest
> as if it were a mystery he would not reveal to anyone.
> Sometimes I think my life is what I keep escaping.
> Staring at my hands, I almost expect them to turn
> into driftwood, bent and polished by the waves,
> my only proof I have just returned from a long journey.

Despite its shifts in narrative structure and diction, the poem has thus far presented itself quite seamlessly. But in the final passage the speaker combines her seemingly disparate concerns in an even more relentless and risky fashion. The stories of the two bars continue to converge and are fused with the speaker's meditation on blood—on bloodletting as well as bloodgiving—as a metaphor for her own process of self-discovery and physical and spiritual renewal. And finally, due in part to a sort of Whitmanesque lyricism that emerges in the poem for the first time, and in part to a reemergence of Mitchell's insistence that "A Story" directly address its reader, the poem achieves a convincing quality of communion, the synthesis of private utterance and public statement that it has from its beginning sought to attain. Mitchell's conclusion is spellbinding:

> The night Tom Littlebird killed Richard Highwater
> with a knife no one knew he carried, not even
> during five years he spent at Stateville,
> I thought of men and women who sell their blood for
> a drink of sleep in a doorway or for a bus ticket
> into a night which is also a long drink to nowhere,
> and I thought of the blood I was given
> when I was nineteen, one transfusion for each year of my life,
> and how I promised myself
> if I lived, I would write a poem in honor of blood.
> First my own blood which,
> like the letter that begins the alphabet,
> is a long cry AAH! of relief.
> Praise to my own blood which is simple
> and accepts almost anything.
> And then for the blood that wrestled
> all night with my blood
> until my veins cramped and the fingers of one hand went rigid.
> Praise to the blood that wanted to remain alone,
> weeping into its own skin,
> so that when it flowed into me, my blood contracted
> on the knot in its throat. For you
> who raised a rash on my arms
> and made my body shiver for days, listen,
> whoever you are, this poem is for you.

I can think of few other recent poems which can as rightly be called a "story of deep delight." And yet one hopes that our decade's interest in narrative will help us to produce a number of poems which are equally impressive. The resurgence of interest in narrative strategies in verse has helped to create a rich and exciting environment for the poets of the 1980s, and *The Reaper* has played an important role in establishing the tenor of our times, however strongly one might disagree with certain elements of Jarman and McDowell's narrative program. There are many stories yet to tell, and many ways to tell them.

(1989)

8.

Weldon Kees: A Photo and Two Afterlives

It is not so much the best-known photograph of Weldon Kees; instead it seemed to us the only one. Many of us knew the photo even before we knew Kees's poems, for it appeared in front of the selection of Kees in Stephen Berg's and Robert Mezey's influential 1969 anthology, *Naked Poetry.* (It is also, of course, the picture which appeared on the cover of the University of Nebraska Press's first paperback edition of Kees's *Collected Poems,* yet at the time we first saw it that book had long been unavailable, and the 1975 revised edition would not come along for several years.) Kees stands in profile, an unlit cigarette in his mouth, jacket collar turned up so that you're sure a gale-force wind off the Pacific is battering him as he looks down over San Francisco Bay; he is staring out at Alcatraz, you think, and beyond it to the arches of the Golden Gate. He's got a pencil-mustache, which, from the vantage point of the beard-crazy seventies, had an almost archaic suavity—there's a bit of David Niven in his pose, or Gable. It's a still from a noir flick, and in it you can almost feel the shadows lengthening, the soundtrack theremin commencing its sinister wail; something terrible is going to happen, soon.

This was, in short, a forlorn and mysterious photo, in keeping with the mysteries which we would soon learn had surrounded the life—and disappearance—of Weldon Kees. And to this day, to many of us who started writing poetry in the listless seventies, the photo seems to embody all the enigmatic complexity and contradiction of its subject; he can't be conjured up except through the photo, no more so than Chatterton can be called up except through Wallis's famous painting of his suicide, the dead poet sprawled in pre-Raphaelite majesty beneath his garret casement. And Kees, in a certain sense, *was* our Chatterton, playing for a generation of American poets the same role of forebear, martyr, and enigma that Chatterton played for the Romantics. Like Chatterton before him, Kees was not the subject of studies but of tributes, speculations, poems. Just as Wordsworth conjured up Chatterton as "the marvelous Boy, the Sleepless Soul that perished in his pride,"[1] so my own generation saw in a Kees a figure of, in Mark Ford's words, "an hallucinatory, beckoning ominousness."[2] Something terrible is going to happen soon: if Kees's poems know anything, they know this much, brimming as they are with a sense of imminent personal and cultural apocalypse. And yet, thanks to the offhand elegance of Kees's formal experiments and his ever-present and ever-corrosive wit, this sense of impending doom seems, in several small but crucial ways, bearable. When the end time comes, the poems tell us, we can at least try to keep our cool; like Hitchcock heroes, we shall face our demons with suits unrumpled, with every hair in place, and with a collection of wisecracks as our shield. But unlike Hitchcock heroes, there's little chance that any of us will triumph, and Kees said it plainly.

This is our Kees, the mythic and prophetic Kees, his apotheosis now complete. He arrived, ex-nihilo, from the shadows where he beckoned for a moment in his trenchcoat—and soon he will be gone, replaced by a very different and surely more real Kees, whose letters we can read, thanks to Robert Knoll; whose deftly written short stories, thanks to Dana Gioia, can now be placed on shelves beside his poems; and whose biography, through the efforts of James Reidel, will soon replace the Kees Enigma with the sturdiness of scholarship. So the second afterlife of Kees—his revised and expanded apotheosis—has now begun. And yet, before its memory disappears completely, I would like to mourn Kees's *first* afterlife. What was it about Kees that spoke so eloquently to us? How and why did Kees the figure of cult veneration emerge? Surely a generation of *poets* is an exceedingly small group, as tiny and endangered as a "generation" of white rhinos or snail darters. And it is as arcane-sounding a label as that of a "generation" of Assyriologists or ska trombonists. But among this generation of several dozen poets born from roughly the end of World War II to the start of the Vietnam War, Kees has exerted a subtle but steady impact, one which I can speak of partly through examining some poems of homage to Kees and partly through some anecdotes about my own encounters with the Kees Enigma.

It is sadly appropriate to begin with Larry Levis, who now dwells with Kees among the shades. Born in 1946 and a student of Kees's editor, Donald Justice, Levis surely discovered Kees early in his career, and though his mature poems are rangy, Whitmanesque, and narrative and meditative in their concerns in a way that little resembles Kees, his "My Only Photograph of Weldon Kees" is a wry and heartfelt homage. Appearing in Levis's 1981 collection, *The Dollmaker's Ghost,* with a section of similar homages to Lorca, Akhmatova, Zbigniew Herbert, and Miguel Hernandez, the poem is partly a stylistic imitation of Kees, partly a meditation on the famous photograph, and partly a set of speculations about Kees's disappearance. In other words, it combines nearly all of the factors that made Kees fascinating in his first afterlife. Here is the poem in full:

My Only Photograph of Weldon Kees

—For D.J.

10 P.M., the river thinking
Of its last effects,
The bridges empty. I think
You would have left the party late,

Declining a ride home.
And no one notices, now,
The moist hat brims
Between the thumbs of farmers

In Beatrice, Nebraska.
The men in their suits,
Ill-fitting, bought on sale . . .
The orange moon of foreclosures.

And abandoning the car!
How you soloed, finally,
Lending it the fabulous touch
Of your absence.

You'd call that style—
To stand with an unlit cigarette
In one corner of your mouth,
Admiring the sun of Alcatraz.[3]

We can pick out echoes of several Kees poems here: the syntax of the opening seems modeled on the telegraphic gruffness of "Homage to Arthur Waley," and the "orange moon of foreclosures" is lifted almost wholesale from "1926." The poem's narrative set-up—the speaker walking some nocturnal waterfront—replicates the opening of "Relating to Robinson," and the shift from this to an address to Kees recalls the speaker's chance encounter with Robinson in that poem. The form of the poem is similarly Keesian in that it is written neither in free verse nor in a strict form, but in three-beat accentuals—in fact, a minor Kees poem, "The Turtle," employs an identical meter and is also written in quatrains. Clearly, Levis knows Kees well, well enough to write something that partakes of several elements of his style while at the same time not devolving into mere pastiche or imitation.

Yet the speaker's knowledge of Kees's manner stands in sharp contrast to his sense of Kees himself. He can allude to aspects of Kees's life and character—to Kees's birthplace in Nebraska, to Kees the jazz musician in his "solo" freefall from the Golden Gate—but such knowledge seems now as ephemeral as the unnoticed "moist hat brims / Between the thumbs of farmers." His portrait of Kees must be maddeningly free of tangibles, much in the way that Kees's "Aspects of Robinson" must describe Robinson's possessions rather than allow Robinson himself to appear. All that is left are the events leading up to Kees's disappearance, and these too are lacunae, the stuff of speculation and little more: "I think / You would have left the party late / Declining a ride home . . . / And abandoning the car!" What fragments can Levis shore against such ruins? Only enigma—"the fabulous touch / Of your absence"—though enigma is seen as a "style," a mystique. And, of course, the photograph, which becomes by the end of the poem a thing of Rilkean numinoisty: Levis seems to hope that if he looks at the photo with enough intensity and concentration it will somehow offer the key to the Kees Mystery. Something in it, some detail, will reveal everything, will act as what Barthes calls *the punctum.* Perhaps it's the unlit cigarette. Perhaps the sun, and the shadows cast on the Bay by Alcatraz. But Levis also understands that there may be no key at all; unlike Berryman from a different bridge, Kees did not wave goodbye.

The contrast between Levis's clearly demonstrated intimacy with Kees the poet and his utter consternation when he tries to grasp something of Kees the man is for me the source of the poem's poignancy. Surely the selves of Sappho and Shakespeare are similarly lost to us, but it seems to Levis especially ironic and cruel that the self of Kees is so unavailable to his admirers: after all, he is almost our contemporary, and his sensibility seems to speak to us with a deep and discomforting resonance. Yet both the poems and the life seem to testify to us that Kees did not *want* to be known. And so, by the end of his poem, Levis is back to the photograph he alludes to in his title, striving, like some archeolinguist in battle with Linear B, once again to crack the code. Levis's wrestling with the Kees Enigma is something many of his readers shared in Kees's first afterlife, though few expressed the nuances of this struggle so eloquently. And once presented with the Kees Enigma, a reader does all he can to solve it. This brings me to a second poem, similarly representative of the search for Kees but far different in its tone, Simon Armitage's "Looking for Weldon Kees."

Armitage, born in 1963, is one of the best of a younger generation of British poets whose ranks include Michael Hoffman, Glyn Maxwell, John Ash, and Jo Shapcott. Like his peers, he writes an irreverent and pyrotechnical verse, much influenced by Paul Muldoon and to some degree by the

New York School. Armitage is the sort of poet more likely to embrace the whimsical side of Kees, as displayed in poems such as "Obituary" and "Abstracts of Dissertations," rather than the existentially brooding Kees of "For My Daughter" and "The Smiles of the Bathers"—the Kees, in other words, who appealed to Levis. And yet the Kees Enigma is finally just as confounding for Armitage as it is for Levis. Here is the opening of the poem, published in Armitage's 1992 collection, *Kid:*

> I'd heard it said by Michael Hoffman
> that *Collected Poems* would blow my head off
> but,
>   being out of print
>   and a hot potato
>   it might be a hard one
>   to get hold of;
> more than a case of shopping and finding
> nothing on the shelfs between Keats and Kipling.
>
> There was too much water under the Golden Gate
> since the day that dude became overrated
> the dawn
>   he locked both doors
>   of his Tudor Ford
>   and took one small step
>   off the face of the planet.
> No will, no note, no outline of police chalk
> on the deck around his drainpipes and overcoat,
>
> not even a whiff of spontaneous combustion
> to hang his vaporizing act on. Simultaneously, Robinson,
> who
>   had been through the hostel
>   with a host of problems
>   was back in town
>   and giving me the runaround.
> We went back years, me and that man Robinson,
> the illiterate son of a Maltese policeman. . . .[4]

The ebullient use of rhyme and the slightly nutty stanza form are typical of Armitage's work. So too is the absurdism, here emerging in a cheeky send-up of American detective fiction slang and some outrageous allusions: the second stanza, for example, finds a way to lampoon *both* Neil Armstrong and the Tudor Ford of Lowell's "Skunk Hour." At the same time, Armitage pays homage to Kees's similar parody of detective fiction: think of poems such as "Crime Club," "The Scene of the Crime," and "The Testimony of James Apthorp." The motif arrives at its weirdest permutation in the appearance of Robinson as "the illiterate son of a Maltese policeman." But what better way to address the Kees Mystery than to offer this skewed satire of hard-boiled fiction?

As the poem continues, it alternates between descriptions of the speaker's lengthy search for a copy of *Collected Poems* (this was long before Kees became a Faber poet) and the various shadowy appearances of the Maltese Robinson, with whom the speaker has had "more ups and downs / than San Francisco," a Robinson who leaves "his monogram daubed on my car windscreen / his Pidgin English on my answering machine." Just as our speaker has about given up in his search for the book, having been told by a book-finding service that "American books were a different ball game," Robinson leaves a parcel with his doorman "about the size and weight of a book." "No point," says Armitage, in "opening it up / blowing it up / or disclosing it"—a final blistering irony. The end of the poem continues this conundrum, but with a more straightforward homage to Kees, coopting a line from "Relating to Robinson":

> at night as I chanced it through the subway
> I thought I made out Robinson ahead of me.

"Tube," of course, would neither rhyme nor scan. For all its high jinks, "Searching for Weldon Kees" ends in precisely the same fashion as Levis's more saturnine homage. We can know Kees only through some shards of documentary evidence and through the work, which in Armitage's poem is itself nearly impossible to locate. He commences his search for Kees because of the rumors and mysteries surrounding him, not because he has yet read him, and the possible gift of the book by (Maltese) Robinson may provide Armitage with his final line, but by no means does his search come any closer to reaching its end. Indeed, several other poems which appear later in *Kid* make a character called Robinson their subject. In them Robinson seems neither the "Maltese" Robinson of "Searching for Weldon Kees" nor much like the Robinson of Kees's poems; in a wry postmodern twist, Armitage's Robinson becomes a sort of Elvis impersonator version of the figure, composed partly of parody and partly of very genuine homage.

There are a good many other poems addressed to or inspired by Kees which were published between the late 1970s and the present. Some of these efforts, following the lead of Justice's "Sestina on Six Words by Weldon Kees," take Kees as a prosodic model: a recent issue of *Prairie Schooner,* for example, contains a poem by Kathleen West entitled, "Imperfect Monorhyme after Lines by Weldon Kees."[5] But many others contend with the Kees Mystery and do so with a fervor similar to that of Levis and Armitage. John McKernan's "When the Ghost of Weldon Kees Visited," which appears in a recent *Paris Review,* even has the shade of Kees appearing to a group of students in an Omaha high school.[6]

What caused Kees to enjoy his first afterlife and to be the subject of such puzzlingly urgent homages? I think there are three reasons. First, there are the poems themselves, which are good by any standards but which seemed especially enticing to a generation of poets who even at an early age grew skeptical about the work of the poets then in fashion: the giganticism and self-importance of Lowell, Berryman, and the other middle-generation poets who were Kees's immediate contemporaries did not speak to all of us. Nor did the atavistic surrealist pieties of the Deep Image writers and the vatic yammerings of writers from the Beat and Black Mountain crews. Kees, although his voice is often acerbic and chilly, was a poet much easier to approach, and his inventiveness with traditional form in an era dominated by free verse also helped him to stand out. And furthermore, Kees knew something about the importance of irony—not the lofty and effete irony of the Modernists but a more sly and compelling irony such as that of Cavafy and Milosz, writers who first appeared in serviceable translations in the early 1970s and whom many of us read at the same time we were discovering Kees. It would be possible to write an interesting essay comparing Kees and either of these two writers: their work possesses a remarkably similar sort of tone to that of Kees—and a similar moral authority.

The second and third reasons are less about Kees's work than about the Kees Mystique. What we knew of Kees made him out to be a romantic and even dashing figure, a modern-day cavalier who tried his hand at everything important in the arts and who seemed to master it all: he exhibited with the Abstract Expressionists; he played jazz; he knew about film and about psychology; and he did not teach in a creative writing program, was not caught up in the benumbing po-biz professionalism that seemed to afflict so many of our teachers (who, even if we wanted their jobs, we never wanted to *be*). And the "fabulous touch" of Kees's disappearance made this image of him even more haunting, especially when we heard the rumors that Kees might be not be dead—that, for example, he had run off to Latin America, Butch Cassidy–style. All of this created a heady concoction for a bunch of impressionable young poets, and we drank it eagerly. Finally, there was the pleasure of knowing ourselves to be members of a tiny but fervent cult. An anecdote will serve as example. When I was in graduate school in Tucson in 1979, I had an interesting encounter with a book rep from Kees's publisher, the University of Nebraska Press. I was browsing in Sixth Street Books, the town's only literary bookstore, a Quixotic enterprise of the novelist Tom Cobb, which was soon to close. Tom introduced me to the book rep as "a Kees freak," and the rep allowed that Kees freaks must be exclusively a Tucson institution, for in the last two years, he said, *all* of the sales of Kees's *Collected Poems* (I believe it was something like twelve copies) had come from Tom's bookstore. Needless to say, this wasn't good news for Kees, but it certainly made a callous graduate student feel as though he were a member of a fairly exclusive club.

Perhaps because even finding an edition of Kees's poems was in those days fairly difficult, and perhaps because Kees had been the subject of virtually no critical treatments, there was nothing to counter the seductiveness of the Kees Enigma, and those of us who read him at that time needed to create from the absence of any information about Kees a distorted and even mythological portrait—much in the way that Baudelaire's generation constructed its own version of Poe or the British of Swinburne's and Wilde's day formed an iconic version of Whitman. And it wasn't simply the life of Kees which invited such portraiture: the work itself seemed to demand this. The haunted figure of Robinson, partly the stuff of satire and partly and discomfortingly Kees's alter ego (and for that matter our own—Robinson is, after all, a sort of repellent Everyman), invites for readers a kind of parallel attempt to draw a portrait of Kees: not a portrait that can be drawn from life, but from speculation, hunches, fragments. In other words, each reader hoping to discover Kees in those days had to summon up a different version of the poet and, for that matter, a different version of Kees's afterlife.

The best way I can illustrate this claim is to offer an account of my own creation of a Kees, a character I invented some twenty years ago now. This Kees may not exactly be "representative" of Kees's afterlife, and he certainly doesn't much resemble the real Kees. But my creation of him seems to me an important event in my development as a poet. Had I not created my Kees, I think I would be a very different sort of writer today.

I first read Kees as an undergraduate in the early 1970s; although Kees's reputation was perhaps at its lowest ebb at this time, none of his books being in print, he had the good fortune to be well-represented in two of the era's most widely read anthologies—Berg and Mezey's *Naked Poetry* (although even then I sensed that Kees was interesting not because of nakedness but because of his various disguises) and Mark Strand's *Contemporary American Poetry,* which had the cheek to give Kees more space than figures such as Ginsberg and Bly. Strand also made a tasty selection, offering some of Kees's best work: "For My Daughter" is there, as well as "Homage to Arthur Waley" and portions of the Robinson sequence. The selection was intriguing enough to cause me to withdraw Kees's *Fall of the Magicians* from the University of Minnesota library, and I remember that the book's library card made me feel as though I were in good company—in the twenty-five years it had been in the stacks, it had been taken out only twice, once by Allen Tate, professor of English, and once by James Wright, assistant professor. A few years later I picked up the 1975 revised edition of Kees's *Collected Poems,* and I remember going back to it often, although many of Kees's most significant qualities were lost on me, especially his quirky mastery of form. Like many poets of a generation schooled exclusively on free verse, I had a vague understanding of Kees as someone who experimented with difficult meters and received forms, but scansion was as foreign to me as Sanskrit, and all I knew of sestinas was that they were a little on the long side. Still, what appealed to me about Kees was his voice more than his technique; "one of the bitterest voices in history," said Justice in his introduction to the *Collected Poems.*[7] And to a young poet seething with collegiate angst and addled by multiple readings of *Nausea,* this voice had a strong and familiar appeal. It would be a long while, however, before I would be able to separate the intricacies and profundities of Kees's despair from the more superficial ennui that I knew about. Suffice it to say that Kees seemed sort of down on things; I could relate to that.

But by 1977 I had read enough of Kees to better understand his tone, to see him not as a kind of 1940s version of Leonard Cohen but as a writer of a truly terrifying aspect. I was in graduate school at the University of Arizona by then, and I was lucky to have the poets Steve Orlen and Jon Anderson team teach my first poetry workshop there. Steve was a hardcore Kees fan and on one night began the workshop by reading "The Testimony of James Apthorp" and "The Smiles of the Bathers." Having been a student of Donald Justice, Steve also gave us a tantalizing introduction to the various Kees Myths. The main one, surely, was the rumor that Kees had not jumped from his bridge but instead had gone off to Mexico; that he'd even continued writing from there, publishing stories in trashy men's magazines under the pseudonym of Michael Weldon; that Justice's attempts to locate Michael Weldon—who, according to his fiction editors at *True* or *Stag* or wherever, actually *did* live in Mexico—came to nothing. Kees was starting to sound more and more like a character in *The Long Goodbye.* These stories may not have made the poems any better, but they certainly made them more enticing. And I imagine that they were the direct cause of that formidable twelve-copy surge in Kees's book sales.

Not long after Steve's workshop, I hit upon a notion for a poem. Why not assume that Kees *had* gone to Mexico? What would his life be like there? How ironic it might be if his afterlife there were in some way a happy one. (This would be akin to discovering that Robinson were the Lost Dauphin or that Boris the Parrot were the Firebird.) Why not let Kees himself speak in the poem? So "Weldon Kees in Mexico, 1965" was born, in which Kees is *re*born, or at least seems reasonably well-adjusted. Although it may be shameless of me to quote in full my own monologue, the poem is distant enough from me now that someone else seems to be its author:

Weldon Kees in Mexico, 1965

Evenings below my window
the sisters of the convent of St. Teresa
carry brown jugs of water from a well
beyond a dry wash called *Mostrenco.*
Today it was hard to waken
and I've been dead to the world ten years.
They tread the narrow footbridge
made of vines and planks, sandals clicking:
brown beads and white wooden crosses
between hands that are also brown.
Over the bridge they travel in a white-robed line
like innocent nurses to a field hospital.

Exactly ten. I've marked it on the calendar.
And Maria, who speaks no English,
is soaping her dark breasts by the washstand.
Yesterday she said
she'd like to be a painter and sketched,
on the back of a soiled napkin,
a rendition of a cholla
with her lipstick. She laughed,
then drew below each nipple
a smudged rose. Weldon

would have been repelled
and fascinated, but Weldon is dead.
I watched him fall to the waves
of the Bay, the twelfth suicide that summer.
He would have been fifty-one this year,
my age exactly, and an aging man.

Still, he would not be a fool
in a poor adobe house, unwinding
a spool of flypaper from a hook
above the head of his child bride.

When she asks me my name, I tell her
I am Richard, a good midwestern sound.
She thinks Nebraska is a kingdom
near Peru, and I
the exiled Crown Prince of Omaha.
I've promised to buy her a box of paints
in a shop by my palace in Lincoln.
We'll go back, Maria and I,
with the little sisters of Saint Teresa
who are just now walking across the bridge
for water to be blessed at vespers.[8]

Clearly, there is little that sounds like the *manner* of Kees here, although the nuns trooping by like "nurses to a field hospital" might be a vaguely Keesian simile. I suspect that I was trying to sound like Norman Dubie in the poem, whose monologues were all the rage in those days and who uses a slightly oddball syntax which I must have been trying to replicate. I have no idea where the nuns came from; they now seem a bit ludicrous—a conga line of Sally Fields clones. Note, too, that the twenty-something author has his fifty-one-year-old speaker regard himself as something of a Methuselah, little suspecting that someday even Keith Richards would see fifty-one as youthful. It is an inane but sweet-tempered poem, and it has a couple of decent moments. The scene with the flypaper is handled well, and the foot-bridge is also a nice touch: the reader's so caught up with the preposterous image of the nuns that the heavy-handed symbolism of the bridge seems almost beside the point. True, the figure of "Maria" is a fairly crass male fantasy, but a memorable enough one that the late Howard Nemerov can allude to her—dismissively—in his introduction to James Reidel's selection of Kees's reviews.[9]

And yet, despite the poem's very obvious flaws, writing it meant a great deal to me. It is one of the earliest poems included in my first collection and one of the first of my efforts to seem truly my own, even though the poem is, admittedly, a Norman Dubie knockoff alleging to speak in the voice of Weldon Kees. But aren't all poetic selves fabrications, even when invented for urgent and complicated reasons? You of course want that invented poet to resemble yourself, but sometimes there are many trial-selves who must be invented first. My Weldon Kees was one such self, and I still feel some affection for him.

And it goes without saying that this Kees is not the one who in my photo gazes out toward Alcatraz, collar turned up and Lucky Strike dangling. My Kees I can claim in some small way to know. But this other Kees, even as he takes his rightful place among the significant poets of his time, will still in many crucial ways elude us. Are we so foolish as to think it might be otherwise?

(1996)

9.

Snodgrass's Borrowed Dog: S. S. Gardons and "Remains"

In a canny essay about portraiture and self-portraiture entitled "Borrowed Dogs," the photographer Richard Avedon begins with the tale of how his family took snapshots of themselves when he was a child. Photographs were meticulously planned, almost to the point of absurdity: "We dressed up. We posed in front of expensive cars, homes that weren't ours. We borrowed dogs. . . . It seemed a necessary fiction that the Avedons owned dogs. . . . I found eleven different dogs in one year of our family album. There we were in front of canopies and Packards with borrowed dogs, and always, forever, smiling."[1] This anecdote is a deft introduction to Avedon's thesis, a point which should be obvious to all of us—that all self-portraits are really a form of performance. Revelation is imparted not so much by disclosure as it is by the subtle mingling of disclosure with the smoke-and-mirror props the artist selects; and such props can range from the stylized hand gestures of Egon Schiele's numerous self-portraits to the costume-shop burnooses and turbans which Rembrandt sports in certain of his. Schiele, Rembrandt, and the Avedon family—all but the appropriated Spots and Fidos—are *acting.* So I have begun by reiterating what is self-evident, that the artist varnishes the truth, distorts it for the sake of what is (we hope) some high aesthetic purpose. The artist is revealed, surely, but only through a scrim of "necessary fiction."

And yet, as anyone who has taught undergraduates the work of the Confessional poets knows, such a distinction between literal truth and performance is one that the unsophisticated can often fail to grasp. Thus, during a class discussion of Lowell's "Skunk Hour," I once had a student wonder aloud why the Castine, Maine, police hadn't arrested Cal Lowell for peeping into the "love-cars" parked on the hill above the town. Weren't the cops vigilant enough to keep an eye on the visiting crazy poet and peeping tom? After all, Lowell himself confesses that his "mind's not right." On another occasion, I received an essay on Plath's "Daddy" which began, "Sylvia Plath, a Jewish woman born in Germany to a Nazi father. . . ." These students may not have been very informed, nor did they apparently pay much attention to what was going on in class, but in a certain sense their assumptions were logical, if not sensible. If Confessional poetry emphasizes a stance of intimate personal disclosure, then shouldn't we assume that the poet is telling the literal truth about himself? No wonder college students voted overwhelmingly for Reagan in 1980 and 1984.

There's little excuse for this sort of gullibility among college literature students, and even less of an excuse for a sadly similar sort of gullibility on the part of critics who have written about the Confessional group, for the prevailing tendency in their writings is to see autobiographical poems *as* autobiography. For whatever reasons, the Confessional poets have attracted the sorts of critics who have regarded Lowell, Berryman, Plath, and related figures such as Sexton and Snodgrass as rather helpless chroniclers of their personal lives' traumas and miseries. Dabbling just a bit in psychoanalytical criticism, suspicious of the New Critical methods of literary analysis against which the Confessional poets rebelled so strongly, and generally indifferent to other current modes of literary theory, these critics have come to regard the poems of the Confessional school as simply more compressed versions of the self-accusations and troubled meditations which occur in many writers' diary entries. As a consequence of this tendency, we have gloating, gossipy, and histrionic treatises such as Jeffrey Meyers's recent *Manic Power: Robert Lowell and His Circle.* Although he purports to be writing a serious study, Meyers is instead engaged in a *New York Post*–style sensationalizing of the lives of the Lowell circle. Such tabloidization by Meyers and other critics is often accompanied by a similarly simplistic reading of the poems. Meyers's appraisal of Confessional poetry is usually limited to remarks such as these:

> They helped to establish the dangerously fashionable notion that living on the edge of suicide—or falling over—was the most authentic stance, almost an absolute requirement of the modern sensibility. John Bayley observed that their menacing, morbid verse is "almost wholly interior-ized, the soul hung up in chains of nerves and arteries and veins." Their poems are arrested in their own finality, "like a suicide hitting the pavement."[2]

What critics such as Meyers seem not to notice is that there are borrowed dogs aplenty in the self-portraits which constitute Confessional verse. Although the borrowed dogs have, perhaps, moved a bit into the background of the photograph, they remain integral to its composition. Granted, there are times when the poet tries slyly to conceal his borrowed dogs. Lowell's insertion of his prose memoir "91 Revere Street" exactly in the middle of *Life Studies* is on one level meant to validate the "truthfulness" of the poems which follow it, but does this mean that Lowell has tethered himself to the literal truth? Hardly. And it is, needless to say, the robust and picaresque character of Henry that makes *The Dream Songs* great. While the introspective and deeply neurotic John Berryman is the puppeteer who commands the quixotic Henry, *The Dream Songs* belong to their performer, not to the man who toils with the strings of the marionette. In sum, the author of the Confessional poem identifies with the poem's speaker, but it is simplistic to regard author and speaker as always one and the same. The costume of the speaker and the borrowed dogs employed do not often flatter the performer of the poem, but they frequently serve to enhance the poem's tension, complexity, and ultimate artistic success. This can be seen in the sequence which is one of the most interesting of all the "borrowed dog acts" of the Confessional movement, S. S. Gardons's *Remains.* It's not a secret—as it was meant in some degree to be in the fifties and early sixties—that the author of Gardons's poems is W. D. Snodgrass, who, as Gardons, wrote some of his most harrowing and memorable verse. Gardons's poems began appearing in journals in the late 1950s at roughly the same time during which Snodgrass's own early poems surfaced, those which were eventually gathered in his first volume, *Heart's Needle.* Only a handful of Gardons's efforts were published, but they appeared in respected places, most notably in Hall, Pack, and Simpson's influential formalist anthology, *New Poets of England and America,* which featured the first anthology appearances of James Wright, Robert Bly, and—near the end of the alphabetically arranged selections, far removed from G-men such as Gardons and W. S. Graham—one W. D. Snodgrass. We're told in Gardons's contributor's note that he is a Texan, attended Rice University, and now works in a gas station: quite a significant contrast to the information given about the other contributors, who are bejewelled with the 1950s' most prestigious vitae—Prix de Romes, Guggies, and Fulbrights; teaching gigs at East Coast universities. Gardons, then, is not a typical 1950s academic formalist, is not, in fact, an academic at all. Perhaps this is why, unsullied by the need to goose-step to some English department's publish-or-perish marching orders, Gardons chose not to be a terribly prolific writer and certainly not a very public one. In fact, his single slim volume of poetry was probably published posthumously, in a fine press edition of two hundred copies, in 1970. The collection, entitled *Remains,* contains a prefatory note which elaborates on the earlier information given about Gardons and relates a mysterious disappearance which is at least as interesting as those of Weldon Kees or Jimmie Hoffa:

> S. S. Gardons lived most of his life in and near Red Creek, Texas. For years he worked as a gas station attendant, though he took a few university classes in Houston, and later became an owner of a cycle shop.

> Also a musician, he played lead guitar in a well-known rock group, Chicken Gumbo. This sequence of poems was collected by his friends after his disappearance on a hunting trip in the mountains. From the condition of his abandoned motorcycle, it was impossible to determine whether he suffered foul play, was attacked by animals, or merely became confused and lost, or perhaps fell victim to amnesia. At present the case is listed as unsolved.[3]

Of course, the identity of the true author of the Gardons poems was never, as A. Poulin Jr. reminds us in his foreword to the second edition of *Remains,* "a very well-kept secret among the literary grapevine."[4] Poulin's BOA Editions released *Remains* under Snodgrass's own name in 1985, and in Snodgrass's recent *Selected Poems* the Gardons oeuvre appears in its entirety. In Snodgrass's endnotes to this volume, we are given the ostensible reason for the abandonment of the Gardons disguise: after the death of Snodgrass's parents, he was able to release the poems under his own name. And indeed, the portraits of the mother and father who figure in *Remains* are merciless ones, hardly the sort of characterizations that even the most estranged of sons would want his parents to see.

So there we have it. Gardons was created in part to perpetrate a po-biz hoax or in-joke, and in part to shield Snodgrass's parents from hurt. Now that Gardons is out of the way (perhaps even eaten by wolves), can we simply, though belatedly, add an intriguing sequence of poems to the Snodgrass canon and forget about the subterfuges their author employed in originally bringing the poems to print? The New Critic lurking in us all would of course say yes and ask that we see *Remains* as a sequence of eight *very* well-wrought urns and that we leave issues which speculate upon the identity and intentions of the poems' author to bad-boy dabblers in deconstruction. But the fact remains that *Remains* presents us with some vexing problems pertaining to the interrelationship between Gardons and Snodgrass, problems which must be solved if we are to truly understand the poems. Why, for example, does Gardons often seem to be a better writer than Snodgrass? And why is it that the poems of *Heart's Needle*—especially its famous title sequence, upon which much of Snodgrass's reputation rests—are in many ways less engaging than the more forceful and dramatically complex poems of *Remains?*

That a writer's best work can result from a kind of literary hoax is not as surprising as it may initially seem. There is, as the psychologist Louise J. Kaplan points out in her recent study of Thomas Chatterton, a long tradition of "imposter-poets," whose literary production reaches its fullest expression in what might at first seem elaborate practical jokes.[5] Kaplan argues that the fatherless teenager Chatterton had no benevolent authority figure in his life and therefore chose to create one in the form of his bogus fourteenth-century monk, Thomas Rowley; Kaplan further contends that the poems of Rowley are far more significant and expressive than the satiric poems which Chatterton published under his own name after his Rowley hoax had been exposed.[6] Surely the twentieth century's best-known imposter-poet is the Portuguese writer Fernando Pessoa, who referred to his distinct alter egos—Alberto Cariero, Alvaro de Campos, and Ricardo Reyes—not merely as pseudonyms but as *heteronyms.* He concocted elaborate biographies for each and even confessed that one of the trio, Cariero, wrote better Portuguese than could Pessoa himself—a claim that is borne out when comparing the lack-luster poems which appeared under Pessoa's own name with the dazzling productions of Cariero and his heteronymic brothers. The imposter-poet not only borrows dogs for his self-portraits but goes to elaborate lengths in order to make us think the borrowed dogs are his—he fakes their pedigrees, gives them new names, and somehow, in the act of borrowing, creates something of depth, a joke of deadly seriousness.

Perhaps it is this very seriousness which most distinguishes Gardons from Snodgrass. Although the persona of *Heart's Needle* confronts some very troubling personal issues—divorce, separation from a beloved young daughter, and the speaker's own aging—his approach to these subjects never strays too far afield from the elegance and wit which characterize so much of the poetry of the 1950s. The Snodgrass of *Heart's Needle* is prone to melancholy but is finally more interested in *checking* his sorrow through self-deprecating humor than he is in straightforwardly expressing his grief. Thus, we have the tone of "April Inventory," perhaps Snodgrass's best-known poem. It's all there in the opening stanzas:

The green catalpa tree has turned
All white; the cherry blooms once more.
In one whole year I haven't learned
A blessed thing they pay you for.
The blossoms snow down in my hair;
The trees and I will soon be bare.

The trees have more than I to spare.
The sleek, expensive girls I teach,
Younger and pinker every year,
Bloom gradually out of reach.
The pear tree lets its petals drop
Like dandruff on a tabletop.[7]

This is wonderfully modulated phrasing, of course, but the net effect is as if Richard Wilbur had rewritten one of the anxiety-ridden comic soliloquies we encounter in Woody Allen films. Somehow, the tone and the form of the poem are at odds: is the speaker telling us that things are much worse than they seem, or is he simply exhorting himself to "lighten up"? Although Hayden Carruth greeted *Heart's Needle* with praise for its "genuine feeling" and Donald Hall spoke of the book's "true feeling," "April Inventory"'s *feelings* are in fact expressed in a rather muddled fashion—as a catalogue of somewhat wimpy ironies masquerading as a record of the poet's struggle toward wisdom.[8] Yes, I know I'm being unduly harsh toward the poem, but contrasting it with the terse eloquence of "Viewing the Body," a short lyric at the center of *Remains,* shows that my characterizations are not wholly groundless. Gardons, too, has the capacity for irony, but irony of a much more brutal sort. One doesn't even need to know that it is Gardons's sister in the casket to see that the Hardyesque snarl of the tone arises from a very immediate sense of grief and pain:

> Flowers like a gangster's funeral;
>   Eyeshadow like a whore.
> They all say she isn't beautiful.
>   She who never wore
>
> Lipstick or such a dress,
>   Never got taken out,
> Was scarcely looked at, much less
>   Wanted or talked about;
>
> Who, gray as a mouse, crept
>   The dark halls at her mother's
> Or snuggled, soft, and slept
>   Alone in the dim bedcovers.
>
> Today at last she holds
>   All eyes and a place of honor
> Till the obscene red folds
>   Of satin close down upon her.

Instead of the posh tetrameters we find in "April Inventory," Gardons employs a stuttering but brilliantly effective trimeter: spondees and trochaic substitutions are everywhere, and they help to give the poem its gruff dignity. The strained effort to pepper "April Inventory" with the occasional colloquialism ("In one whole year I haven't learned / A blessed thing they pay you for") contrasts sharply with the blistering conversational bite of a passage such as Gardons's "Never got taken out / Was scarcely looked at, much less / Wanted or talked about. . . ." (It's worth remembering here that Gardons went to the "college of life" and not to the Iowa Writer's Workshop.)

"Viewing the Body" should not be seen as Gardons's best poem, no more than "April Inventory" should be regarded as Snodgrass's worst. Yet the two poems are very typical of their respective authors' tones and concerns. Gardons tells it like it is; he has a fine eye for the right, dramatic detail and is always the outraged, impulsive witness to human cruelty and suffering. Snodgrass is introspective, analytical, discursive. Gardons's principal creation is a sequence of poems that explores the grisly dynamics of a pathological family unit; there are six main characters. *Remains* reads like a novella or one-act—it could be turned into a marvelous opera libretto. The principal effort of Snodgrass's *Heart's Needle* adopts a different kind of model; the title sequence is a poetic diary, unfolding over the course of a year. Only two figures are involved, the speaker and his young daughter, to whom he addresses the poems. *Heart's Needle* is meditative and rangy; its reader is meant to be a kind of eavesdropper. In *Remains,* however, the reader is led to a seat in the audience, the houselights dim, and before him the Gardons clan struts their stuff. They are not a happy family; the playlet reminds us not of the Waltons but of O'Neill's tortured Tyrones.

Gardons and Snodgrass, then, are not one and the same, and the other differences between the author of *Remains* and the poet of *Heart's Needle* could easily be brought forth. But my purpose in the following pages will be instead to talk of Gardons's poems themselves. Gardons does, after all, deserve to be better known. Although I don't think Gardons would have begrudged Snodgrass and other poets their Pulitzers and writing fellowships, one sometimes wonders if Gardons would have welcomed a little more attention: to be a cult figure within today's already miniscule poetry audience is to have a very small readership indeed.

Gardons would certainly agree with Snodgrass's contention, expressed in his essay "Tact and the Poet's Force," that "the poet faces the same problem faced daily by the individual conscience. We know that we must restrain some part of our energies or we destroy ourselves. Yet, as we turn these energies back against ourselves, they too may destroy us."[9] This statement could serve as the thesis of *Remains.* Gardons confronts a world where the Middle American virtues of restraint and tactfulness are almost invariably perverted into forces of repression and destruction. The effects of such a transformation are studied in excruciatingly vivid detail, and try as he might, Gardons seems ill-equipped to offer alternatives to the pattern. All of the family members who populate Gardons's poems are victims of this process. Gardons and his parents are psychologically maimed by it, and his sister, who had never left home, has died from its effects, from an asthmatic condition which is interpreted by Gardons as psychosomatically induced. The results of this process are so crippling that Gardons repeatedly wonders if his sister is not, in fact, better off dead. In "The Survivors," he addresses the dead sister during a visit to his parents' home. "Nothing is different here," he concludes. Perhaps not: in an earlier poem he imagines his sister in a gray and Attic sort of afterlife. Its TV set notwithstanding, the parents' house is depicted as a similar kind of underworld.

> The Venetian blinds are drawn;
> Inside, it is dark and still.
> Always upon some errand, one by one,
> They go from room to room, vaguely, in the wan
> Half-light, deprived of will.
>
> Mostly they hunt for some-
> Thing they've misplaced; otherwise
> They turn the pages of magazines and hum
> Tunelessly. At any time they come
> To pass they drop their eyes.
>
> Only at night they meet.
> By voiceless summoning
> They come to the livingroom; each repeats
> Some words he has memorized; each takes his seat
> In the hushed, expectant ring
>
> By the television set.
> No one can draw his eyes
> From that unnatural, cold light. They wait. . . .

How did the Gardons family come to be this way? By looking at the sequence's structure, some explanation can be arrived at, and we can see what efforts Gardons makes at coping with these horrors. Much of the blame is placed upon the parents. In the diptych portrait which opens the sequence, we are introduced to "The Mother" and to the subject of "Diplomacy: The Father." The two poems bristle with merciless invective. The mother is portrayed as domineering, unforgiving, and silently vengeful. Although the father is, as the title of the poem implies, diplomatic and deferential, these qualities are seen as flaws—conflict avoidance pursued to the point of cowardice. Need it be added that opposites attract and that a sort of perverse symbiosis has been created by this union?

Still, it is the mother who controls the Gardons home. The metaphors employed to describe her are celestial, but also dark and brooding. Such a combination makes for some very unsettling writing, as in the poem's opening stanzas:

> She stands in the dead center like a star;
> They form around her like satellites
> Taking her energies, her heat, light
> And massive attraction on their paths, however far.
>
> Born of her own flesh; still, she feels them drawn
> Into the outer cold by dark forces;
> They are in love with suffering and perversion,
> With the community of pain. Thinking them gone,
>
> Out of her reach, she is consoled by evil
> In neighbors, children, the world she cannot change,
> That lightless universe where they range
> Out of the comforts of her disapproval.

Rather churned-up rhetoric, but we ain't seen nothin' yet. In the stanzas that follow, the rhetorical flourishes continue to crescendo:

> If evil did not exist, she would create it.
> To die in righteousness, her martyrdom
> To that sweet domain they have bolted from.
> Then, at last, she can think that she is hated
>
> And is content. Things can decay, break,
> Spoil themselves; who cares? She'll gather the debris
> With loving tenderness to give them; she
> Will weave a labyrinth of waste, wreckage
>
> And hocus-pocus; leave free no fault
> Or cornerhole outside those lines of force
> Where she and only she can thread a course.
> All else in her grasp grows clogged and halts.

This goes on for two more stanzas. If the Gardons household is a kind of underworld, then the mother has been selected to play Satan—a distinctly Miltonic

Satan, in fact, for the Latinate phrasing and rhetorical flourishes turn the poem into a sort of pastiche of the infernal councils which open *Paradise Lost.* Compare the above descriptions to Satan's scheming in Book I:

> And all is not lost; the unconquerable will,
> And study of revenge, immortal hate,
> And courage never to submit or yield:
> And what is else not to be overcome?

It's an outrageous scheme which Gardons pursues in the poem, but he is too purposeful, too angry, to let the writing become merely an outlandish tour de force. Gardons believes in the integrity of his project, however unfair and unflattering a portrait "The Mother" may seem to us.

Regrettably, the father's poem is not nearly as powerful; perhaps it is not intended to be. The problems of style Gardons chooses to confront in the poem are tricky ones; if cosmic-sounding Miltonisms are the proper style for describing the vampirish mother, then a kind of jargon-polluted gassiness is the language sought for the father, who is not simply the henpecked husband. His adamant neutrality, his pose of diplomacy, is seen as just as blameworthy and manipulative as any of the mother's stratagems, for it is the source of his misuse of power:

> Your fixed aim,
> whatever it costs, must still be for a balance
> of power in the family, the firm, the whole world through.
> Exactly the same
>
> as a balance of impotence—in any group or nation
> as in yourself.
> Suppose some one of them rose up and could succeed
> your foe—he'd *be* your foe. To underlings, dispense
> all they can ask but don't need; give them till they need
> your giving. One gift could free them: confidence.
> They'd never dare ask. Betray no dedication
> to any creed
>
> or person—talk high ideals; then you'll be known
> as, in yourself,
> harmless. . . .

The father may not dwell in Milton's hell, but he certainly would be assured a place in Dante's, probably in Circle Eight, with the Hypocrites, Flatterers, and Fraudulent Counselors. The Flatterers, you'll recall, are condemned to swim in bullshit for eternity. Unfortunately, although bullshit may be the essential weapon which the father employs for maintaining a balance of power within the family and within his professional life, it is not poetry's most effective stylistic device. The workings of the father's mind are evoked through an impossibly intricate verse form, an eight-line stanza rhyming a/b/c/d/c/d/a/c. Generally, lines 1, 4, 5, and 6 are written in pentameter, lines 3 and 7 in hexameter, and lines 2 and 8 in dimeter, with line 2 comprising a refrain which is repeated in every stanza, "as in yourself." The poem is *Remains*'s longest effort, and it is apparently one which has always given Gardons trouble: between the 1970 and 1985 editions of the sequence he substantially revised the poem. Yet even in his latest version the problem persists: how does one write an interesting poem about garrulousness and evasiveness without the poem itself becoming garrulous and evasive? Gardons's colleague Snodgrass confronts similar problems in testing the prosodic limits of the imitative fallacy in the monologues of *The Fuehrer Bunker*—the poems of the inhumanly analytical Himmler appear on graph paper; Magda Goebbels poisons her children while reciting a kind of nursery rhyme—yet these later efforts are considerably more successful than is the father's poem.

In the sequence's next three poems, there is a marked change of approach. The ironic grandiosity and pyrotechnical displays of the portraits of the parents are replaced by a hard-boiled realism and a more businesslike use of form. The earlier poems' invective turns to pathos as we are introduced to Gardons himself and to his sister. "A Mouse" begins with a memory from childhood. The tone is saved from bathos by Gardons's barely suppressed fury:

> I remember one evening—we were small—
> Playing outdoors, we found a mouse,
> A dusty little gray one, lying
> By the side steps. Afraid he might be dead,
> We carried him all around the house
> On a piece of tinfoil, crying.
>
> Ridiculous children; we could bawl
> Our eyes out about nothing. Still,
> How much violence had we seen?
> They teach you—quick—you have to be well-bred
> In all events. We can't win.

The poem then takes a rather preposterous turn, equating the sister with the wounded field mouse and the "old insatiable loves" of the parents with the predatory games of a cat, who "pats at you, wants to see you crawl / Some, then, picks you back alive; / That needs you just a little hurt." Still, we feel that Gardons has earned this garish conceit. He even seems to get away with the tricky business of implying that he, too, can be identified with the figure of the tortured mouse:

And then the little animal
Plays you out; the dulled heart year by year
Turns from its own needs, forgets its grief.
Asthmatic, timid, twenty-five, unwed—
The day we left you by your grave,
I wouldn't spare one tear.

This sort of corrosive deadpan continues in the previously quoted "Viewing the Body" and in "Disposal." The latter achieves its power by simply listing some of the dead sister's personal effects and has the tone and structure of certain poems of Larkin's, such as "Mr. Bleaney." Snodgrass has written admiringly of Larkin's work, and Gardons too seems to have studied him. In fact, the ending of "Disposal" is one of the few poems I can think of which actually outdoes Larkin in the dyspeptic hiss of its closure:

Spared all need, all passion,
Saved from loss, she lies boxed in satins

Like a pair of party shoes
That seemed to never find a taker;
We send back to its maker
A life somehow gone out of fashion
But still too good to use.

The method of sequence changes again in the following poem, "The Fourth of July." More dramatically and narratively complex than the previous poems, its ironies are enacted upon a larger stage than before. Gardons and his second wife are on a visit home to his family's rust-belt mill town, a place Gardons conjures up through the use of by now familiar imagery of the infernal. It's no wonder the sister could not breathe in this environment, for as Gardons tells us, "the sulphurous smoke / That is my father's world" has permeated everything. Although its steel mills are closed because of a workers' strike, the town remains "stifling," "smoke-filled," and after the evening's fireworks display a politician "fumes." When a "blonde schoolgirl" is crowned "Queen of this war-contract factory town," Gardons imagines his sister, now dead for year, as celebrating the anniversary of her death in the underworld, "a tinsel wreath on her dark head." Yet these lavishly macabre descriptions serve merely as the backdrop to the more dreadful ironies which are presented to us in the Gardons home. Gardons himself is smoldering, fuming in a silent rage. He and his wife are sleeping in his older sister's room, still furnished with her possessions. To express his anger is his only hope for defeating his domestic hell, but silence is a Gardons family tradition. And besides,

> What can anybody say?
>
> In her room, nights, we lie awake
> By racks of unworn party dresses, shoes,
> Her bedside asthma pipe, her glasses whose
> Correction no one else will take.
>
> Stuffed dogs look at us from the shelf
> When we sit down together at the table.
> You put a face on things the best you're able
> And keep your comments to yourself.

Furthermore, Gardons bears the burden of his guilt for having brought his pregnant wife into this clapboard isle of the dead. Her birthday is less a celebration than it is a rite of initiation into the Gardons family's underworld:

> It is a hideous mistake.
> My young wife, unforgivably alive,
> Takes a deep breath and blows out twenty-five
> Candles on her birthday cake.
>
> It is agreed she'll get her wish.
> The candles smell; smoke settles through the room
> Like a cheap stage set for Juliet's tomb.
> I leave my meal cold on the dish.

By the conclusion of the poem, nothing is resolved. Gardons's grim observations have become a kind of litany:

> It is an evil, stupid joke:
> My wife is pregnant; my sister's in her grave.
> We live in the home of the free and the brave.
> No one would hear me, even if I spoke.

"The Survivors," the poem which follows "The Fourth of July," continues to explore the same sorts of concerns. But by addressing the poem to his sister, Gardons is able to overcome to some extent his misanthropic rage. The ending of the poem, although it is no less ironic than the conclusion of "The Fourth of July," is suffused with regret. The purpose of the sequence's previous poems has been as much to condemn the family's twisted values as it has been to elegize the sister. Yet "The Survivors," despite its title, ends by belonging to the sister. Gardons's rage and obsession with decay turn—almost involuntarily—into a poignant farewell:

> In the cellar where the sewers
> Rise, unseen, the pale white
> Ants grow in decaying stacks of old newspapers.
> Outside, streetlamps appear, and friends of yours
> Call children in for the night.
>
> And you have been dead one year.
> Nothing is different here.

In its tentative way, "The Survivors" also introduces the theme which concerns Gardons in *Remains*'s final poem, "To a Child." Although Gardons's sister could not escape her suffocating fate, and although Gardons himself believes he will never recover from the cruelty he suffered as his parents' child, it is possible that other children will grow up to be normal and healthy. Although Gardons cannot save himself, perhaps he can save his own daughter and, in attempting to do so, change *Remains*'s bleak expressions of blame and betrayal into something more nurturing than stark pathos and anger. Although "To a Child" concerns itself with renewal, it is less an arrival at redemption than it is a coda for previous poems—it asks us to read the sequence as a grim cautionary tale. The epistolary mode recalls *Heart's Needle,* but "To a Child" is a far more turbulent poem. *Don't let this happen to you,* Gardons seems to plead to his daughter. Yet at the same time, he fears that perhaps the die has already been cast because of his own inadequacies as a father and husband. He begins his lecture with the intention to discuss with his daughter "the birds and the bees," but the poem soon becomes an account of his own sexual anxieties, a meditation on death, and an attempt to put his divorce into some perspective. The structure of the poem, however, is a sly one, anything but rambling. Although we at first suspect that the poem's circuitousness is caused by a self-conscious father's reluctance to get to his point about sex, we eventually see that Gardons is striving for catharsis. He wants, more than anything else, forgiveness from his daughter, and admits to his own role in his poisonous family history:

We have walked through living rooms

And seen the way the dodder,
That pale white parasitic love-vine, thrives
Coiling the zinnias in the ardor
Of its close embrace.
We have watched grown men debase
Themselves from their embittered wives. . . .

The line about grown men "debasing themselves," with its ambiguous reference, comes shortly after a passage describing the effects of Gardons's divorce and his separation from his daughter: it indicts himself as well as his father, and Gardons's own admission of guilt might to some degree help to justify the horrific allusion to the mother which immediately follows it:

And we have seen an old sow that could smother
The sucklings in her stye,
That could devour her own farrow.
We have seen my sister in her narrow
Casket. Without love we die;
With love we kill each other.

A dizzying tour de force, this passage. Before we are able to recover from the shocking characterization of the mother as a sow who smothers her offspring—a comparison that has already been made, but in a much less blatant fashion, near the end of "The Mother"—we are again reminded that Gardons feels he has a reason for his wrath: his vicious hyperbole is followed by an abrupt jump cut to the figure of the sister in her coffin. Then Gardons sums it all up with a glib perversion of the ending of "September 1, 1939." Yet this statement's grim conundrum, its terrible double-blind, has been the theme of all of *Remains*'s poems thus far. But as *Remains* ends, in Gardons's most notable lines, he chooses to rebel against this belief. He asks that his daughter see the world with a vision that is different from his own. His phrasing is cautious, his rhetoric tentative, yet the sequence ends with a flourish of genuine grandeur:

You are afraid, now, of dying;
Sick with change and loss;
You think of your own self lying
Still in the ground while someone takes your room.
Today, you felt the small life toss
In your stepmother's womb.

I sit here by you in the summer's lull
Near the lost handkerchiefs of lovers
To tell you when your brother
Will be born; how, and why.
I tell you love is possible.
We have to try.

And thus S. S. Gardons disappears, though surely his influence lives on in certain of Snodgrass's later works—in the monologues of *The Fuehrer Bunker* and in the character of "W.D.," the alter ego who ambles about in many of Snodgrass's most recent poems. Such creations are merely borrowed dogs of a different color. Snodgrass and Gardons would both concur, I'm sure, with a remark of Machado's. "In order to write poetry," he said, "one must first invent the poet who will write it." From necessity, from what could only have been a deep inner need which could not find expression in the poems of W. D. Snodgrass, the poet S. S. Gardons was born. And Gardons was a powerful and original writer, superbly capable. In fact, if W. D. Snodgrass had never existed, then S. S. Gardons would surely have invented him.

(1988)

10.

Illegible Due to Blotching: Poetic Authenticity and Its Discontents

No book of poetry of the past decade has attracted quite the same attention as Ted Hughes's *Birthday Letters.* Released simultaneously in Britain and the United States in January of 1998, the book sold out several printings on both sides of the Atlantic within weeks, was reviewed respectfully and frequently, and even became the subject of front-page news items and feature stories, something unheard of for a book of poetry, even one by a well-established poet such as Hughes, who was Britain's poet laureate and who died of cancer within a few months of the book's publication. Of course the reason for the book's popularity has as much or more to do with the public's craving for scandal and gossip than it does with literature. As everyone knows, *Birthday Letters* is addressed to Hughes's late wife, the American poet Sylvia Plath, whose poems are anthologized for the college market at least as frequently as those of Donne and Chaucer and whose turbulent relationship with Hughes, culminating in her suicide after Hughes had left her for another woman, seems a motivating force behind many of Plath's best-known poems. Hughes had for over three decades kept a public silence about the pair's relationship, save to act as editor of several volumes of Plath's posthumously published poetry and prose. But now, with *Birthday Letters,* readers were finally to get Hughes's side of the story. It's no wonder, then, that by March of 1998 the volume had sold over 125,000 copies in the United States alone—during a time when print runs for poetry are normally less then a tenth of that amount.[1] Sales continued to climb in the following months, and Hughes sold the movie rights to the volume. The Merchant-Ivory team has a film adaptation of the book in development, and leaked portions of Ivory's script, entitled *The Dead Bell,* have made their way onto several of the websites devoted to Plath. Merchant-Ivory has even signed on, with Hughes's apparent blessing, the actors who will portray the pair. British actor Gary Oldman seems to have been selected for the role of Hughes, and, after actresses such as Nicole Kidman and Jody Foster had been rumored to be in contention for the part, the role of Plath was awarded to Gwyneth Paltrow. The May 1998 issue of *Vanity Fair* quotes Hughes's reaction to hearing Paltrow read for the part of Plath: "She *was* Sylvia. When she read 'Lady Lazarus,' my hair stood on end—it was as if a time machine had shuttled me back half a lifetime ago."[2]

Unfortunately, however, the public may have to wait a very long time before seeing *Birthday Letters* on the big screen. The movie is likely to be put on hold indefinitely now that the strangest chapter of all in the Hughes-Plath saga has begun to unfold. The British daily *The Observer* was the first to break the story early in June, and it has since rocked the literary world, becoming a scandal which even threatens to shake the foundations of several British governmental ministries. On June 8, 1999, *The Observer* revealed what had for five decades been a secret known only to a handful of operatives in the British Intelligence Service, MI5. Neither Ted Hughes nor Sylvia Plath ever existed.[3] The pair were in fact the product of a hugely elaborate literary hoax—or more properly a literary conspiracy—originally concocted by MI5 in the 1950s as one of the more Byzantine operations of the Cold War and continuing in an ever more elaborate form into the recent past, when the escalating costs of the hoax prompted the Blair government to downsize the project by alleging that "Ted Hughes" had died. That the intelligence community would be willing to perpetuate a hoax of this particular type and magnitude may at first seem to beggar the imagination. But the reasons for the continuing existence of MI5's Hughes-Plath operation are in some respects self-evident ones, typical of most government agencies. What started as a simple project of minor disinformation and espionage turned instead into a governmental white elephant fed by a bloated bureaucracy. Although the exact budgetary figures remain secret, it is likely that the MI5 division responsible for perpetuating the Hughes-Plath hoax, code named Operation Ariel, at one time employed between 100 and 150 full-time workers, operating from a secret suite of offices in Whitechapel. Over the years this group has been responsible for creating the entire oeuvre, published and in manuscript form, of Hughes and Plath; for training and coaching the agents assigned to act the parts of Hughes, Plath, and their family members; and for sustaining the campaign of disinformation designed to prevent readers and scholars from discovering the government's ruse. It appears that the secrecy of the operation began to unravel this spring when retired MI5 operative Michael Weldon, one of the four agents who over the years had been assigned to impersonate Hughes, made a deathbed confession of his role in the conspiracy to freelance journalist Wilfred Olsen. Olsen then sold the story to *The Observer,* and the rest is history, though history of a most improbable sort, proving once again that fact is stranger than fiction.

Operation Ariel seems to have begun in the mid-1950s, when a group of MI5 specialists on "cultural intelligence" surveyed the postwar British literary scene and in a top-secret white paper came to several troubling conclusions, one of which was that poetry in England was in a bad way. British literature, like the British empire itself, was in decline, and of all the literary arts, poetry seemed the most moribund. T. S. Eliot, the only poet of international stature dwelling in the U.K., was not a native Briton and had lapsed into poetic silence. The younger generation of poets was indifferently talented; Philip Larkin and Thom Gunn, its most promising figures, were problematic, at least as far as the government was concerned. Larkin, a balding and misanthropic Hull librarian, was decidedly unsexy, hardly the dashing and Byronic figure who MI5 felt would be required for the salvation of British poesy. And Gunn, although he surely cut a sexier figure than Larkin, was sexy in the wrong way: agency surveillance and phone taps revealed what several operatives had long suspected—Gunn was an "invert." The white paper concluded by noting with alarm that poetry in the Soviet Union and in several of its Eastern-bloc satellites was thriving. A "poetry gap" existed, and MI5 arrived at a novel means to close it. Seeing that no suitable young British poet existed, a small special-operations unit of the agency set about creating one, and so, toward the end of 1955, "Ted Hughes" was born, savior-to-be of British poetry. The name was suitably manly, and the character was given a background deemed appropriate for a poet designed to act as the bard of a democratic and classless postwar Britain. "Theodore Hughes" and "T. H. Hughes," the poet's original monikers, were rejected as sounding elitist. A cover story for Hughes was devised—an upbringing on a Yorkshire farm, a B.A. from Cambridge—and an operative was selected to act the part of Hughes in public. Hughes's verse, however, would be authored by a committee of specially trained agents operating out of a small basement office in Whitechapel. Within its first two years the operation was judged a rousing success, so much so that MI5 sought to expand its range by creating an American poetess to act as Hughes's companion. It is at this point that Operation Ariel became a joint MI5 and CIA operation. In order to symbolically present the spirit of Britain and America's close alliance in the Cold War, Sylvia Plath was devised, and several young CIA operatives, most of them recent graduates of Seven Sisters schools such as Smith and Vassar, were sent to London to assist the project. Various individuals of the Operation Ariel office team devised the poems which later appeared in Hughes's first two collections, *Hawk in the Rain* and *Lupercal,* as well as those poems which were gathered in Plath's debut volume, *The Colossus.* As the poems were composed, microfilm versions of their drafts and finished versions were left at various drop-off points for the operatives impersonating Plath and Hughes.

Although none of the members of Operation Ariel's office team had written much verse prior to their assignment to the project, perusal of some literary journals and anthologies gave the team its models. Some of the poems were cowritten by project members; others were the work of operatives working alone. Winnifred Eimers, a young CIA recruit who is now living in retirement in Florida and who at one point played a crucial role in the CIA's botched efforts to assassinate Castro, and a young Cornishwoman named Millicent Shollworth seem to have been the most prolific authors of the Hughes and Plath oeuvre. It is Shollworth, in fact, who may be the indirect cause of the formation of the Plath cult—which seems to have arisen for reasons of expedience having little to do with Operation Ariel's original intent: Shollworth, born into a family of radical socialists and fluent in both Russian and Polish, made contact with Soviet agents during a 1961 trip to Frankfurt. Alerted to the success of Operation Ariel and suffering major setbacks in their own poetry fabrication operations, the Russians sought both intelligence information and creative support. Shollworth provided them with both and for two years acted as a double agent before defecting to Russia in February 1963. Shollworth is one the most brilliant and devious figures of Cold War espionage, and her defection hurt Operation Ariel greatly, for MI5 quickly realized that no other of its operatives could turn out Plath poetry of quite the same intensity and quality. Embarrassed at the loss of its best poetry operative to the KGB, M15 decided to call in from the cold its agent impersonating Plath and close down the Plath division of Operation Ariel entirely. A cover story was then devised in which Plath would kill herself in reaction to Hughes's infidelity and as a consequence of her long history of mental instability. There would be no more Plath poems.

Yet the fact that there would be no more Plath poems did not stop the Plath Juggernaut, a consequence wholly unforeseen by MI5. The public, attracted both to the Plath fabrications themselves and to the glamorously tragic circumstances which had been invented to explain her death, could not get enough of the dead poet, and since 1963 the primary purpose of Operation Ariel has been to simultaneously propagandize for the Plath industry and to conceal the Plath-Hughes conspiracy; the 1963 decision to kill Plath off by suicide is one that many in the agency came to rue. As one anonymous operative who worked on the project during the crisis year of 1963 told the BBC last month, "We would all have been better off if we'd done her in some other way. No one makes a cult of someone killed by a falling brick or run over by a lorry." Although the staff of Operation Ariel has grown ever larger over the years, Plath's estate has generated a considerable income through book sales and reprint permission fees, and this has turned out to be an unforeseen boon to the agency. In his most recent

Observer piece, journalist Wilfred Olsen alleges that in the mid-1980s at least some of this money was laundered by M15 operatives Tomás Disch and William A. Logan through a Cayman Islands numbered account and was used by MI5 and the CIA to fund various covert activities in Latin America. Both Logan and Disch were later found garroted in a Guatemala City brothel, probably the victims of a Sandinista hit squad. In other words, Lady Lazarus helped to purchase Contra rifles and was responsible for more deaths than her own imaginary one. Over the years, the project's Plath-related activities have tended to overshadow those centered around Hughes, so much so that assignment to the project's Hughes bureau was seen by many in the agency as the kiss of death, the province of has-beens and burnt-out cases charged primarily with penning children's books and laureate doggerel about royal christenings. The agency's neglect of its Hughes activities' production in recent years eventually became a source of embarrassment for MI5, and the creation of *Birthday Letters* last year was meant to rectify this problem. It was designed to be the poet's final production; thereafter Hughes, too, would be killed off.

Anyone who has watched the news in recent weeks is aware of the repercussions of the Plath-Hughes hoax's exposure, both in London and to a lesser extent in Washington. Investigations have been launched by Parliament, the Blair government has replaced a number of ministers, and it seems only a matter of time before Operation Ariel is shut down for good. In Washington, Senator Jesse Helms, bemoaning the CIA's involvement in a project deemed by him as frivolous, has used the scandal as an opportunity to once again call for the abolition of the NEA. Winnifred Eimers's appearance last week on *Nightline* to explain to Ted Koppel how she composed certain of the Plath poems garnered ratings which hadn't been seen since the Simpson trial. The media's feeding frenzy about all things Ariel in recent weeks has been so rabid as to overwhelm those voices, largely from the academy, that have speculated about what all this means for contemporary literature. After all, two of our era's principal poets, one of whom has been seen by many as a feminist and literary martyr and whose poems have been the most enduring example of what has come to be known as "Confessional" poetry, have been shown to be forgeries. Critics of a Foucauldian bent have seen the Plath-Hughes hoax as further proof that it is culture and power dynamics which create literary texts, not authors. "This hoax makes the best argument yet for anti-essentialism," wrote Language poet Charles Bernstein when the scandal broke.[4] And surely the literary reputations of Plath and Hughes will now undergo a reappraisal. Here is how Richard Howard regards the situation: "The easy felicities of the Plath author's more canonical strophes, for many readers, myself regrettably included, have always carried with them the faintly detestable aroma of mere *applied* poetry. I have never regarded the oeuvre with the enthusiasm typical of the Plath author's legions of admirers. Today the work must be regarded with an even more assertive suspicion and—dare I say it?—disdain."[5] Yet for others the significance of the Plath-Hughes canon remains undiminished. As actor David Duchovny put it, on a recent airing of CNN's *Crossfire* devoted to the scandal, "Plath's poems have changed my life, and my way of thinking. I guess I'll always return to them; it doesn't matter if they were written by her or by a committee of British bureaucrats or by a coven of literary-minded extraterrestrials." And Duchovny may indeed speak for many of us as we continue to survey the consequences of our knowledge that Sylvia Plath and Ted Hughes exist only in the form of their poetry. Perhaps that particular form of existence is all that readers require; perhaps not.

Ah, postmodernism. Forgive me, gentle reader, for in the course of this tale adding certain embellishments to the facts. I admit to the possibility that Ted Hughes may have indeed existed, that Sylvia Plath may have existed as well, and that they themselves, or individuals quite similar to them, may have at one time or another written at least some of their poems. But in an era in which all of our negotiations with fact, all of our confrontations with what once was known as reality, have become ever more convoluted and daunting; in which virtual realities have cheerfully annexed the last remaining provinces of self-evident truth; in which pomo fragmentation, pastiche, and a Pavlovian tic of irony as the proper response to all human endeavors inform or afflict us all, the question is no longer "Is it real or is it Memorex?" It is instead that *everything* is Memorex, and what shall we do now? This condition creates all manner of hilarity, strangeness, ethical relativism, and what might be called factual relativism. During the weeks in which I first worked on these pages, a university where I once taught allowed a Holocaust denier with spurious academic credentials to give a speech on its campus—after all, shouldn't "all sides" be represented regarding this "issue"?; Bob Hope died at the hands of an AP wire-service report, was eulogized in Congress, and then, in the fashion of Christ and Osiris, was miraculously resurrected; a fired reporter of *The New Republic* admitted that twenty-seven of the forty-one stories he had written for the magazine were fabrications; serial killer Henry Lee Lucas, who had confessed to some two hundred slayings but probably inflated that figure, finally was given a date with Old Sparky—although there is little evidence that the particular murder he is being executed for is actually one of his productions; a group of teenagers in an Atlanta suburb was arrested for passing counterfeit twenties, using as their printing press the same model of three-hundred-dollar ink-jet printer with which I will copy this essay; and the radio blaring from the used-car lot across the street from me two times in as many days oozed "Unforgettable," a wretched "virtual" duet sung by Nat "King" Cole and his daughter, Natalie, its recording completed several decades after the former's death. This bit of necrophilic treacle was then replaced by a news report of the death of Khmer Rouge generalissimo Pol Pot, perhaps the most infamous practitioner of moral relativism of our time, who declared 1976 the Year Zero and then murdered two million in order to commemorate the birth of this blessed New Order. But wait—there seems to have been a factual glitch even here: several of the journalists who were brought to view and video the remains claimed that the corpse rotting in the jungle heat beneath their klieg lights could not be that of Pol Pot. Wrong morphology, something about facial scars that are missing. The "real" Pol Pot apparently had less hair, and what there was of it was gray; he was presumably too busy eluding capture to enroll in the Hair Club for Men or purchase some Grecian Formula. Is it possible that Pol Pot's death was faked? The decomposing body may have been a real one, but it was a Memorex Antichrist. And who would manufacture this stinking simulacrum?

Seeing of course is never believing, which is why the Zapruder film is the century's most studied example of cinematic art. And what, by the way, *is* art? If I were to aim my mouse to close this document, fire up my printer, and copy on the ink jet a pair of twenties, would I be able to call them poems? I am, after all, an author of poetry and not a counterfeiter, and with a poet's characteristic hubris see myself as one of the last remaining custodians of the authentic. But then I must remind myself that authors no longer exist, having all gone the way of the dinosaur around the time of Foucault's famous 1969 essay, in which they become instead rather dreary and ineffectual cultural products, "linked to the juridical and institutional system that encompasses, determines, and articulates the universe of discourses."[6] Foucault dances upon the grave of my kind, declares his own version of Year Zero, and tells us that we have been replaced by a new sort of creature, which he christens "the author function." It's an intriguing term, sounding more like an option you can order on a luxury car than anything you could regard as bardic. In other words, were I to print up my counterfeit twenties, I couldn't even claim them as my own, although, ironically, I *could* make the claim that the bills were not in fact counterfeit, in the same way that Andy Warhol could assert that the various hangers-on from his Factory whom he sent out to impersonate him on lucrative campus speaking tours were just as good as the real thing. And who's to say that Andy wasn't right? He would have known best, after all.

But I'm telling you things which you already know and have known for quite some time. As Hugh Kenner put it twenty years ago in a study which he entitled *The Counterfeiters,* "We are deep, these days, in the counterfeit, and have long since had to forego easy criteria for what is 'real.'"[7] Yet no longer are we merely "deep" in the counterfeit: today we are in over our heads. But is this water real or is it Memorex? Words once synonymous with truth and actuality today seem quaint—"authenticity," snorts right-wing pundit George Will in a recent column, "that's a '60s word"—while words such as counterfeit, hoax, forgery, fabrication, plagiarism, deception, and fake have come to seem woefully inadequate in defining the degrees, subtleties, and purposes of the falsehoods we perpetrate and which are perpetrated upon us, as well as the necessary fictions, the anodyne masks, and various alternative realities which some of us who dwell outside the mainstream must inhabit. Drag queens will sometimes tell you that their personae are just as real as their other selves, and who is to say this claim isn't true? Like the Eskimos with their twenty words for different kinds of snow, our culture demands a taxonomy of the bogus. As a gay friend of mine put it as we waited in line for a screening of *The Truman Show,* there is "good bogus" and "bad bogus," much in the way that there is good cholesterol and bad cholesterol. And there are ever so many shadings of bogus which range between these poles.

One small example of why this is the case can be seen in the continuing controversy over the Araki Yasusada hoax—which is, I should add, a real hoax, not a phony hoax in the manner of my Hughes-Plath conspiracy. Of course there are some Yasusada proponents who would claim he is not, strictly speaking, a hoax, though even they will admit that a corporeal Yasusada never existed. Who is Yasusada? There seem to be two prevailing opinions. The first offers the more certain definition. He was born in Kyoto in 1907 and studied Western literature at Hiroshima University but left before finishing a degree. He worked as a military postman in Hiroshima and survived the atomic-bomb blast of 1945, which killed his wife and one of his two daughters. The surviving girl, Akiko, perished in 1949 as a result of radiation sickness. Yasusada himself died of cancer in 1972. He was fluent in Western languages and was an eager but unpublished participant in several Japanese avant-garde literary movements, most prominently in the "Layered Clouds" group. He was influenced by classical Japanese poetry, as well as by modern Western writers, of whom two of his favorites were Roland Barthes and the Beat poet Jack Spicer. His importance as a poet began to be recognized when, as his translators/editors Tosa Motokiyu, Ojiu Norinaga, and Okura Kyojin write,

> The notebooks of the Hiroshima poet Araki Yasusada were discovered by his son in 1980, eight years after the poet's death. The manuscripts comprise fourteen spiral notebooks whose pages are filled with poems, drafts, English assignments, diary entries, recordings of Zen dokuson encounters, and other matter. In addition, the notebooks are interleaved with hundreds of insertions, including drawings, received correspondence, and carbon copies of the poet's letters.[8]

This biographical sketch, with small variations, appeared along with translations of the Yasusada documents, which were published with some frequency in a number of quarterlies, among them *Grand Street, Conjunctions,* and *Stand,* and—in the po-biz equivalent of making the cover of *Rolling Stone*—as a special supplement in *American Poetry Review,* which also reproduced a pencil portrait of Yasusada and included biographical sketches of his three translators. As Marjorie Perloff later noted in what will probably be the definitive essay on his work, Yasusada had a Zelig-like capacity to be a poet for every aesthetic, every poetic party line. Those craving what—thanks to Carolyn Forché's problematic Norton anthology, *Against Forgetting*—has come to be called "a poetry of witness" had a bona fide Hiroshima survivor to champion, a *Hibakusha* who also happened to be a little more talented (at least for Western sensibilities) than other Hiroshima survivor poets whose work had appeared in translation. Avant-gardists had a genuine specimen, too. Language poet Ron Silliman singled out for rapturous praise a Yasusada effort entitled "Telescope and Urn," largely on the basis of its arresting first line, "The image of the galaxies spreads out like a cloud of sperm." Yasusada was, said Silliman, "a poet whose work simply takes my breath away."[9] The cause of multiculturalism was also of course served by Yasusada, for although he was influenced by Anglo-European Modernism, his Zen-inflected oxymorons seemed to wonderfully represent a non-Eurocentric "other-ness." And even so-called "mainstream" poets, who would choose to remain aloof from the identity politics and aesthetic factionalism of today's poetics, found something to admire in the emotional nakedness and confessional vulnerability of certain of the Yasusada poems. Yasusada was poised on the edge of posthumous fame: Wesleyan University Press was about to issue a book-length selection of his poems and notebook entries; he was also to be represented in the second volume of Pierre Joris and Jerome Rothenberg's massive anthology of twentieth-century world poetry, *Poems For The Millennium.*[10] Were the MacArthur Foundation awards not limited to living writers, Yasusada would likely have added that prize to his resume as well.

The other definition of Araki Yasusada is best conveyed by the following announcement printed in the pages of the September/October 1996 issue of *American Poetry Review:*

> To Our Readers:
> We regret the publication of "Doubled Flowering: From the Notebooks of Araki Yasusada" in our July/August issue. Neither Araki Yasusada nor the three names identified as his translators, "Tosa Motokiyo," "Okura Kyojin," and "Ojiu Norinaya," are actual persons. The facts in the note, "Introducing Araki Yasusada" as well as the "Portrait of Yasusada," are a hoax. All of the materials came to us from Kent Johnson of Highland Community College in Freeport, Illinois, an actual person who represented himself as the close friend of the ill and incapacitated "translator" Tosa Motokiyu. Kent Johnson has admitted the above ruse, and has claimed the materials were written by an unnamed American poet whose name he refuses to reveal. Still other persons may be involved, as the hoax was carried out with the aid of a post office box in Sebastapol, California, an address in Tokyo, an address in London, and a disconnected phone number in Springfield, Illinois.[11]

So there you have it. The feces had hit the (Japanese) fan. And the reactions to this occurrence are perhaps as interesting as the Yasusada poems themselves. The editors who had been duped were of course furious. Wesleyan deep-sixed the book-length manuscript, "concerned about the ethical issues involved."[12] Poet Arthur Vogelsang, an editor of *American Poetry Review,* was quoted in an article in *Lingua Franca* as calling the Yasusada hoax "a criminal act," and *Conjunctions* editor Bradford Morrow did an about-face regarding the poems he had earlier published, castigating them as "coy, self-satisfied, glib."[13] The Japanese media saw the case as another example of Japan-bashing, and a group of Asian American writers cosigned a statement denouncing the Yasusada writings as racist.[14] With hindsight it was pointed out that many of the Yasusada documents should have been suspect from the start. Yasusada seems to have sung the praises of certain writings by Barthes, Celan, and Spicer before they were even written, and Hiroshima University, which Yasusada was supposed to have attended in the twenties, was not founded until 1949.[15] And the material itself should have been a giveaway: John Solt, an Amherst professor of Japanese culture, characterized it all as "Japanized crap," crudely devised to fit Western preconceptions of Japanese culture.[16] Also, certain of the documents are so implausible as to have been intentionally comic: could Yasusada *really* have preserved so many English-language exercises done for an instructor named "Mr. Rogers," a Scotsman who seems to have done his teaching in a kilt? ("What is the meaning of those broom-like forms attached to the front of his skirt?" asks Yasusada.) Would he *really* have attempted to engage in a correspondence with Jack Spicer, who himself engaged in an imaginary correspondence with García Lorca and "translated" Lorca poems which were in fact his own creations? And what about that pencil portrait of Yasusada published in *American Poetry Review* and later in *Lingua Franca ?* A friend of mine who is a connoisseur of Hong Kong action films swears that the sketch is actually one of Hong Kong movie mogul Run Run Shaw. But perhaps Yasusada merely resembles him—yet to speculate about this may be another way of saying that all Asians look alike. One writer even claimed that "Araki Yasusada" is an anagram for "Klaatu, niktu, barata," Patricia Neal's famous command to Gork the Robot in *The Day the Earth Stood Still,* although this is plainly not the case.[17] No wonder that editors and readers felt taken in; they should have known in the first place.

Furthermore, the scandal around the hoax seems to have refused to go away, and—again—for some fascinating reasons. A year after the news broke, I found myself at a party during a writers' conference where I was teaching along with Arthur Vogelsang. (Or someone whom I presume to be Arthur Vogelsang: unlike Andy Warhol, poets haven't the resources to send out impersonators.) Never having been exactly diplomatic in situations such as this, I asked him to talk about the Yasusada hoax and about Marjorie Perloff's recently published *Boston Review* essay on Yasusada, which was largely sympathetic toward Yasusada but rather merciless in regard to certain of the motives of editors he had duped. Like an elderly widow talking to police detectives about the gigolo who'd bilked her of her savings, Arthur spoke of Yasusada with a mixture of astonishment and rage. And could you blame him for this? As for Perloff's essay, he admitted it was pretty smart, smarter still if you were to share Vogelsang's suspicion—also expressed by him in a *Boston Review* symposium on the hoax—that Perloff herself is the likely author of the Yasusada documents.[18] Johnson, according to this and similar scenarios, may be only an "unindicted co-conspirator" who might be working with a whole syndicate of Yasusada hoaxers, whose ranks may include the critic Eliot Weinberger (who is with Perloff one of Yasusada's most fervent supportors, having called him "the greatest poet of Hiroshima and its most unreliable witness"); Johnson's former teacher, the poet Howard McCord; and various others whom not even the resources and doggedness of Kenneth Starr would be able to identify.[19] Johnson, for his part, has responded to all this with some spin-controlling faxes to editors he'd bamboozled, with a slippery interview published in *Denver Quarterly,* and with a continued insistence that if Yasusada doesn't exist, his creator Tosa Motokiyu—who Johnson claims was his roommate in Milwaukee in the 1980s—certainly does, or did.[20] It seems that Motokiyu—or "Moto," as Johnson nicknames him—died of cancer shortly before the scandal broke. Some of these interviews with Johnson are alleged to have been cowritten with an associate named Javier Alvarez, who lives in Mexico City. Never mind that Javier Alvarez is also the name of a Bolivian diplomat who appears in the Yasusada notebooks as a literary acquaintance of Yasusada's and who died in the Hiroshima bomb blast. Perhaps this is another Javier Alvarez—or perhaps Javier has been miraculously resurrected. (If Bob Hope can do it, why can't he?) There's also a Russian critic named Mikhail Epstein involved in this process, but let's not go into that. Johnson's spin control in these documents is an interesting mixture of current theoretical dogma and chicanery. The most telling passage occurs in a fax to British poet Jon Silkin, whose *Stand* was one of the journals taken in by Yasusada. With small variations, what follows is the phrasing Johnson adopts in several such situations. After listing some famous examples of other writers who adopted alter egos, among them Pessoa, Kierkegaard, and Pushkin, Johnson tells him,

> These writers, as I'm sure you know, wrote and published important portions of their works "as" others. For them, anonymity was not a "trick," but a need, something intrinsic to their creative drive at given times. Likewise for Moto, anonymity—and its efflorescence into multiple names—was a gateway to a radically sincere (I use that word with care) expression of empathy. Rather than being "fakes," I would offer that the Yasusada writings represent an original and courageous form of *authenticity*—one that is perhaps difficult to appreciate because of the extent to which individual authorial status and self-promotion dominate our thinking about, and practice of, poetry.[21]

"Radically sincere . . . empathy"—Johnson may be using such terms guardedly, but even the most charitable reader of this statement would have to characterize it as singularly self-congratulatory. Does this mean that to write in a Hiroshima survivor's voice is an act of only partial empathy, while going to the trouble to make your survivor an outright forgery is empathy of a more groundbreaking and courageous sort? This is not an arch question under these circumstances, because there is evidence that Johnson pondered it for a long while. While looking through some old quarterlies the other day I came across a 1987 issue of Michael Cuddihy's now-defunct *Ironwood,* and there, on the page facing a poem of my own, begin three poems "From the Notebooks of Ogawara Miyamora"—by Kent Johnson.[22] All three of these were later reprinted under Yasusada's name, including one alleged to be Yasusada's final poem, written on his deathbed. So in 1987 Johnson seems only to have been writing monologues in the voice of a Hiroshima poet.

Dramatic monologues are certainly not anything new or "radical" in literature (although one might question the appropriateness of an Anglo poet speaking in the voice of a *Hibakusha,* just as I myself now might question the appropriateness of the poem of mine that faces Johnson's, in which I decided to turn one of my closest friends, a perfectly healthy individual, into a deaf-mute). But somewhere along the line Johnson decided that it wasn't enough to impersonate his *Hibakusha;* instead he had to *be* him. We are back to the question of what is real and what is Memorex: is "Trilobites," which appears in *Ironwood* under Johnson's name and is written in the persona of Ogawara Miyamora, a less successful or empathic poem than the identical version which later appears as Yasusada's? Johnson would seem to think so, though there's a certain smugness and reliance on post-structuralist cant in the way that Johnson makes his points to the editors that gives you to suspect that it's all an effete game for him. "Radical empathy" seems not to include carrying the Yasusada part to its logical conclusion and, for example, purchasing a couple grams of plutonium from some renegade Soviet scientists in order to more authentically method-act the effects of Yasusada's radiation sickness. This is radical empathy without the hair loss and diarrhea, radical empathy as a problem of technique, as just one more aspect of "author function." But here I am launching an ad hominem attack against Kent Johnson, even as he keeps insisting that he's not to blame; after all, he reminds us, he's not Yasusada, not Motokiyu, not Javier Alvarez, Mikhail Epstein, nor Ogawara Miyamora. The only person he has not insisted that he isn't is—tellingly—Marjorie Perloff. I'm reminded at this point of a line of Lynda Hull's: "larger and larger circles of misunderstanding."

Before I close, I want to try to narrow some of these circles, and the best way to do so is to separate the Yasusada materials from the controversies they've engendered and to try to come to some provisional conclusions about Yasusada, which might in passing also say something about the state of contemporary poetry. It is easier to do this now that all of Yasusada's work has been published by Ron Silliman's Roof Books as *Doubled Flowering: From the Notebooks of Araki Yasusada.* This is presumably the same manuscript that Wesleyan got cold feet about, and it is to Silliman's credit that he, unlike others who had initially lauded Yasusada but then condemned him when the hoax was revealed, has chosen to stand by his initial enthusiasm for the poems. As Silliman's jacket blurb puts it, "the 'scandal' of these poems lies not in the problematics of authorship, identity, persona, race, or history.

Rather, these are wonderful works of writing that also invoke all of these other issues, never relying on them to prop up a text." Silliman's confidence in Yasusada is strong enough that he can allow such praise to appear on the jacket beside this statement by Hosea Hirata, a Princeton professor of East Asian studies: "Knowing its fictitious nature, with a slight sense of disgust, I find Yasusada's poetry evil, and eerily beautiful." (This is titillating stuff, certainly much more provoking than the blurbs on your average book of poetry, where someone like Richard Wilbur diffidently notes that the stanzas didn't put him to sleep.) Roof's willingness to face the Yasusada controversy head-on implies that one will finish the book on Silliman's side rather than on Hirata's. I am not sure that this is finally the case, but no one who seriously studies the book and reads the texts in their intended sequence will be unimpressed. It is weird, sorrowful, and wry by turns. In its attempt to use the convention of the notebook transcriptions, arranged more or less chronologically, the book is more a novel in verse than merely a sequence of poems, and read as a whole the volume possesses an integrity (at least of a structural sort) that poses a challenge to Yasusada's detractors, one that might not have been apparent to them during their brief encounters with him in the quarterlies. It is also, in the manner of Borges's *Ficciones* and Nabokov's *Pale Fire,* a witty parody of academic scholarship, current literary translation practices, and patterns of literary influence. Most importantly, however, Yasusada emerges from the notebooks as a wonderful and masterfully constructed character, who tries with great poignancy to salvage his ruined life through art. Taken in their intended context, his elegies are shattering, and as he attempts to create a sort of homegrown avant-garde poetry, largely in isolation, he recalls some of the century's great outsider artists. When reading *Doubled Flowering,* I found myself thinking of Rousseau (who was also a postal clerk) and Joseph Cornell more than of other poets, yet at one point in the notebooks Yasusada writes a letter to an associate in which he talks of translating Dickinson—perhaps the greatest outsider poet of them all. And like each of this trio, Yasusada is decidedly eccentric, crankily devoted to his art, given to naïve flights of wild enthusiasm, and a little bit buffoonish. Taken as a whole, Yasusada is a memorable creation, at times even a brilliant one. The pose does not work all the time, however, and Roof and Johnson have made a major blunder by attaching as appendices to the volume several self-justifying essays and interviews about Yasusada's creation by Johnson, "Motokiyu," "Javier Alvarez," and "Mikhail Epstein," as well as Perloff's revised version of her *Boston Review* piece. To put it bluntly, it does no good for Yasusada to ever have the man behind the curtain appear, for whenever Johnson himself opens up his mouth he strikes us as a windy and slightly paranoiac jerk.

Perloff comports herself much better, but the inclusion of her essay suggests mixed motives on Johnson's and Silliman's parts. By printing all of the Yasusada materials under a single cover, Silliman is asserting that the texts should be allowed to speak for themselves, yet at the same time Perloff's essay seems transparently intended to give the volume a bit of critical cachet. They want to have it both ways, and this is not a good means to present an author whose reputation for duplicity precedes him. (I'm of course referring here to Johnson rather than Yasusada.)

I want here to examine two poems from *Doubled Flowering,* both of which derive from Yasusada's experience of the Hiroshima bombing and his daughter's subsequent illness and death from radiation sickness. They exhibit all of the hallmarks of Yasusada's style save for the loopy humor and gaga avant-gardism of later works such as his "exercises" for his English teacher, Mr. Rogers. Like most of the Yasusada documents, the two poems are accompanied by the "editors"' inclusion of footnotes, a practice which—surprisingly—serves to enhance their impact and appearance of verisimilitude. Here, then, is exhibit number one:

Loon and Dome

January 1, 1947

The crying girl sounds like a loon . . .

Why does her mournful sound call to mind the sky
through the dome of the Industrial Promotion Hall?[1]

You told me there you were pregnant with her
as we strolled through the plaster chambers
of the giant Model of the Heart.

I have waited all week, you quietly said,
to be with you here in this magical place
and to tell you something beautiful.

(It was your sentimental heart
that always made me laugh,
and this stain on the page is spilt tea.)[2]

[Yasusada note in margin] Insert breast plate stanza here?

Nomura, the long wake of our daughter
vanishes, ceaselessly, in our union.

[1. The Hiroshima Industrial Hall, a prominent city landmark because of its windowed dome, was one of the few structures left recognizable after the bombing. Its skeletal remains have been preserved as a memorial.
2. In the original, there is, indeed, a stain covering the first half of the poem.][23]

The associative movement of the poem is lyrical and compelling. The ill daughter's moaning is likened first to the loon's plaintive cry, and this in turn evokes Yasusada's memory of strolling with his late wife, Nomura, in the industrial hall, where she told him she was pregnant with their daughter Akiko, the same daughter who now lies wasting away. The contrast between Yasusada's mournful present existence and his recollection of the couple's moment of intense intimacy in the "magical place" of the industrial pavilion's giant model of the heart is an affecting contrast, in keeping with the emotional directness and bittersweet elegiac intent we find in translations of classical Chinese and Japanese poetry. The language of the poem evokes these models as well; it is fussy and a bit awkward: "translationesque" is the best way to describe it. But of course the charm of many of the poems of Pound's *Cathay* and Waley's and Rexroth's translations can be attributable to a similar awkwardness and syntactical inversion; think of the famous line in "The River Merchant's Wife": "at fourteen I married My Lord you." Yasusada's rendering of this moment of lyrical grace may indeed be "Japanized crap," but it evokes for those of us who grew up on such translations a powerful tradition and does so inventively. Inventive, too, is the metaphorical rhyme between the industrial pavilion dome—famous from photos of the Hiroshima bombing's devastation—and the giant rendering of the heart. (I suspect this heart model derives not from an actual prewar Hiroshima attraction but from a walk-through heart in Chicago's Museum of Science and Industry, a place which a Midwestern teacher of creative writing such as Johnson would know as the subject of innumerable undergraduate poems.) But perhaps the most interesting aspect of the poem is its resolute resistance to closure. In exploiting the convention of the poem's unfinishedness by so strongly insisting on the fiction of the poem as a manuscript page, Yasusada and his editors leave us wandering with him among the ruins of obsession. The final three stanzas, along with the endnotes, offer us three abandoned efforts to conclude the poem. First we have the parenthetical stanza with its reference to the spilt tea, which the editors—with a marvelous pedantry—tell us actually does stain the manuscript. This sort of gesture is used elsewhere in the manuscript to great effect. A letter to an associate of Yasusada's, printed *en face* to "Loon and Dome," is half "illegible due to blotching"; the marred passage thus appears on the page in fragmentary fashion, its white space and lacunae bringing to mind the manuscript shards of Sappho and the Greek Anthology poets. Then we have Yasusada's reference to the unwritten "breast plate" stanza and finally the poem's lines of even more emphatic address to Yasusada's dead wife—lines which I suspect the author designed to be of great earnestness but which are also quite woefully bad. Yasusada ends with a clumsy mixed metaphor, in keeping with none of the patterns of imagery which the poem had previously developed—unless the "long wake" of the couple's daughter is meant to somehow evoke the wavelike blast pattern of the explosion and/or Yasusada's obsessive return to the memory of the visit to the industrial pavilion. The effect of this triad of would-be conclusions is, however, quite compelling. The poem ends elliptically, with none of its sorrows relieved—yet this seems fitting.

Such qualities are also present in a poem alleged to have been written shortly after Akiko's death:

Trolley Fare and Blossom

—For My Daughter Akiko, 1930-1949
May 18, 1949

How can I tell you now
that the fire's warmth was pleasurable
on my body?[1]

Your body enveloped by it
and somehow, still, by mine.

The round urn, so finely cut,
each blade of grass bent black
against a black moon. You, weightless,
within it.

How embarrassing, I thought, cupping it before me,
if in the middle of the ceremony I
stumbled, kabuki-like, and fell!

Thus, bearing you and weeping,
I paid the trolley fare.

How to tell you now
of this simple happiness,
of the children laughing in a ring
at Hiroshima's heart, the brushstrokes
falling fast and light?[2]

You, Akiko, thick branch
of which this scentless blossom
is breaking.[3]

[1. This refers, at least literally, to his daughter's cremation.
2. The poem, guarded in a ricepaper sheath, is in calligraphy. See frontispiece.
3. A somewhat amateurish sumi drawing (we believe by Yasusada himself) of a flowering branch runs down the right side of the page.][24]

As anyone who has handled cremated human remains is likely to tell you, one carries them gingerly, with an awkward delicacy that Yasusada heartbreakingly conveys. The worry that he may "stumble, kabuki-like" and fall as he is presented with the ashes is a brilliantly apt way to describe the speaker's feelings, even as the statement also comes to us in Yasusada's characteristically clumsy "translationesque" and even as his choice of metaphor evokes an Orientalized exoticism of the kind which Solt no doubt had in mind. Yet I would propose that the passage is effective enough to transcend such quibbles. And, furthermore, the image of Yasusada later weeping with the funerary urn on the trolley is harrowingly described, a scene of abjection and pathos reminiscent of early Kurosawa films. Yet, in characteristic fashion, Yasusada cannot conclude the poem with this image, for its imagistic finality betrays the relentlessness of the speaker's grief. Instead, the poem goes on for two more stanzas, with Yasusada continuing to construct tropes to describe his experience, however tentative and provisional these metaphors may be. And once again this sense of unfinishedness is amplified by the footnotes, which bleed into the poem's text much in the same way that we are told that Yasusada's own "amateurish" sumi drawing does. The description of the poem as "guarded in a ricepaper sheath" comes to us as itself a wry comment upon the text: the visual impression which the poem leaves us with, one of seeing the poem's calligraphy through the translucence of its ricepaper covering, reminds us that we must read the poem palimpsistically. In effect, the "manuscript"'s condition asserts that we must read the poem itself as a kind of shroud. Such palimpsistic devices abound in the Yasusada manuscripts, of course. Each poem is a text layered upon several other texts, and the mask of the Yasusada character again and again appears to slip, offering us glimpses of other personae, be they the imaginary translator/editors; the probably real Kent Johnson and/or his coconspirators; or, if you want to get post-structuralist about it, "writing" itself, and all the heavy-metal smoke-and-mirror and dry ice interplay of sign and signifier which this implies.

In conclusion, I want to make some generalizations about Yasusada which may be worth our attention. This is a subjective and by no means definitive list.

1. Yasusada is a better poet than Kent Johnson. I feel that it is safe to make this claim even without my having read any of Johnson's other poems. Yasusada is also, as an outright forgery, a better poet than Johnson writing through the persona of Ogawara Miyamora in his *Ironwood* poems. Nothing that I have seen of Johnson himself makes me think he would be a poet of character or of talent; Yasusada, however, is both.

2. Yasusada is a better poet than Ted Hughes. Birthday Letters is written by a poet of talent and character, of old-fashioned sincerity rather than "radical" sincerity. But Yasusada is the better writer, and he shows us again that sincerity, talent, and character are not always enough to make good poetry. Compare "Loon and Dome" to the following passage from Hughes's book, which J. D. McClatchy rightly compares to something you'd find in a Harlequin rather than in a Faber:

> We half closed our eyes. We held them wide
> Like sleepwalkers while a voice on tape,
> Promising, directed us into a doorway
> Difficult and dark. The voice urged on
> Into an unlit maze of crying and loss.
> What voice? "Find your souls," said the voice.
> "Find your true selves. This way. Search, search."
> The voice had never heard of the shining lake.
> "Find the core of the labyrinth." Why? What opens
> At the heart of the maze? Is it the doorway
> Into the perfect vision?[25]

Even in "translation" Yasusada is better. Can anyone read this and *not* suspect that Hughes's poems are the product of versifying secret agents?

3. Yasusada gives good "author function." In other words, he plays with our presuppositions of authorial sincerity and authenticity; deconstructs the piety of reading with the willful suspension of disbelief—something which we can only do intermittently in Yasusada's case, knowing what we do of his pedigree; parodies literary scholarship; lampoons the politics of translation;

and makes such ironies some of the most prominent formal elements of his writing.

4. Yasusada reminds us again how woefully ignorant American readers are of contemporary world literature. The Yasusada hoax would never have been successful if we knew anything about modern Japanese writing. Charles Simic, probably our most internationalist poet, has noted that the Yasusada hoax shows once again that ours is "a country where confident provincialism reigns supreme."[26] (I should add that in the same essay Simic trashes Yasusada's "Loon and Dome," yet I think his appraisal of the poem is wrong.)

5. Yasusada is one of the better literary hoaxes of this century and even compares favorably with some of the more famous literary hoaxes of previous centuries. I'd rank Yasusada as a better bogus poet than Australia's Ern Malley; as good a fabrication as Bill Knott's Saint Geraud, Kenneth Rexroth's Marichiko, and W. D.Snodgrass's S. S. Gardons; but not as good as Pessoa's heteronymic alter egos, Ricardo Reyes, Alvaro de Campos, and Alberto Cariero. Johnson's Yasusada will likely be one of those hoax-authors whose work is remembered for its literary value—like Chatterton's Rowley and MacPherson's Ossian. Johnson even fits the profile of these eighteenth-century forebears: like them, he is a unknown writer from the sticks who no doubt took a great delight in hoodwinking the literary establishment. Being called a criminal by Arthur Vogelsang may not be exactly the same sort of thing as MacPherson being vituperatively shit-canned by Dr. Johnson, but both denunciations are, in their way, indicative of a kind of literary celebrity. Yasusada is probably destined to be a hoax of lasting literary value and not one of those hoaxes, like the counterfeit Hitler diaries, the forged JFK and Marilyn Monroe correspondence, or William Ireland's faked Shakespeare play, *Vortigen: A Tragedy,* which are remembered for their audacity rather than their artistic success. For a time in the eighteenth century, *Vortigen* was admitted to the Shakespeare canon, even though, as Hugh Kenner remarks, it is "unreadable and absurd."[27] Yasusada may be absurd, but he is never unreadable.

6. Yasusada is a monster. This is not a statement made "guardedly": Yasusada is a monster. I agree with Perloff's belief that Yasusada is a "brilliant" creation. But he is not, it seems to me, the product of what Johnson terms "a radical empathy." The problematic ethics of creating a faux Hiroshima survivor, claiming he is real, and then foisting him upon a gullible reading public have to be seen as sins of hubris against the gods of morality and the muse. Yasusada is, finally, a version of the Golem or of Dr. Frankenstein's unholy offspring: he should never have come into being. And yet, as *Star Trek*'s "prime directive" would remind us, Yasusada now exists as a "sentient life form" and must be accorded all of a life form's rights and privileges. Knowing

Yasusada's creepy origins, readers can choose to ignore him if they so desire. But others can see Yasusada as a case of loving the sinner but hating the sin and read him with the appreciation which his best poems warrant. Mary Shelley felt a similar ambivalence about her own "monster." In her preface to the 1831 edition of *Frankenstein* she tells us that, after more than a decade of mulling over the moral and artistic implications of her creation, she has now decided "to bid my hideous progeny go off and prosper."

So the Yasusada case shows us again—not that we needed to be reminded of it—that the motives for artistic creation are always infuriatingly complicated, and are made even more complicated as we attempt to ascend the Virtual Mount Purgatory of Postmodernism. Is art still the lie that tells the truth? Probably. Is art still the lie that helps us *bear* the truth? Perhaps. Or is art still, as Picasso had it, the lie that helps us to *appreciate* the truth? Maybe so. Hideous progeny, go off and prosper.

Postscript

Several noteworthy events have occurred since I presented an earlier version of this paper at the third annual international "Being and Nothingness" conference on postmillennial poetics, held last summer at St. Jauss College, a small Jesuit school in Minnesota. In the discussion following the presentation an audience member identified himself as Okura Kyojin, one of the Yasusada translators, and asserted once again that it is Tosa Motokiyu and not Kent Johnson who is the author of the Yasusada notebooks. This individual further contended that Johnson's reports of Motokiyu's death are in fact falsehoods and that Motokiyu is presently living in the Phoenix area: he even promised to furnish "Moto"'s address and phone number. But by the time I left the podium and tried to talk with him after the lecture's conclusion, "Kyojin" had disappeared. A private investigator I later employed to find Motokiyu in Phoenix could not locate him. Also, because the "Being and Nothingness" conference was covered extensively by the national media, I later received a number of interesting letters from readers of the Yasusada documents. Most of these letters expressed disdain for the Yasusada hoax, but others showed a strong partisanship in his favor. I've even been told that a number of Yasusada reading clubs and study groups have been formed. But two of the letters I received were a bit unsettling. One came from a representative of the Boston legal firm of Abrams, Abrams, and Weingarten, which I later discovered specializes in slander and copyright law and whose clients have included Courtney Love and Tonya Harding, as well as Simpson trial notables Mark Furhmann and Kato Kaelin. Abrams is now representing "Ted Hughes" and the Plath estate, and a letter similar to one which has gone out to almost every writer who has published anything about the Hughes-Path forgeries threatens legal action if I continue to claim in any way that its client does not exist. If the public is given the impression that Hughes is a fabrication, the letter suggests, his heirs will be deprived of book royalties. A publicity release also arrived from a public relations firm representing Kent Johnson, inquiring whether the university where I teach would be interested in hosting *Yasusada: An Evening of Doubled Flowering,* a one-man dramatic presentation by Johnson in which he plays Yasusada, in the manner of Hal Holbrook's Mark Twain and Julie Harris's Emily Dickinson. For an additional fee, the firm will arrange for a koto player to furnish incidental music for the play. It's an interesting proposition, surely, but the fee is much larger than my department could likely afford.

(1998)

III.

11.

John Flanders on the Anxious Highway: First Books and the Politics of Poetry

The late Richard Yates was arguably the most depressing novelist of his time. An old-fashioned writer in the realist tradition, his work has been likened to that Chekhov and Flaubert, and his best-known novel, *Revolutionary Road,* resets *Madame Bovary* in the American suburbs of the 1950s. The change of setting makes the story no less forlorn. Most forlorn of all, however, is Yates's fifth novel, *The Easter Parade.* The book's opening clause is typically Yatesian: "Neither of the Grimes sisters would have a happy life. . . ."[1] You always know where you are in a Yates novel: things begin badly, get worse, and continue to worsen with a slow relentlessness that is painstakingly described. His characters are usually alcoholic, are often borderline psychotics, and are always depressive. They tend to have good intentions, but in Yates no good deed goes unpunished. It's the lucidity of Yates's prose and his deadpan descriptions of the manifold ways in which fate grinds us down that give Yates's writings their particular pungency. These qualities, and the lack of any popular success during a long and prolific career, have led critics to characterize Yates as a writers' writer, yet I suspect Yates believed that to be stuck with such a label was to be damned with faint praise and to labor in obscurity. In Yates's work nearly every characterization of what we might call "the writing life" is accompanied by a set of scathing ironies, and the writing life never helps his characters to lead a better life. More typically the opposite is the case, as when the protagonist of *Disturbing the Peace* ends up on the locked ward after a mental breakdown that takes place while he is teaching at an event that sounds quite a bit like the Bread Loaf Writers' Conference. Now, not even Yates would have been of the opinion that writing conferences make you crazy, but he certainly didn't see a literary career as ennobling. A secondary character in *The Easter Parade* is more typical of Yates's literary folk. He's the managing editor of a magazine called "Food Field Observer," and he and Emily Grimes discover their mutual attraction while working on a photographic spread about pork chops. One thing leads to another:

After their fine first night together, when it seemed abundantly clear that this particular long, skinny man was the kind she had always wanted, she prowled along his bookshelves, wearing his bathrobe, until she came to three slim volumes with the name John Flanders on their spines. He was out in the kitchen making coffee.

"My God, Jack," she called. "You were a Yale Younger Poet."

"Yeah, well, it's kind of a lottery," he said. "They have to give it to somebody every year." But his self-effacement didn't quite ring true: she could tell how pleased he was that she'd found the book—he almost certainly would have showed her to it if she hadn't.

She turned it over and read one of the endorsements aloud: "'In John Flanders we have an authentic new voice, rich in wisdom, passion, and perfect technical control. Let us rejoice in his gift.' Wow."

"Yeah," he said in the same proud-bashful way. "Big deal, huh? You can take it home with you if you'd like. In fact, I'd like you to. The second book's ok, too: probably not as good as the first. Only for Christ's sake don't mess with the third one. It's lousy. You wouldn't believe how lousy. Sugar and milk?"[2]

Not long after this exchange Jack allows that working for "Food Field Observer" is a "better deal" than academic life, and this statement proves to be prophetic. Emily accompanies him to Iowa City, where his teaching stint at the Writers Workshop ends badly; his drinking worsens, the couple breaks up, and when we last hear about John Flanders it is years later, when the protagonist comes across a negative *New York Times* review of his fourth book. We are presented with the entire review, including some quotes from Jack's poetry ("'I watch you fooling with the dog and wonder / what does this girl want from me'") and characterizations such as "'one is tempted to dismiss poem after poem as commonplace and sentimental.'"[3]

John Flanders is not as one-dimensional as my descriptions about him may lead you to believe, and let's remember that fiction writers simply love to lampoon everything having to do with poetry. And yet, as a former Yale Younger Poet myself, I have over the years thought about John Flanders often enough so that he has in my mind, by a slow and somewhat involuntary process, joined the ranks of real Yale Younger Poets. Jack Flanders, was he one of Stanley Kunitz's choices? Or was it James Dickey who picked his book? Didn't I give a reading with John Flanders once? Somewhere in the Southwest, I think. Was it Southwest Texas State, Permian Basin campus? Didn't our books get reviewed together somewhere? I seem to remember the reviewer liked his stuff better than mine, but he wasn't crazy about it. And so on.

And I find myself thinking about John Flanders yet again as I sit head-phoned in a radio studio. Before me, inside a glass booth, is an engineer who is sporting the curious combination of a nose ring and a pocket protector. I'm in the Chicago NPR bureau, and I was late for the appointment because some terra-cotta tiles on a building on East Wacker—not far from where the studio is located—came loose and crushed two pedestrians. I've had to weave my way through ambulances and news teams. (Who was the poet who was killed by a falling brick? I think it may have been Rostand.) At any rate, the news bureau has emptied; everyone but the engineer and me can be found downstairs watching to see if more tiles will fall. I'm trying to hear the voice of "Anthem"'s Renee Montaigne emerge from Washington, and the voice of the 1999 Yale Younger Poet, Craig Arnold, makes its way to me from Salt Lake City. We're here to talk about poetry and about winning prizes such as the Yale, and it seems that Craig, whom I have never met, has chosen me to serve as the former Yale winner he wants to engage in such a conversation. ("Anthem" likes to think that two artists are better than one—more like a salon, I suppose.) The booth is not so soundproof that I can't hear the sirens outside, and Craig's voice arrives so thick with static that it seems to be coming from the Mir space station. Knobs are being fiddled with, engineers in DC and Salt Lake are exchanging jargon, and within all the white noise I have time to brood. By po-biz standards, getting on NPR is a big deal. "Anthem" is carried by a great many public radio affiliates, and even though it's generally broadcast at obscure times on the very early weekend mornings, more people will hear Craig and me on this one occasion than will likely ever read our books of poetry over the course of our careers. But then I'm reminded that radio waves and lines of verse have never much harmonized. The only radio personality I can think of who also had an interest in poetry was accused of treason and condemned to a madhouse. He may well have belonged there, just as Rush Limbaugh might. But that is another story.

The technical difficulties are fixed, and our three-way conversation begins. I've been prepped for it with a manuscript copy of Craig's forthcoming book, entitled *Shells;* with W. S. Merwin's introduction to the volume; with some newspaper clippings from NPR that amount to a kind of press kit; and, last but not least, with a CD by Iris, the punk band that Craig Arnold plays with, writing most of the songs. The clippings are of the "Univ. Utah Student Wins Award" variety, offering little that is of use to me; the Iris CD is more interesting, a sort of arty glam rock deriving from T. Rex and Ziggy Stardust–era Bowie. The conversation seems to be going well at first. We talk about the Yale Prize and its prestigious tradition, about the "state of poetry" today, and I ask Craig to read a representative poem from his collection, entitled "Scrubbing Mussels." It's a spare, precisely crafted, and engagingly sensual piece in the manner of early Heaney. He reads it well:

> Easy at first to think they're all alike.
> But in the time it takes your brush to scour
> away the cement their beards secrete to stick
> to the rock, to one another, you find the lure
>
> of intimacy a temptation. Palm
> cupping each shell, you learn a history
> from what you scrape off—limpets, worm-
> castings, their own brown crust—the company
>
> they've kept, how many neighbors, on the fringes
> or in the thick. This patriarchal shell
> suffered a near-mortal crack—hinges
> skewed by a scab, its valves will never seal
>
> perfectly, ever. This one lost a chip
> of its carapace—the nacre gleams, steel plate
> in a war veteran's skull. Here's a couple
> tangled by their beards. But do they mate?
>
> You can't remember how they reproduce.
> Now and then you'll find one open, startle,
> fling it aside, your fingers too close
> to what you hoped would stay hidden, the veil
>
> lining the shell, flushed pink, not orange,
> no, not yet. Once they are cleaned, and more
> or less alike, they're ready to arrange
> in the skillet, large enough for a single layer,
>
> with chopped onions and garlic, maybe a pinch
> of tarragon—no salt, they will provide
> the salt themselves—butter, a half inch
> or so of dry white wine. Replace the lid,
>
> turn on and light the gas. Make sure the match
> is thoroughly stubbed out. If you've been tempted
> at any point to see in them an image
> of yourself, you must make sure your mind is emptied
>
> of all such madness. Mussels cannot mind
> the slowly warming pan, the steam, or feel

real pain, which requires sympathy, a kind
of tenderness. The worst, most capable

monsters admit a feeling for the flesh
they brutalize—the inquisitors who cry
with the heretic they rack for a confes-
sion, the kind cop who stops the third degree

to offer coffee, a smoke, the death camp
doctor who celebrates a patient's birthday,
slips him an extra piece of bread—all symp-
athetic men. Think how delicious they

will be, the shells relaxing, giving up their humble
secrets, their self-possession. Your demands
are not so cruel. Don't follow their example.
Slice the lemon. Make sure to wash your hands.[4]

The quatrains are graceful, and the tone strikes exactly the right balance between intimacy and rhetoric. Arnold plays a sly game with our presuppositions, warning us against the dangers of the pathetic fallacy while at the same time embracing them, yet he never allows the poem to grow arch. This casual but fervent prosodic control is typical of Arnold's poetry; he's a writer with a rock and roll heart, but he's also been to Yale, where J. D. McClatchy and John Hollander were his teachers and instilled in him a healthy respect for traditional forms. Later, I read some of my own work; we speak about the influence of pop music and culture on contemporary poetry, and the conversation takes its disastrous turn only near its conclusion, when Renee asks me how winning the Yale "changed my life." I hem and haw a bit about how the prize allowed me to get academic jobs I otherwise wouldn't have had much chance of getting, how being a YYP suddenly turned me from a poet with less than a dozen readers to one with a few hundred, and then I'm spouting all the cynical clichés about poetry's lack of audience and importance in today's culture and sounding like William Bennett on a bad hair day. My metaphor-making machinery starts to work overtime and to malfunction. I drag out the one about publishing a book of poetry today as being something akin to dropping a rose petal in the Grand Canyon and liken the receipt of the Yale Prize to those South Sea Island movies of my youth, where the sacrificial virgins are feted and pampered for a year—and then tied up and heaved into the volcano crater. Craig and Renee respond to this harangue by laughing uneasily, and before my monologue is even over I'm regretting my cheesy attempts at wit and berating myself for coming off as so embittered when I know that in truth I've been exceedingly lucky. My role in this event should have been to celebrate another poet's good fortune, but instead I've been railing against the way that our discipline has been neglected and probably using this as a codified way of complaining about how *I* have been neglected. The good news from all of this is that by the time the interview is broadcast several weeks later my ranting has been edited out, and I come across as sounding almost reasonable and almost intelligent. Maybe not as intelligent as singer Bob Mould, who is also interviewed that day on "Anthem," and maybe not as interesting as the woman who has restored the orchestral score to the silent version of Cecil B. DeMille's *The Ten Commandments* and who comes on immediately before Craig and I do. No, I am not John Flanders, nor was I meant to be. For now, at least.

And yet, in the weeks which follow the radio interview I find myself wondering if nearly all of us who labor in the vineyards of contemporary poetry aren't John Flanders or John Flanders wanna-bes. In the strangely atomized world of contemporary poetry, small to begin with and made to seem even smaller thanks to the aesthetic rivalries and pettiness within the discipline, a career such as that of John Flanders would be regarded as a success story—after all, he's won a major prize, taught at a prestigious writing program, won Guggenheim and Rockefeller fellowships, and over the years published steadily. This is not a bad fate for a fictional alcoholic who is only a secondary character and arguably a much better fate than that endured by some of the century's genuinely great poets: Franco's thugs aren't going to dump him in a mass grave outside Granada; he's not going to be last seen scavenging a garbage pit in the gulag in search of food; he's not apt to die in exile, throw himself from a bridge in Paris, San Francisco, or Minneapolis, or jump ship in the gulf of Mexico. Better to go down dignified, as Frost would have it. And better, too, I suppose, not to bite the hand that feeds you. The fact that today there are more and more poets, each scrambling for a slice of an ever-shrinking pie, may not be a cause for celebration, but it certainly isn't a tragic state of affairs. Better to have your manuscript of *Sestina for Frida Kahlo and Other Poems* be rejected for the umpteenth time than to be given a blindfold and a last cigarette by the Guardia Civil. Better to pony up to the Xerox machine yet again and purchase another fistful of priority-mail stamps than to listen to the noise of the gas being pumped through the showerheads while the kapos bolt tight the iron doors. Better to be John Flanders, but what if, for whatever reasons, you end up fearing you can't even be that? There are many more poets, many more first-book manuscripts, and many more credible and publishable books than will ever appear in print. And of the ones that are printed, many are dreadful, and many of the ones that are not dreadful will attain no readership at all. The poetry audience is so atomized at this point that within a few years the publication of poetry books may be limited almost exclusively to something like the Xeroxed course readers that college instructors make their students buy at Kinko's. Imagine a future in which poetry publication amounts to creative writing teachers assigning vanity-published Xeroxed "books" of their poetry to their own students, thereby bringing the poet-teachers a small readership and income and thereby offering models—of a sort—for their students to emulate. This is a hectoring and small-minded prophecy, I know, but I've known more than one college creative writing instructor who has assigned their own poetry to students, and who's to say that market forces or wounded vanity won't drive more of them to do so as verse gets harder and harder to publish? And let's face it: poetry is probably not as adaptable as many of the other arts; it thrives as much upon tradition as it does upon change, and this condition has made the discipline endangered for many of the same reasons that the giant panda, the white rhino, and the cassowary are threatened. To change the circumstances of its writing or methods of transmission may well be akin to taking away the diet of bamboo shoots which allows the giant panda to survive. Cyberspace may not be an atmosphere in which poetry will thrive or even long exist. But I'm no oracle. All I know is that poetry is in a strange place. How does one go about publishing anything, let alone a first book, in a situation as bizarre as ours sometimes seems? And what case can still be made for the value of first books? In the pages which follow, I want to posit some provisional answers to these questions.

In attempting to answer such questions I first pick from my bookshelves twenty-five first books, all of them published within the past several years, all of them ones I have read, if not remembered well. Aside from the occasional review copy or book sent to me by its author or publisher, they are all collections which looked interesting enough to me to bring home from the bookstore. I'm less prone to spend money on first books than I used to be, and sometimes I'll pick up a collection largely because of the track record of its publisher. I still purchase nearly all the books on the Wesleyan, Pitt, and Chicago University Press lists, and among the smaller independent presses I'll buy almost anything that comes my way from Copper Canyon, Graywolf, and BOA. Some of the books come from houses identified with an avant-garde tradition, such as Sun and Moon; others from presses whose lists run to more traditionalist fare (Story Line, Louisiana State). Most of the books are contest winners, since these days very few first volumes get published without having aced a competition. Of course the first collections from commercial houses are few in number, and one has to wonder if their existence owes something to insider connections. There's a first book from Knopf whose author is an editor at Norton, and another collection (picked up from the remainder table) bearing the imprint of Random House, whose author is a subeditor at the Magazine Tina Brown Used to Edit. You can speculate about what young poets are writing about these days from a scan of the titles, but in doing so you might conclude that the vast majority of them present a strong argument for Zoloft: by far the largest percentage tends toward expressions of fin de siecle ennui: *The Misunderstanding of Nature, The End of Desire, Disfortune, Sweet Ruin, Body Betrayer, The Broken World, Some are Drowning, After Estrangement, Crash's Law, Perfect Hell, Junk City, And Her Soul Out of Nothing, Apology for Want,* and *What Silence Equals.* Movement, travel, and geography are alluded to frequently, but often in a strangely unsettling fashion—as wrong turns, pauses in journeys, sinister meetings at crossroads, or talismanic hejiras: *Brief Landing on the Earth's Surface, After We Lost Our Way, Threshold, Shift, Cities in Motion, Anxious Latitudes, Walking Distance, Journey Cake.* The titles are all, in other words, pretty blue, although the only color which seems to appear in them is red—*Red Signature, Red Under the Skin,* and *Red Roads,* which conveniently fuses a pair of motifs. Titles containing wordplay of a more witty sort are rare, but there are a few *Bright Moves;* there's *A Little Star,* a *Wild Kingdom* and a *Candy Necklace.* Single-word monikers are rarest of all, and they are either portentously earnest—*Refuge, Torque*—or seem to come from the bookshelves of the Exxon boardroom—*Capitalism, Refinery, Debt.* This list may lead you to conclude that the best way for an unpublished manuscript of the nineties to make it out of the slush pile is to employ a title along the lines of *Lost on the Anxious Red Highway.*

Still, I seem to be one of those people willing to shell out fifteen bucks for a ticket on the anxious red express. This is because the pleasures of reading an interesting first book are substantial. A first book doesn't always have to be good to be interesting; in fact, some of the most promising first collections contain a fair number of turkeys. What we see in an engaging first book is a young poet's record of self-discovery: the more cumbersome task of self-acceptance is more generally taken up in a poet's subsequent collections. First and foremost we see this process taking place through the poet's choice of models and masters. Who has the poet read, and how well does the master's voice get replicated? James Wright's *The Green Wall* and Adrienne Rich's *A Change of World,* their Yale volumes, are covered all over with Frost, and in some instances—because even in their youth these writers are more generous in spirit than their chosen master—they write Frost almost as well as Frost (although of course they can *help* being Frost while Frost himself cannot). In much rarer cases, you see poets in their first books already extending rather than replicating or refining the lines of their masters, as in the case of Stevens's and Crane's supernoval expansions of the aesthetic possibilities of French Symbolism in *Harmonium* and *White Buildings* and, later, in Ashbery's supercharging of Stevens in his *Some Trees* or in Bishop's humanizing the mechanistic eccentricities of Marianne Moore in her *North & South.* Second, we see in first books inklings of the lived life, those moments when the stuff of autobiography transforms itself from self-examination into the sterner material of obsession and transforms obsession into a guiding aesthetic. The speaker of the title poem of Philip Levine's first collection, 1963's *On the Edge,* who was "born in 1928 in Michigan [where] / nobody gave a damn" is a voice whose pissed-off snarl is still familiar to us in Levine poems which end the millennium. And of course, for better or for worse, it is the child of "Tintern Abbey" who fathers the Big Daddy of "The Prelude." "Where have I come from?" is the question which seems to be asked most frequently in first books of poetry, and this explains if not justifies the preponderance of first books and MFA theses which devote their opening sections to poems about childhood and family history, moving in later sections to two categories which can best be described as "poems vaguely about sex" and "poems about everything else." You may laugh here, but you've probably written that book yourself or want to; I and all my grad-school buddies tried to write it too. We were different from that smaller class of youthful writers who answer the question of "Where have I come from?" by testifying to a descent into the underworld, whether this means the shellfire over the trenches that is the soundtrack to the war poems of Graves, Sassoon and Blunden; or the Tet-offensive napalm blasts of Michael Casey's *Obscenities* (the first book to be published by a Vietnam Vet and the best-selling Yale Younger Poet volume of all); or, in the eighties and nineties, the AIDS pandemic, which has informed the aesthetics of an increasingly long list of collections, ranging from the stately requiems of Mark Doty's *Turtle, Swan* in 1987 to the hauntingly discordant vampings found in D. A. Powell's recently published *Tea.*[5]

Resonant first books may be born from trauma or from what Stevens called the pleasures of mere circulating; they are made partly through self-consciousness and partly through serendipity; they're apt to have clunkers, but the best ones have intriguing clunkers; slickness isn't always an asset, nor is earnestness, despite its increasing endangerment in an poetic ecosystem which has lost its ozone layer to pomo irony. First-book poets have to rely overwhelmingly on nerve, half the time being willing to try anything once but the rest of the time hewing to tradition with an unwavering ardor. Poets in midcareer and beyond tend to regret or mildly condescend to their first collections, as Robert Hass does when speaking of his own first book, *Field Guide;* "I can't say much about the poems, what strikes me now, predictably enough, are their limitations, and the memory of the human situations out of which they were written"—this about one of the most compelling first collections of the past few decades.[6] But we readers don't have to view first books so sternly: a lively first book offers the reader the delightful luxury of being able to check at the door all the retrospective regrets and second thoughts which we bring to the work of more established poets. Lack of craft or youthful excess are a first book's primary failings, and these hardly rank as High Crimes and Misdemeanors. Everything is promise, and every good first book you read may be the debut of another Bishop, Stevens, or Hass. But you must also be wary of making predictions. I'm reminded of a certain poet of my own generation whose Yale volume was characterized by its judge, Richard Hugo, as evidence of his "already entering the company of Wright, Levine and Stafford." (This crystal-ball gazing did him no service, and I suspect that at this point, now that two of this trio dwell among the shades, he's actually a little relieved that he never joined their company.) For every Bishop or Stevens there's a battalion of John Flanderses, and for every John Flanders there's a legion of everyone else. Your standards have to be high but flexible.

Consider Exhibit A, Jeff Clark's *The Little Door Slides Back.* I pulled this from the bookstore shelf solely because I liked the title; the book is a prizewinner in one of the more prestigious competitions (the National Poetry Series), and I suppose this automatically endows the collection with a bit of cachet. Unlike the winners of most of the other major competitions, this is an untweedy West Coast production all the way. Sun and Moon is the press, and Language poet Ray DiPalma, the judge, does Clark no favor with his jacket blurb, which informs us that "the ironic threnodies, 'demonologues,' and antiphonal writing collected here afford the reader far more than a finely articulated gathering of poems" and that the book "offers a further sense of the perplexing consolations that bring us, in our flight from platitudes and tethered monodies, to seek out the poem in the first place." I can't say what this means, but I like the book too. Clark is a *young* younger poet, born in 1971. And although he decorates his house with some trendy bric-a-brac he's purchased from the Language writers, he can more accurately be described as a Big-S Surrealist, who drinks his Dada straight with no chaser. His is not the lapidary Deep Image of seventies magazine verse, but the undiluted grunt and howl and murmur of Artaud and Company. Here's a poem from a series called "Demonologues":

> I had a ward I adored and tortured in four ways
>
> I mocked his wish to be rid of me
>
> I made it impossible for him to sit still
>
> How shall I say it   Proprietor
>
> Of his parts Lord   I was Lassitude
>
> He was like a horse to me I locked him in and then starved him
> As for my horse Lord I starved him and introduced ticks to his body
>
> It was dark inside all day except when at noon and three and six
> It was dark inside save at noon and three and six I opened the door
> It was only lit when I opened the door and showed him an apple
>
> And yet I believed I thought now and then I loved my horse Lord
>
> Thus the more barbarous of my treatment the less his vision and voice
> The more barbarous my acts the less his face and thought disturbed
> The more the horse moaned the less I was inclined to Lord the *less*[7]

This is a creepy piece of work, a kind of bent Sadean prayer; it's a continent removed from the plangent quatrains of Craig Arnold's "Scrubbing Mussels"—but it's equally intriguing. Like Arnold, Clark finds his voice through paying homage to his masters while at the same time very idiosyncratically adapting their methods to his own concerns. Clark is not a miniaturist: he favors longer sequences that try to push the nomenclature of surrealism into a troublesome psychological realm that little resembles the wise-ass whimsy into which American surrealism has for the most part evolved. The book's centerpiece is a blistering and guttural autobiography in verse entitled "Some Information About 23 Years of Existence." Like Hejinian's *My Life,* which it certainly derives from, it purports to be a year-by-year record of the speaker's life, yet it is an account of deep memory and occluded impressions rather than a collection of events and facts. The poem acknowledges Michaux as an inspiration, but if you're ambitious enough to look up the work of his which serves as Clark's model, you'll discover it's not a poem but instead a kind of hallucinatory parody of a curriculum vitae, which Michaux once contributed to a magazine. Here's a representative section of Clark's poem, "1984":

> My impressions are dim impressions. I console myself thus:
> "My impressions are merely *not of this dimension.*"
>
> —Alas, they are of this dimension and are like corduroy in
> the palace cloak room.
>
> Ruptures.
>
> Church Of Evangelical Freedom: Sunday mornings, Wednesday
> evenings. Hilarious faux-tongues to the left and to the right.
> Inward guffaws.
>
> Sometimes a small wind on the back of the neck.[8]

Consider Exhibit B: Talvikki Ansel's *My Shining Archipelago,* the Yale Younger Poet volume which precedes Craig Arnold's and the final selection to be made by the late James Dickey. Ansel, too, is at her most impressive when writing extensive sequences, and like Clark, her prevailing subject is the self's intricate relationship to the workings of memory. But Clark's dissembled and electroshocked stance toward recollection is replaced in Ansel's work by something more reflective and Proustian. Hers is a book of endless lost Edens, many of them lost even before we have the capacity to recognize them as such. Fittingly, ecological destruction plays a major role in this recognition, and Ansel possesses some of Bishop's capacity to see in the natural world a relentless succession of metaphors for our fallenness, yet—also like Bishop—her means of making this point are quietly insistent: her metaphors and descriptions are exact but strange, forlorn but never weepy. In contrast to the droves of Bishoplings who inhabit the pages of the Magazine Tina Brown Used to Edit, she understands something of Bishop's consciousness and knows that the point is not simply to ape Bishop's style. Of course, Ansel has an advantage over her competition in that she's actually lived in Brazil, in the Matto Grasso rainforest to be exact, where as a member of a research team she banded birds. This is the subject of her book's longest effort, a sequence of eighteen loosely rhymed and peripatetic sonnets entitled "In Fragments, In Streams," which brings its speaker to a primeval land too unlike the known world to be sentimentalized or even conventionally described, despite the offhand shapeliness of Ansel's sonnet-making. Paradise and terrible reckonings are offered to the speaker at the same time, and although the speaker closes the sequence in the gray light of a New England winter, the rainforest is a place and state of mind which she will never leave. What remains is abiding obsession and unquenchable thirst: it's the haunted Amazon of Carpenter's *The Lost Steps* and Herzog's *Fitzcaraldo,* green mansions swarming with ghosts. But it is also piranhas, morpho butterflies, and a gecko shooting across the pages of *War and Peace* as it's read in a hammock by lamplight. Here's section XIV:

> Along the road, the bright painted crosses
> on the steepest banks, overturned buses,
> people waiting in the rain. A deep
> gouge with smaller rivers running down it,
> mud slick as ice, and driving we slide
> sideways. My last day in the forest
> I tilt my head back in the stream, the palms
> silhouetted against the sky, under
> my butt the water hollows out sand;
> why did I come here? Everything slips
> away. On the road, a man with a gun,
> a dead chachalaca slung at his waist;
> back in the city, rain clouds stud
> the gray sky, my clothes are reddened with mud.[9]

The collection ends with another group of sonnets, which further these themes and tragicomically comment upon them. They're a coda to *The Tempest,* spoken by Caliban after leaving Prospero's island and making his way to England. In them the stammer of ferality collides with Elizabethan English. It is, so to speak, a savage poem, but clearly it is Prospero who commits the savagery: he's no sorcerer, just a nasty ur-imperialist who exercises his power through insults and floggings. He toys with poor Caliban "like a Boy will a June bug / on a stick." Here's a representative section:

> The tulip, too, was in those days a novelty—
> Ruffle-edged, flared, flamed with names
> Of Dukes and Duchesses, Queens—all from an
> Onion-like Bulb. My days were ordered rows
> Of leeks: wake, eat, tidy and weed, harvest.
> Into portions He first divvied my days—as if
> I didn't know to Wake: wood-time, dig-time,
> Piss-time. Schedule and Rules, farewell sleeping
> Until the need to wake. Before my Dreams
> Were spent he made me rise, pull Dill seed
> Before it dried. Not everything can come
> From Books, lines of ink-grid numbers; I place

Carnations in the earth, they break Forth
Mysterious in Spring: some here, Red; there, Striped.[10]

I'm not about to make predictions as to whether Arnold, Clark, or Ansel will rise to the top of the prosodic food chain, but I know that theirs are first books which I will read again and that the three are poets whose careers I look forward to following.

Yet here I speak of three books out of the many book manuscripts that seek publishers, three success stories among endless stories of disappointment, hubris, and naiveté, linked only by Xerox ink, contest fees, and priority-mail SASEs. If you're circulating a first book you know the drill; the manuscript goes out and comes back, goes out and comes back, the process a benumbing ritual which is apt to go on for years or even decades before the book is finally published or left in a desk drawer. The environment in which first books of poetry are nurtured and brought forth has always been strange, but at the present moment the situation might be more properly described as bizarre, for reasons having more to do with the economics of publishing and the sometimes troubling pedagogical methods of graduate writing programs than anything having to do with aesthetics.

True, the general quality of first-book manuscripts is surely much higher today than it was in earlier decades, but a general level of competence probably doesn't make the number of truly distinguished manuscripts much higher than it was when the Yale series had its heyday in the fifties and sixties. Just as significantly, the number of publishing opportunities for young poets—or even for poets with proven track records—hasn't grown in such a way as to keep up with the numbers of manuscripts making the rounds, and it certainly hasn't much affected the sales figures for books of poetry, especially first books, which have remained more or less the same for decades. Crane's *White Buildings* and Stevens's *Harmonium,* the finest first collections of the 1920s, garnered dismal sales. It took three years for Crane to sell out Liveright's first printing—five hundred copies—of *White Buildings,* and perhaps a quarter of these were reviewer and complimentary copies.[11] Crane in a letter expresses a fair amount of satisfaction with these stats, telling his correspondent that these sales are better than the ones normally expected for a collection of verse. Knopf's similarly puny print run of *Harmonium* took eight years to sell out: lucky for Stevens he kept his day job.[12] Liveright and Knopf were in the twenties small commercial houses, specializing in serious literature and comparable in today's market to a university press or to one of the more high-profile small presses such as Copper Canyon or Graywolf. Today's poetry publishers tend not to move many more first books than they did in Crane's and Stevens's day.

Here, for example, are the first-year sales figures of the recent debut collections published by two of the better-known university press poetry programs, furnished by confidential sources, who gave them to me on the condition that they and the names of the poets remain anonymous:

Press 1	Press 2
Title A:	Title A:
paper, 576	paper, 753
cloth, 151	cloth, 157
Title B:	Title B:
paper, 718	paper, 562
cloth, 118	cloth, 128
Title C:	Title C:
paper, 743	paper, 689
cloth, 104	cloth, 255
Title D:	
paper, 903	
cloth, 108	
Title E:	
paper, 580	
cloth, 194	

Bear in mind that cloth sales are made almost exclusively to libraries and that a good many poetry publishers do not even bother with a cloth edition anymore. Furthermore, the presses in question, like almost all other university presses, don't print dust jackets for their cloth editions, under the assumption that libraries will simply throw them away. Yet this also makes commercial sales of clothbounds for the most part impossible in these days of barcodes and flashy jacket designs all vying for attention on a bookstore shelf. One of my Deep Throats also told me that no first book in his series had gone into a second printing and closed his communiqué with an apology: "Depressing, I know . . . but also illuminating." Now, collections which are contest winners should be expected to fare a lot better, but such is not the case. I contacted a recent winner of one of the highest profile first-book awards and was given—again on the condition of anonymity—the following breakdown: the first-year sales (combined paper and cloth) were fourteen hundred, not counting returns. Presumably about half of these sales were to libraries, as the contest is a well-known one, meaning that many of the larger public and university libraries would be expected to have standing orders for the series titles. This makes for bookstore sales of about seven hundred, not counting returns. Interestingly enough, during the year this collection won the contest, precisely seven hundred manuscripts were submitted. Odd as these figures may be, there's a certain symmetry to them. But in the case of some of the other competitions the numbers are even more askew. Contests such as the Academy of American Poets' Walt Whitman Award and Pittsburgh's Starrett Prize have been known to receive over a thousand submissions in some years, yet the annual bookstores sales of a title in these competitions will rarely pass a thousand. Let me again rely on some anonymous sources, who provided me with first-year sales figures for six contest-winning first books:

Title A: paper, 840 cloth, 175	Title D: paper, 686 cloth, 173
Title B: paper, 519 cloth, 126	Title E: paper, 782 cloth, 128
Title C: paper, 1165 cloth, 403	Title F: paper, 847 cloth, 111

The authors of titles C, E, and F can console themselves with the knowledge that their first collections have sold faster than those of Crane and Stevens: these books are now in their second printings. But Crane and Stevens did not have the advantage of the subsidies which attend poetry publication these days, nor of our more extensive and convenient distribution systems. The Whitman Award can exist in part because the Academy distributes a free copy of each year's Whitman title to its members, assuring a larger print run for the book. The Starrett Prize titles sell reasonably well for poetry books, since Pittsburgh's distribution is better than that of most other university presses. But of the fourteen titles listed above, only three have gone into second printings. And first books which garner large sales often do so for reasons which are not purely literary. Casey's *Obscenities* sold well because it was the first book of poetry to be authored by a Vietnam veteran and thus was reviewed in popular magazines that otherwise pay no attention to poetry. Julia Kasdorf's *Sleeping Preacher* found a sales niche among the Mennonite communities where its poems are set, no doubt because the book's ambivalent stance toward the speaker's heritage created something of a scandal. Nothing like the *Peyton Place* effect to move a little poetry, and the poems must have seemed especially titillating within a community in which having cable is regarded as a sin.

Despite these depressing sales figures, contests proliferate. In addition to designer-label competitions such as the Yale, Whitman, Wisconsin, and Starrett, there are the National Poetry Series, AWP, and Juniper Prizes, on the occasions when they're offered to first-book poets. Then there's an increasing number of knock offs, some of which look legitimate, some of which look as though they're following in the tradition of Mickey Rooney and Judy Garland getting together in a forties musical and saying, "Let's make a play!" *Poets and Writers* brims with announcements of these sweepstakes, and with photos of their intense-looking winners, who generally are given a thousand bucks for their book in lieu of royalties and are assured its publication, although distribution of the collection is probably another matter. They may be sponsored by a small press with a misguidedly imaginative name such as "Silverfish" or by a fairly obscure university press affixed with an august-sounding prize name in order to wheedle some cachet—what, for example, does T. S. Eliot have to do with a state college in Missouri? I don't mean to condescend here. Some of these contests are first-rate, the winners selected by prestigious poets in the same way that they are in the better-known competitions, and in many instances the books are elegantly produced. Most of these competitions are somebody's labor of love; none of them that I know of is a scam. Yet all of them are likely to be tickets to oblivion: if you're a poet you already know as much. Furthermore, in most instances winning a contest from a publisher is no guarantee that the same publisher will even offer you first refusal rights for your next book. For that you'll have to enter another contest which accepts second books, and the process will begin all over again. If you're circulating a book manuscript your options are many, but they are puzzling, prohibitively expensive, and almost always frustrating.

What can be done about this? I'm not sure that much *can* be done. Some of the causes of the present state are due to forces no one would want to control. One reason why there are more first books than ever being shopped around is due to the growth of MFA programs and the creative writing industry, causing almost everyone who writes a graduate thesis in poetry to wrongly suspect that their thesis is a publishable book. Thus, first books of poetry have come to be seen not only as writerly productions but also as a kind of creative writing union card, the only likely means by which a teaching job may be obtained. This means that even the most talented young poets circulate books before they're really done, having been encouraged to do so by their teachers, who themselves may have a host of self-interested reasons for wanting their po-biz spawn to do well. These conditions create venial rather than cardinal sins against the muse, and there's nothing wrong with a young poet trying to publish a less-than-brilliant manuscript, provided that one knows the odds; nor is there anything wrong with a teacher encouraging a student to publish (assuming, of course, that the teacher sincerely believes in the student's work). But this does make for an unusual situation, in which a substantial percentage of people who read a first book of poetry are also people who have a manuscript which they themselves are sending around. A former student of mine who won the Yale Prize told me that she wasn't surprised that her book sold modestly: after all, she said, most of the people who read a Yale or Whitman winner are "poor graduate students" who have little disposable income and will read library copies of the collections rather than purchase them. And perhaps the disposable income they do have is being used up in postage, copying, and entry fees for the contests. Another student of mine recently won what I considered to be a fairly hefty writing grant from her state arts board. What was she going to do with the money? I asked her, thinking she'd take some time off from work or travel to some exotic locale in search of inspiration. But instead she was using the grant almost exclusively to bankroll the costs of sending her manuscript out. A few years of doing this can easily set you back thousands of dollars. Short of prohibiting people to write and publish or arranging public hangings of the creative writing instructors who wrongly encouraged you and the editors who wrongly rejected you, nothing can or should be done about these problems, although problems they surely are. And it would hardly make sense for publishers to issue fewer first books, given that so many decent first collections are ignored, unreviewed, or unpublished.

I suspect that the only way in which the situation of first books of poetry can be improved is through what arts-administration types call "audience development" and through efforts to cure first books of poetry of what might be termed the Rodney Dangerfield syndrome—first books don't get no respect. One might think that contests and prizes would be useful in addressing these issues, but in fact they aren't. Contests are now so numerous that to win one doesn't do much to draw attention to the winner. In fact, in the small and envy-saturated world of po-biz, being a prizewinner may just as frequently leave you a sitting duck. "Does anyone care who the Yale Younger Poet is anymore?" asked J. D. McClatchy in a review of one of Richard Hugo's selections in the series. The answer of course was no, and he then went on to attempt to show why, turning the book and the recent fate of the Yale Prize into sushi. Unfortunately, the book was written by a friend of mine, who learned that bad reviews are the ones you're apt to best remember. One important thing to recognize is that book contests are likely to receive larger and larger numbers of submissions each year and that it seems only fair to consider entrants as potential readers of the winning manuscript. Imagine a book contest in which a portion of the entry fee was used to mail copies of the prizewinning collection to all its contestants. Most rejected applicants would be intrigued, if not always delighted, by an opportunity to read the book that bettered them and would not carp about a few extra dollars being tacked onto a reading fee for such a purpose.

Getting first books onto the shelves at Borders, B&N, and the handful of remaining independent bookstores is a problem whose solutions are less simple, especially if the book is brought out by a little-known press whose distribution is spotty. But in seeking to get more attention paid to first books we would do well to remember that there are contests—and then there are contests. Poetry-prize winners of the sort I have been discussing, even prestigious ones such as the Yale and the Whitman, draw a readership made exclusively of other poets. Contrast this with the additional sales figures which books—even poetry books—will command when they win one of the major national book prizes such as the Pulitzer, the National Book Award, or the National Book Critics' Circle Award. Or consider how new editions of a poet's backlist get rushed into print when he or she is appointed the poet laureate. Britain's Booker Prize countdown is a major news event there, and sales for even its shortlisted books increase exponentially. The Brits now sponsor an equivalent award for poetry, the T. S. Eliot Prize (not to be confused with the Missouri version of the same), and its bestowal is accompanied by some of the same sort of hubbub which attends the Booker. As few first books of poetry ever win the big-enchilada book prizes such as the Pulitzer and the National Book Award (Alan Dugan's and Marilyn Hacker's first collections are the only ones I know of that have done so), and as the big-enchilada prizes assure the sale of lots of books, some enterprising publishers and other interested parties should create and endow one for first collections—not a prize to *publish* a first book but to recognize a distinguished book among the many that are brought out each year. I'm envisioning something along the lines of the PEN-Faulkner Award for first books of fiction. A handful of first-book prizes along these lines already exists—*Ploughshares* oversees one, as does the Poetry Society of America, and there's a sort of junior-grade version of the Kingsley Tufts Award which its judges dole out to first-book poets and which is meant to bask in the reflected light of its fifty-thousand-dollar prize for midcareer poets. But none of these awards has anything like the status of the National Book Award—or even of the PEN-Faulkner.

Finally, Americans might draw upon the British model for another innovation and devise through an organization such as the Academy of American Poets or the Poetry Society of America a distribution system like that of the Poetry Book Society, which combines the best elements of a book club with a selection process for its offerings that functions as a de facto prize competition. Subscribers to the Poetry Book Society are mailed copies of each season's main selections, chosen by a rotating board of established poets, and also offered the chance to be sent books from a lengthy list of alternate selections. It's a system which ensures that a number of first books are always among its offerings, and the catalogue which accompanies the society's offerings contains reviews of all of the main selections and alternates. Once a system such as this was in place, poetry publishers would soon discover that it would offer a much better use of bound galleys than the current one: most of them go straight into the wastepaper baskets of book-section editors and quarterlies or make their way to used bookstore shelves months in advance of their publication dates—when did you last see a first book of poetry reviewed in *The New York Times Book Review?* I haven't the arrogance to think that suggestions such as these, however sensible they may be, are likely to be acted upon by anyone. But they're reasonable suggestions, practical suggestions, and if justice were indeed poetic someone would listen to them.

To reach the end of this story I must go back to its beginning, to the winter of 1980 to be exact. I've been writing poetry, badly but earnestly, in the way that most young poets do it, for nearly ten years, and during that time, simply through trial and error rather than through anything like skill or talent, I've grown better. I've in fact reached the point where I've started sending to the contests a poetry manuscript, an inchoate and sprawlingly self-indulgent little behemoth which I know is a mess but which I'm convinced will grow better, somehow, through time. I'm in graduate school at the University of Arizona, and my classmate William Olsen and I spend every weekday afternoon swimming with our teacher, the poet Jon Anderson. We're terrible swimmers, thrashing around in a tiny backyard pool like shark victims during the moments just before they're pulled down in the *Jaws* movies, but the swimming matters less to us than the poetry talk, and after a few months of this we've finally convinced the reluctant Jon to help us structure our book manuscripts, and we in turn have agreed (eagerly) to read his own recent work, the new poems which later become a section of his selected volume, *The Milky Way.* Each week for three weeks we spend an evening in a windowless seminar room, sheaves of poems spread out on the table. Bill and Jon have been the first in rotation, and I've seen us go after their manuscripts for hours at a time, and with a manic intensity. Their books shrink and expand, get shuffled and reshuffled, only to shrink again. Poems metamorphose from dreck to brilliance or shrink to nothing under their scrupulous eyes; the dialogue between them possesses some of the intricate intensity you imagine goes on in a battlefront headquarters, but we're peering over stanzas instead of ordinance maps, and I'm heady with the vitality of their talk but unable to keep up my end of it. And finally it's my turn. Jon has my poems scattered across the table; some of the poems I regard as my best have turned into sand thanks to his comments, and others, through his juxtaposing them with other poems, suddenly don't seem half bad. He shuffles and reshuffles the pages. In an hour or two he's arranged them into piles, and before long into sections, and not long after that a manuscript is born, so unlike my previous version of the book that I now seem less a different writer than I feel like I'm a *real* writer for the first time. He's given me a gift which still seems to me of incalculable worth, even though the book will change enormously in the years before it's finally published. But at that moment something like my poetic self was born, for all its limitations and for all its manifold possibilities for self-delusion: a self distinct from David Wojahn, but David Wojahn nevertheless. And as I sat before my smudged typewritten pages, spread out and affixed with Jon's slashes, xes, question marks, and exclamation points—some of the poems now mine as never before; and others dross, a snake's shed skin, that distinct smell of old-fashioned, low-tech Xerox paper wafting up from them—I felt wholly myself and outside myself at once and knew that if I were truly to be a poet I would have to again and again devise ways to honor gifts such as these, ones which had just been bestowed upon me not through efforts of my own nor even of Jon's, but through some force far more mysterious, something very much like grace. I wish there were a way to put this less grandly, but I count that moment among the happiest of my life.

(1999)

12.

Like a Rolling Incognito Lounge: Rock and Roll and American Poetry

Since the advent of Romanticism, we've grown numbingly used to regarding movements in art as attempts at cultural and sometimes political revolution. And if the notion of the avant-garde is now, as the century draws to a close, coming to be seen as a quaint and exhausted one, replaced by the more cynical forms of pastiche, homage, and outright cultural cannibalism that may be defined as postmodernism, this is not to deny the power and initially revolutionary nature of the dozens of cultural movements of this century which we link with Modernism. In what follows, I would like to focus on two of those movements and on how they've cross-fertilized one another: modern and contemporary American poetry and rock and roll music. Granted, the two movements are seldom discussed in the same breath, and even today there remain a few high-cult Tories who refuse to dignify rock and roll with the status of art (the late Alan Bloom warned of the "androgynous" Mick Jagger's influence on the young—forgetting, one supposes, that Jagger was nearer to Bloom's age than to a teenager's). And although the revolutionary nature of both Modernism in poetry and rock and roll music eventually dissipated, turning the former into a highly specialized mode of discourse practiced mainly in college creative writing programs and the latter into a hugely successful corporate enterprise which only dimly recalls its anarchic roots, the two movements continue to share some essential characteristics and comparable patterns of development.

Both movements began inauspiciously, even accidentally. In 1908 a young professor at a backwater college in Crawfordsville, Indiana, was fired from his job after a young woman had spent the night in his rooms. So Ezra Pound went to Europe, and stayed. The rest, as they say, is history. More than forty years later, Memphis record producer Sam Phillips, at this point making a decent but not princely income recording Black bluesmen such as Howlin' Wolf and Rufus "Bearcat" Thomas, is reported to have wistfully—and indelicately—stated that if he could "just find a white boy who can sing like a nigger," he could "make a million bucks."[1] In 1956, when Phillips sold Elvis's Sun Records contract to RCA, he came very close to realizing his goal, though RCA got a bargain on par with the original sale of Manhattan Island. The rest, again, is history. Both movements created their aesthetic through outright plagiarism: Pound shoplifted late Symbolist poetry, particularly that of Laforgue, in order to create free verse Imagism and let the notebooks of the Orientalist Ernest Fennollosa teach him the Chinese he needed for the poems of *Cathay;* figures such as Arthur "Big Boy" Crudup and Big Mama Thornton were Elvis's Laforgure and Fennollosa. Both movements created their most memorable and ambitious work within the first two decades of their inception. The 1920s brought *The Wasteland,* Stevens's *Harmonium,* Williams's *Spring and All,* Crane's *The Bridge,* and Pound's *Draft of XXIII Cantos.* The 1960s were a similar watershed for rock. Bob Dylan's *Highway 61 Revisited* and *Blonde on Blonde* albums possess for rock music the same classic status that *The Cantos* and *The Wasteland* have within the Modernist canon. The sixties also saw the release of vastly influential albums by the Velvet Underground, the Rolling Stones, and the Beatles, productions analogous to the major works of Modernist poetry. But both movements rather quickly lost their sense of revolutionary mission. The tenets of literary Modernism, shorn for better or for worse of implicit extremist political and cultural agendas (both leftist and rightist in nature), were sanitized by the New Critics, who saw to it that Modernism would exist mainly within the safe confines of universities or in the pages of the *Partisan* and *Kenyon* reviews. The 1970s saw a similar change in popular music. The seductive menace of the young Elvis and the early Rolling Stones and the outright nihilism of groups such as the Velvet Underground and the Stooges were replaced by travesties such as disco, a movement that even the Stones themselves tried to cash in on. And of course we know what the seventies did to Elvis. In later phases of both Modernism and rock, adversarial movements emerged which tried to reverse this retreat toward complacency and conservatism. The Beats, the New York School, and the Deep Image poets arrived by the end of the 1950s, all fueled with the notion that they, and not the New Critics, were the true inheritors of Modernism. Similarly, the late seventies saw the emergence of punk rock and post-punk, and the green teeth of the Sex Pistols' Johnny Rotten were a far cry from the gold lamé dresses of Donna Summer. Punk self-consciously sought to recapture from rock its original sense of danger: fittingly, the cover design of the Clash's *London Calling,* the most enduring album of the punk movement, follows slavishly the design and color scheme of Elvis's first RCA album, with one important difference—the cover photo shows bassist Paul Simonon smashing his instrument against a London stage. Of course, both Beat poetry and punk soon became domesticated, part of the mainstream. Allen Ginsberg became everyone's uncle, and Robert Bly would like to regard himself as everyone's shrink. One-time punks such as Elvis Costello now fancy themselves as crooners or, like Sting, have squandered their artistic integrity in an effort to be taken seriously by the establishment. Modernist/late-Modernist poetry and rock music are now institutions rather than movements—one occupying a small and somewhat insecure niche within the world of the university, the small and university poetry presses, and the little magazine; the other occupying a considerably bigger and more secure niche within the world of the record industry, the concert promoter, and the rock-video channel.

Twentieth-century poetry and rock are thus paradigms of how avant-garde movements have been assimilated into mainstream culture in this century, but my purpose is not to discuss this process in depth, however interesting such a topic may be. Nor is my purpose to discuss rock *music* as it relates to contemporary poetry. I'm instead interested in examining how rock has had an impact on the themes and subjects of recent poetry and on how the sensibility and lyrics of particular rock artists have influenced poets of my approximate generation. I want to accomplish these goals by discussing some poems that are representative of rock music's influence and by examining how the verse of a particular American writer of the 1980s, Denis Johnson, has been significantly influenced by the work of Bob Dylan, a figure who, to paraphrase a poem by Marvin Bell, is not a great poet, exactly, but is a great poet inexactly.

When I speak of rock and poetry influencing one another, I should emphasize that contemporary poetry has received more of a benefit from rock than rock has gained from contemporary poetry. The reasons for this are obvious: rock has been the soundtrack for the baby-boomer generation and the generations that have followed it, a fact which has been exploited by almost any recent film that is set in the 1960s. Coppola uses Doors music to underscore the millennialist concerns of *Apocalypse Now;* Kubrick's *Full Metal Jacket* sets the siege of Hue to the novelty hit "Surfin' Bird." More shameless examples of this device also abound: Lawrence Kasden's *The Big Chill* uses sixties music in its soundtrack to bolster a film which is at best vapid and obvious. For better or for worse, most boomer and post-boomer poets have a greater familiarity with rock lyrics than with the poems they profess to revere, something that was made painfully clear to me a few years ago in a graduate poetry workshop I was teaching. During a rather heated discussion about a very defensive student's garbled piece of Dada, I offhandedly noted that to successfully break aesthetic norms required at least a certain amount of sincerity. "As Dylan says," I told him, "'to live outside the law you must be honest'" ("Absolutely Sweet Marie"). "Well, Professor Wojahn," he retorted, "'you don't need a Weatherman to know which way the wind blows'" ("Subterranean Homesick Blues"—a line that both spawned the Weatherman faction of SDS and made its way into *Bartlett's Familiar Quotations*). A Dylan-duel then ensued, which went on for several minutes. I must say that my student, alas, got the better of me in this battle. Before long I'd exhausted all of my repertoire except for "the pumps don't work 'cuz the vandals took the handles," a line for which I had a tough time finding a context. Clearly neither of us would have been able to sustain an exchange such as this with quotes from Blake, Stevens, or the King James Bible, however more quotable than Dylan such sources may be. Both my student and I shared our generation's tendency to have come to literature to some extent through rock music. How many baby boomers first read Nietzsche because they were told, in Dylan's cryptic liner notes to *Highway 61 Revisited,* that "Nietzsche never wore an umpire's mask"?

Of course, there are numerous rock musicians who fancy themselves poets and who've looked to poetry for inspiration. L.A.'s still somewhat vital punk scene has spawned a number of poetry journals with roots in both rock and literature. John Doe and Exene Cervenka, the leaders of the now-defunct X, the best American punk band, have both published books of Bukowski-derived poetry from L.A. small presses.[2] And it is often pointed out that one of rock's most significant artists, Velvet Underground founder Lou Reed, was a student of Delmore Schwartz. Reed has published many poems over the years, in magazines such as *Poetry* and *The Paris Review,* and his apprenticeship under Schwartz may have something to do with the metrical precision and narrative compression of his best albums, most notably his brilliant 1989 song cycle, *New York.* Unfortunately, when rock figures try to self-consciously do justice to their poetic influences, the results are usually clumsy. Peter Grabriel is as much a failure at doing justice to Anne Sexton's poems—as he attempts to do on one of his albums—as he would probably be at performing one of Rachmaninoff's more difficult piano concertos. The worst song in Reed's very large and very uneven canon is an homage to Schwartz, entitled "My House." Reed calls up the dead poet James Merrill–style on his Ouija board, a feat accompanied by singing that's wretched even by Lou Reed standards and by some singularly clumsy lyrics ("grandly stood the proud and regal name DEEELLLL-MOOORE. . . ."). Poets use rock better than rock artists use poetry.

And rock culture provides ample subject matter for poets. Rock musicians comprise a subculture that poets of the baby-boom generation find attractive and romantic, much in the way that the subculture of jazz musicians appealed to the Beat and New York School poets a generation or two ago. This is not to say, however, that the poetry about rock is merely a rhapsodizing of what some would see as a glamorous lifestyle. If anything, the opposite holds true. Anyone who attempts to catalogue poems about rock music will soon discover that the majority of the poems which treat the subject are either laced with elegiac feeling or are outright elegies. Of course, popular music has created a seemingly endless number of rock star corpses, and contemporary poets appear to possess an apparently inexhaustible will to elegize the noble and not-so-noble dead. The murder of John Lennon spawned countless elegies, even from such unlikely sources as the late Amy Clampitt. Dead Elvis poems are a similar hot item, for Elvis embodies—perhaps too obviously—all of the contradictions and ironies of what used to be called the American Dream: a tragic buffoon, simultaneously old-fashioned gentleman and sneering id-monster; megalomaniac and fool; genius at media manipulation and bewildered dupe of Colonel Tom Parker. What poet could resist such a figure? In the hands of a poet skillful enough to skirt sentimentality and easy lampooning, Elvis can be a riveting subject: Thom Gunn realized this quite early on, for his first poem about the King, "Elvis Presley," dates from the mid-1950s. A second, more harrowing poem, a terse elegy entitled "Painkillers," appeared some twenty-five years later.

William Matthews's elegy for reggae great Bob Marley is a good example of how a rock musician's death provides the occasion for a poem that seeks to fix itself within the grand tradition of the English elegy:

An Elegy for Bob Marley

In an elegy for a musician,
one talks a lot about music,
which is a way to think about time,
instead of death or Marley,

and isn't poetry itself about time?
But death is about death and not time.
Surely the real fuel for elegy
is anger to be mortal.

No wonder Marley sang so often
of an ever-arriving future, that verb tense
invented by religion and political rage.
Soon come. Readiness is all

and not enough. From the urinous
dust and sodden torpor
of Trenchtown, from the fruitpeels
and imprecations, from cunning,

from truculence, from the luck
to be alive, however cruelly,
Marley made a brave music—
a rebel music, he called it,

though music calls us together,
however briefly—and a fortune.
One is supposed to praise the dead
in elegies for leaving us their songs;

though they had no choice; nor could
the dead bury the dead if we could pay
them to. This is something else
we can't control, another loss, which is,

as someone said in hope of consolation,
only temporary, though the same phrase
could be used of our lives and bodies
and all that we hope survives them.[3]

Like so many of Matthews's poems, "Elegy" begins in an offhand and chatty fashion. The opening rhetorical question at first strikes us as a bit glib, cynically self-referential in immediately reminding us that elegies are about elegies and our own fears of dying. Only in the third stanza does Marley's death emerge as the subject of—rather than the *occasion for*—the poem. It's as though Matthews needed to clear his throat of caustic phlegm before getting down to the most urgent business of the elegy. This shift is accompanied by a dictional segue toward a more formal language and a more deliberate use of sonics. The ironic abstraction of "Readiness is all / and not enough" is followed by the Latinate assonance of the lengthy passage which begins with "From the urinous / dust and sodden torpor / of Trenchtown, from the fruitpeels. . . ." These sly rhetorical strategies, insistent upon both the limitations and the necessity of the elegiac impulse, recall certain poems of Auden, one of Matthews's most abiding influences: there are strong echoes of both Auden's Freud and Yeats elegies. But one important difference between these earlier poems and Matthews's effort is that the latter seeks to acknowledge a complicated series of ironies brought about by the contrast between the messianic Rastafarianism of Marley's music—his mystical insistence that the oppressed black masses would rise up to destroy the forces of "Babylon," the white man's power structure—and the plain drab fact of Marley's early death from cancer. Matthews doesn't seek to explore the social and political ramifications of these ironies: he instead uses the poem as both an examination of the inherent contradictions within the elegiac impulse and as an eloquent homage to a great musician. Homage in Matthews's poem does not include any attempt to echo Marley's music or lyrical style in the way Auden's elegy for Yeats imitates the dead poet's manner. Matthews knows he is no Rastaman.

A quite different sort of elegy—different largely because it draws its stylistic energy explicitly from the punk music it is inspired by—is Thom Gunn's "The Victim." The subject of the poem is the murder by ex–Sex Pistols bassist Sid Vicious of his girlfriend, Nancy Spungen, in 1979. The poem, from Gunn's 1982 collection, *The Passages of Joy,* was written well before the same subject was treated by Alex Cox in his film *Sid and Nancy.*

Oh dead punk lady with the knack
Of looking fierce in pins and black,
The suburbs wouldn't want you back.

You wished upon a shooting star
And trusted in your wish as far
As he was famous and bizarre.

The band broke up, its gesture made.
And though the music stopped, you stayed.
Now it was with sharp things that he played:

Needles and you, not with the band,
Till something greater than you planned
Opened erect within his hand.

You smiled. He pushed it through your shirt
Deep in your belly, where it hurt.
You turned, and ate the carpet's dirt.

And then not understanding why
He watched you with a heavy eye
The several hours you took to die.

The news was full of his fresh fame.
He O.D.'d, ending up the same.
Poor girl, poor girl, what was your name?[4]

A creepy piece of work: like numerous other Gunn poems, it looks unflinchingly at violence, treating its subject in the cold but by no means heartless fashion that gives Gunn's best verse its unsettling majesty. Gunn evokes the violence and three-chord primitivism of the punk ethos by employing a verse form almost impossible to bring off convincingly—tetrameter triplets. Yet in this case the form is singularly appropriate. The stridency and insistence of the triple rhymes evokes the histrionic thrash of such Sex Pistols opuses as "Anarchy in the U.K." and "God Save the Queen," as if to fulfill Johnny Rotten's prophecy in the latter song that there's "no future." Yet the methods by which Rotten extols a vague sort of nihilism become in Gunn's poem a remarkably sophisticated narrative device. In twenty-one lines he charts the rise and fall of the Sex Pistols, Sid Vicious's collapse into junkiedom, and his apparently motiveless murder of Nancy Spungen, not long before an overdose brought about his own death. Gunn gives this wretched story poignancy and focus by addressing the poem to Spungen, intensifying the pointlessness of her demise by claiming not to know her name and complicating the narration through his use of the knife/needle motif ("Now it was with sharp things that he played"). In a few broad strokes Gunn—an expatriate Brit in his sixties!—offers not only an elegy for Spungen, but also an elegy for the punk movement as a whole.

Both Matthews and Gunn use their rock sources as subjects rather than as motifs, and one of the consequences of that decision is of course to reinforce the elegy's usual tendency to be more of a public utterance than a personal one. Neither Matthews nor Gunn attempts to claim direct or specific involvement with rock music save as observers or fans. Yet poets have also used rock music in more subjective and psychologically intricate ways. In these cases the poems use rock less as a subject than as a motif against which the poem's central actions are set. If rock has entered our collective consciousness, then it stands to reason that poets will find ways to show rock within the larger framework of their creative lives. After all, don't poets regard all things, finally, as material for poems? Younger poets such as James Harms and David Trinidad take this notion to one of its logical extremes by liberally lacing their poems not just with references to rock songs but with unacknowledged use of rock song titles and even outright plagiarism of lyrics. These expropriations are for the most part cunning rather than crass, a latter-day version of Modernist collage. In Harms's first volume, *Modern*

Ocean, one is initially aware of the poet's debt to figures such as Ashbery and James Wright. But a closer examination of the book reveals some other influences: Harms not only takes some epigraphs from rock songs, but he also lifts titles and sometimes fairly lengthy passages from lyrics of 1980s groups such as the Waterboys and the Smiths. The danger of this technique—and Harms usually avoids this problem—is that the use of rock music motifs can devolve into something that functions as little more than the poem's soundtrack music, a *Big Chill*-ish shortcut to authenticity. Mark Halliday's "Key to the Highway" seems well aware of this problem, and to some degree is able to overcome it. Here's the opening:

> I remember riding somewhere in a fast car
> with my brother and his friend Jack Brooks
> and we were listening to *Layla and Other Love Songs*
> *by Derek and the Dominos.* The night was
> dark all along the highway. Jack Brooks was
> a pretty funny guy, and I was delighted
> by the comradely interplay between him and my brother
> but I tried not to show it for fear of inhibiting them.
> I tried to be reserved and maintain a certain
> dignity appropriate to my age, older by four years.
> They knew the Dominos album well having played the cassette
> many times, and they knew how much they liked it.[5]

This is a masterfully neurotic beginning. The speaker uses the Eric Clapton album as the trigger for a meditation on an event that mixes a Wordsworthian nostalgia for an innocent past with a self-conscious suspicion that such moments may now be forever beyond the speaker's reach. The speaker, slightly older than his brother and his pal, tries to "maintain a certain / dignity. . . ." The speaker's sense of awkwardness and confusion is evoked through a diction that seesaws from the talky ("Jack Brooks was / a pretty funny guy") to the stilted ("I was delighted / by the comradely interplay between him and my brother"). That the speaker feels so out of place while engaged in the quintessential adolescent ritual of empowerment and abandon—joyriding to loud hard rock—further underscores the poem's mixture of the comic and the pathetic. Halliday continues,

> As we rode along in the dark, I felt the music was,
> after all, wonderful, and I said so
> with as much dignity as possible. "That's right,"
> said my brother. "You're getting smarter," said Jack.
> We were listening to "Bell Bottom Blues"
> at that moment. Later we were listening to

> "Key to the Highway," and I remember how
> my brother said "yeah, yeah." And Jack sang
> one of the lines in a way that made me laugh.

Now Halliday shifts toward statement, yet in a somewhat unconvincing fashion:

> I am upset by the fact that night is so absolutely gone.
> No, "upset" is too strong. Or is it.
> But that night is so obscure—until now
> I may not have thought of that ride once
> in eight years—and this obscurity troubles me.
> Death is going to defeat us all so easily.
> Jack Brooks is in Florida, I believe,
> and I may never see him again, which is
> more or less alright with me; he and my brother
> lost touch some years ago. I wonder
> where we were going that night. I don't know;
> but it seemed as if we had the key to the highway.

The style Halliday commenced the poem with, which so effectively mixed dictions in order to create a combination of the wistful, the self-conscious, and the ecstatic—all of it fueled by the reference to *Layla and Other Love Songs*—in the end cannot serve Halliday's ultimate goal. The closing demands—and Halliday himself admits to seek this—a more straightforwardly serious and rhetorically dynamic finish. Although one might argue that the self-conscious nature of the speaker which we have earlier witnessed cannot permit such grandiosity of utterance, it seems clear that a truly effective ending would find a way to obliterate his self-consciousness and ambivalence. But as it stands, we can't quite figure out Halliday's tone. Is he still kidding when he tells us that "Death is going to defeat us all so easily"? Halliday seems himself not to know, and thus ends the poem by moving back to the musical references, a gesture too tentative to work convincingly as a conclusion. Halliday is one of our more gifted young poets, but "Key to the Highway" is not his most successful effort.

A more effective example of how rock music can intensify a poem of psychological speculation and meditation is David Rivard's "Cures." Rivard begins the poem with a relentless self-questioning that is typical of his poetry:

> The part of the soul that doubts, again and again,
> is scratchy as this song, Mystery Train, where Elvis
> relates some dark to himself. Even the light
> in the livingroom seems sullen. We've turned the stereo
> up loud, don't have to talk. After the latest argument,

trading blame is all that is left. After all that,
forgiveness? More punishment? Forgetting?
You curl, knees up, on the couch. Along your bare neck
the skin looks soft—shadows, the barrage
of falling brown hair, soft. I'm in the raggedy armchair,
and the music just washes through these questions,
then pours out the screen door. So this is what we do,
how we feel, each doubt a little larger
than desire, so that nothing
seems enough.[6]

We see the speaker in the benumbed, emotionally exhausted state that can follow a lengthy argument with a partner; the couple is frozen into inaction, though their minds are racing: the "part of the soul that doubts" has amplified the couple's argument into larger and larger significance, in the way that obsessive thinking so often does, yet the nature of that significance seems beyond the speaker's understanding ("each doubt a little larger / than desire"). Now the poem shifts back to the reference to Elvis that was casually dropped in the opening lines:

And for a while,
ten minutes, I've stared at the album cover.
The face with the half-sneered, boyishly charming smile
stares back from the floor. The words echo wall to wall,
then silence as one song ends and we wait for the next.
What do we think? His smoothness and raveling wail will cure us
of all this? These rockabilly blues
from the early Memphis days, a shy country kid,
opening for Pee Wee Crayton at the Flamingo Club.
When all he cared about was shouting the next tune.

Like Halliday in "Key to the Highway," we catch the speaker in a moment of ambivalence brought on by the music. He wants to abandon himself to the songs of the early Elvis, and wants his partner to do so as well. Yet at the same time he suspects such gestures are sentimental and futile, a crude sort of therapeutic device. As the stanza breaks and we reach the poem's conclusion, this ambivalence is given even greater dramatic urgency:

The next tune. But endings are truer,
for all their need: a mansion outside town,
years of Seconal, gaudy stage suits. Ways to simplify
the hundred confusions screaming in the body,
to become a star, or something stranger. . . .
I'd like to go over and brush away the hair

from your face. All the questions,
all the night, as it strikes
the house like a train whistle. And after I get up,
cross the room, you and I aren't sorry
it leads to this kiss. Or to what it brings on,
a soothing that lasts only so long,
like stardom
in America, and now this silence between songs.

Rivard has seamlessly fused the poem's motifs and found a provisional solution to some of the dilemmas which have gnawed at his couple. Like the speaker of Halliday's "Key to the Highway" the narrator of "Cures" longs to regain a portion of lost innocence. He wants his couple to be free of their condition of doubt, wants them to find a means to restore the sense of romance and erotic possibility which an earlier published version of this poem terms "the myth of beginnings." Yet Rivard reveals this desire in order to relate a kind of cautionary tale. The myth of beginnings must be invariably followed by what serves as the title of the earlier version, "The Myth of Endings."[7]

And the speaker comes to see that both myths are at best half-truths or simplistic, just as the often-contrasted images of the youthful Adonis Elvis and the bloated drug-addled Vegas-era Elvis are less truthful than the sadly mysterious "hundred confusions screaming in the body" that motivated the singer's transformation. Neither the myth of beginning nor the myth of ending is true, Rivard seems to say, because in real life we must dwell in the cusp between them and accept what consolations such a condition may offer us. Although the poem concludes with the traditional happy ending's kiss, the couple seems less like Cinderella and Prince Charming than like Milton's Adam and Eve at the close of *Paradise Lost:* the world that looms before them is immense and mysterious—and fallen.

The belief that we dwell in a fallen world, a notion that one would imagine is decidedly out of fashion in contemporary poetry and music, is just one characteristic that links the two figures who are the focus of the final portion of this essay. Yet both Denis Johnson and Bob Dylan share, more than anything else, a kind of apocalyptic Christianity that has continually informed their work and that has both deepened and limited it. Neither figure exhibits a clear theological program. Although Dylan has always expressed religious concerns in his lyrics, only in the past two decades or so has he done this in overtly Christian terms, and his brand of Christianity is by no means, as some of his critics have charged, mere simplistic fundamentalism. Johnson's Christian streak is similarly complicated. Although he is ostensibly a convert to Roman Catholicism, Johnson's theology is by no means doctrinaire. In the case of both artists, religious sensibility seems channeled more than anything else into a sort of Old Testament prophetic stance. The world we dwell in is not only a fallen one, but the End Is Near. Both writers revel in the use of apocalyptic imagery, even when their intentions are autobiographical rather than universal. Here's Dylan in a passage from a song on his 1983 album *Infidels:*

> You're a man on the mountains, you can walk on the clouds,
> Manipulator of crowds, you're a dream twister.
> You're going to Sodom and Gomorrah,
> But what do you care?
>
> . . .Well, the Book of Leviticus and Deuteronomy,
> The law of the jungle and the sea are your only teachers. . . .[8]

Hard to say what this signifies, of course, but you can tell that Dylan means business. Compare this to a similarly apocalyptic passage in the beginning of Johnson's "Passengers," from *The Incognito Lounge:*

> The world will burst like an intestine in the sun,
> the dark turn to granite and the granite to a name,
> but there will always be somebody riding the bus
> through these intersections strewn with broken glass,
> among speechless women beating their little ones,
> always a slow alphabet of rain
> speaking of drifting and perishing to the air,
> always these definite jails of light in the sky. . . .[9]

Such gestures toward vatic prophecy are so common in both Dylan and Johnson that they may arguably be seen as the most distinguishing features of both artists' work. The title song of Dylan's *Highway 61 Revisited* ends with a dialogue between a gambler and a promoter who seek to both create and sell tickets to World War III. "Talkin World War III Blues" is the title of an early Dylan song, and Dylan's first foray into the surrealism that characterizes his best work is the 1962 warning of nuclear catastrophe, "A Hard Rain's Gonna Fall." Even the more personal and cryptic songs of Dylan's canon have an apocalyptic nature: songs from his great period in the mid-1960s invariably seem to focus on moments of personal reckoning for their speakers and characters, reckonings that will lead to absolute change—annihilation or a less-likely rebirth. Such reckonings are implicit in the very titles of many of the songs. Characters end up on "Desolation Row" or "Stuck Inside of Mobile With the Memphis Blues Again." The chastened lover addressed in

"Like a Rolling Stone" needs to "live out on the street" or must perish. The addict speaker of "Just Like Tom Thumb's Blues" undergoes a harrowing *Under the Volcano*–style blackout in Juarez, Mexico. Even Christ figures such as Frankie Lee, in "The Ballad of Frankie Lee and Judas Priest," meet endings which bring no apparent hope of redemption or resurrection.

Similarly, Johnson's characters and speakers live on the edge of annihilation. James Hampton, the schizophrenic subject of "The Throne of the Third Heaven of the Nations Millennium General Assembly," spends his life constructing from tinfoil and trash a throne for Christ to occupy after the Second Coming. "Talking Richard Clay Wilson Blues By Richard Clay Wilson" is a death-house last will and testament spoken by a wife murderer. The narrator of "The White Fires of Venus" prays for extraterrestrials to end human suffering. The speaker of "The Flames," recalling a burning Kansas farmhouse that he once glimpsed from a bus window, regards this visionary sight as emblematic of his own condition. In the case of both Dylan and Johnson, the apocalyptic motifs can grow repetitive and turgid. The fundamentalist Dylan of the late 1970s and early 1980s—Dylan's work reaches its nadir in albums such as "Saved" and "Shot of Love"—is little more than a nut-case blowhard. Similarly, about half of the poems of Johnson's wildly uneven 1987 volume, *The Veil,* meander into vatic self-parody. Too self-aggrandizing and calculated to be labeled as automatic writing, they nevertheless share its tendency to begin in incoherence and to at best be only intermittently interesting: "houses absolutely / hopeless in the red darkness are singing fuck you: / and I have come back into your life again wearing a fake beard."[10] "Red Darkness," from which these lines have been drawn, continues on in a similar vein for six pages.

Because their sensibilities are so similar, it's no wonder that Dylan has been Johnson's major influence. Granted, one can detect a number of other significant influences on Johnson's poetry: the jazzy dictional and syntactical mannerisms of Berryman have clearly had an impact on Johnson, and at times the ragged but formal quality of his prosody, particularly in his many sonnets, seems indebted to poets of the Renaissance, particularly Shakespeare and Wyatt. But none of these figures has haunted Johnson's writing in the way that Dylan has. Johnson is perhaps the first significant American poet who has found in rock and roll music his major influence. Johnson's *The Incognito Lounge* has shown itself to be one of the best and most enduring volumes of the 1980s, and it has influenced dozens of figures who emerged in the later years of the decade, among them Barbara Anderson, William Olsen, Gillian Connoly, Lynda Hull, Richard Katrovas, and Donald Revell. These Johnsonite poets are thus in their own fashion strongly influenced by

Dylan, bastard grandchildren, analogous to the punk-era musicians who learned to sing like Dylan by imitating Lou Reed's own Dylan mimicry. Johnson has forthrightly expressed his indebtedness to Dylan on more than one occasion. When I lived in Provincetown, Massachusetts, in 1983, I remember frequently listening to the public-access radio station's weekly all–Bob Dylan show, hosted by fellow P-town resident Denis Johnson, who spun hard-to-find bootlegs and such rarities as Dylan's important mid-1960s single "Please Crawl Out Your Window." The show was clearly the work of an unapologetic fan. In a 1985 interview about his work, Johnson discusses Dylan in rhapsodic terms. He qualifies his remarks, but only to a small degree: "It may be that I'm just trying to be provocative when I say that he is the greatest poet to write English in our time, but I honestly feel that people have taken those poems into their hearts, and carried those poems into battle. They've died with those poems on their lips. What other poet of our generation can you say this about? He's the one."[11]

One of the most interesting ways in which Johnson has been affected by Dylan is in his prosody. The stridency of Dylan's early electric period, with its combination of 4/4 time and Gatling-gun ejaculation of couplets and near-couplets, seems poor ammunition for serious poetry, but Johnson in his 1985 interview states that in certain poems he is trying to ape these Dylanesque effects. And to some degree the effort works. Here are the ending stanzas of "Minutes":

Would you like
to dance? Then, here, dance with the terror

that now is forever,
my feet are stumps. The band is just
outbreaking now with one that goes
all the evidence / the naughty evidence / persuades
the lovers endearing by the ponds /

the truants growing older in the sleazy arcades /
there's no banishing / of anything
only con- / quering within /
make it enough / make it enough / or eat /
suffering without end.[12]

Johnson uses the italicized passage to give a kinetic immediacy to the sense of existential entrapment that had been explored earlier in the poem. The effect of alienation is created by several devices: Johnson asks that we take the ending lines as song lyrics, as a kind of macabre coda to the poem rather than as part of its text; he uses slashes to even more overtly emphasize the rhymes and internal rhymes, imbuing the poem with a shrill and staccato effect similar to lyrics in rap songs. Of course the origins of such effects are a generation or so older than rap. Readers of the ending of "Minutes" cannot help but be struck by the passage's resemblance to the famous barrage of couplets in Dylan's "Subterranean Homesick Blues" or to stanzas like these from another Dylan song from the mid-1960s, "It's Alright Ma, (I'm Only Bleeding)":

> You lose yourself, you reappear
> You suddenly find you got nothing to fear
> Alone you stand with nobody near
> When a trembling distant voice, unclear
> Startles your sleeping ears to hear
> That somebody thinks
> They really found you.
>
> A question in your nerves is lit
> Yet you know there is no answer fit to satisfy
> Insure you not to quit
> To keep it in your mind and not fergit
> That it is not he or she or them or it
> That you belong to.[13]

Both passages make fairly successful use of Skeltonics, a rhyme scheme generally derided by prosodists but made effective in Johnson's poem because of the dramatic context and in Dylan's song because of the singer's relentless and obsessive delivery.

But of course Dylan has influenced more than Johnson's technique. Dylan's best lyrics are pointedly surrealist, derived in part from his early-1960s reading of figures such as Lautréamont and Rimbaud, whom his friend Allen Ginsberg had urged upon him during the early years of their long-standing association. (Lautréamont's *Maldoror* and Rimbaud's *A Season in Hell* are the probable stylistic models of Dylan's 1971 prose work, *Tarantula.*) Dylan's most sustained surrealist lyrics, such as those in *Blonde on Blonde*'s "Visions of Johanna," are big, messy, panoramic catalogues, having nothing in common with the more domesticated varieties of surrealist imagery practiced in the sixties poetry of Deep Image writers such as Merwin and Bly. Dylan favors cinematic montages, a screen populated by a large cast of characters, some of whom are treated in detail, others of whom appear only as walk-ons. We have figures like the Rainman, the Queen of Spades, the malevolent family that dwells at Maggie's Farm, Nero's Neptune, and the Phantom of the Opera (dressed as a priest). These figures tend, furthermore, to be outcasts, drifters, and losers: there's the Wild West outlaw John Wesley Harding and the characters who provide the title for "Lilly, Rosemary and the Jack of Hearts." When such characters appear in a Dylan lyric, interspersed with clusters of surrealist image catalogues, the songs have a weird hallucinatory verve. Here are the second and fourth stanzas of "Visions of Johanna":

> In the empty lot where the ladies play blind man's bluff with the key chain
> And the all-night girls, they whisper of escapades out on the D Train
> We can hear the night watchman click his flashlight
> Ask himself if it's him or them that's really insane
> Louise, she's alright she's just near
> She's delicate and seems like the mirror
> But she just makes it all too concise and too clear
> That Johanna's not here
> The ghost of electricity howls in the bones of her face
> Where these visions of Johanna have now taken my place.
>
> . . . .
>
> Inside the Museum, Infinity goes up on trial
> Voices echo this is what salvation must be like after while
> But Mona Lisa must have had the highway blues you can
> tell by the way she smiles
> See the primitive wallflower freeze
> When the jelly-faced women all sneeze
> Hear the one with the mustache say, "Jeeze
> I can't find my knees"
> Oh, jewels and binoculars hang from the head of a mule
> But these visions of Johanna, they make it all seem so cruel.[14]

There's a similar surrealist streak in almost all of Johnson's work, and Johnson's particular brand of "complete disordering of the senses" owes more to Dylan than to predictable sources such as Neruda or Éluard. Like the Dylan of "Visions of Johanna," Johnson does not simply manipulate odd metaphors but finds in contemporary existence a horrific sort of alienation that can only be evoked through a reliance on the nomenclature of surrealism. And the settings for the poems of *The Incognito Lounge*—the bars, shopping center strips, and tacky apartment complexes of the Sunbelt—offer surrealism aplenty, Raymond Carver and Edward Hopper landscapes witnessed on hallucinogens. All the hallmarks of the surrealist method occur in the title poem, "The Incognito Lounge"—synesthesia ("She pours some boiled coffee / that tastes like noise"); odd juxtapositions and eccentric metaphors ("this bus . . . wafts / like a dirigible toward suburbia / over a continent of saloons / over a robot desert that now turns purple"); macabre humor ("I go everywhere with my eyes closed and two / eyeballs painted on my face. There is a woman / across the court with no face at all").[15] Yet this is not a dreamscape, but reality seen with an intensity that transforms it into nightmare. That Dylan is the tutelary spirit presiding over this aesthetic will come as no surprise to listeners familiar with Dylan albums such as *Highway 61 Revisited* and *Blonde on Blonde,* which contain lyrics manifesting exactly the same sorts of characteristics: synesthesia ("and he just smoked my eyelids / and punched my cigarette"); eccentric figurative language ("Ruthie says come see her / in her honky tonk lagoon / where I can watch her waltz for free / 'neath her Panamanian moon"); black humor ("Now the preacher looked so baffled / when I asked him why he dressed / with twenty pounds of headlights / stapled to his chest").[16] These lines, drawn from *Blonde on Blonde*'s "Stuck Inside of Mobile With the Memphis Blues Again," all work to characterize a speaker who suffers from the same sort of existential crisis related by the narrator of "The Incognito Lounge." And in neither the poem nor the song do we encounter endings which resolve the speaker's plight. Johnson's speaker, describing a purgatorially long bus ride in the poem's final section, watches a Dylanesque scene of a "pair of uniformed boyscouts / depantsing a little girl," before ending the poem with a description of a baby in a seat beside him reaching out its hand to grab a flying bee. Seeing this scene of small but memorable suffering "marries" the speaker to a "deep comprehension and terror."[17] Similarly, the narrator of "Stuck Inside of Mobile With the Memphis Blues Again" ends his song by plaintively repeating, once again, the conundrum of the song's title. It's also worth noting that Johnson's surrealism is indebted to Dylan in its tic of endowing characters with oddball monikers: *The Incognito Lounge* is peopled by, among others, "Our Lady of Wet Glass-Ring on the Album Cover," "The Lady in the Moon," and "Mr. Young-and-Lovely Negro Busdriver."

Given the intensity of Johnson's admiration for Dylan, it comes as no surprise that he also shares several of Dylan's shortcomings. Both Dylan and Johnson have on numerous occasions sought to present lengthy narratives, yet both are much more successful working within lyric and impressionistic forms. Although many of Dylan's earliest, folk-based songs, such as "The Lonesome Death of Hattie Carroll," are compressed and compelling combinations of story and agitprop, most of his later attempts at storytelling songs are uneven, if not outright embarrassing: one thinks of his preposterous hymn to racketeer Joey Gallo or the ghastly David-Lynch-Meets-Marshall-Dillon Old West mannerisms of "Lilly, Rosemary and the Jack of

Hearts." Johnson is successful at long sequences of interrelated lyrics such as "The Incognito Lounge," but his efforts at sustaining lengthy narratives or monologues are for the most part failures. "The Confession of St. Jim-Ralph, Our Patron Saint of Falling Short Who Became a Prayer," a monologue spoken by a half-crazed eccentric who seems to be both an ex–rock star and an ex–cult leader, is Johnson's longest, most Dylanesque, and least convincing effort. Both figures have a similar difficulty writing convincingly about women. Dylan's women are invariably either madonnas ("Sara," "Wedding Song," "Sad-Eyed Lady of the Lowlands") or, when Dylan has been jilted, whores fit only to be subjects for Dylan's famous skill with invective ("Positively Fourth Street," "Like a Rolling Stone," "Absolutely Sweet Marie"). Johnson has a similar tendency to either idealize ("For Jane," "Surreptitious Kissing," "Proposal") or damn ("Vespers," "All Night Diners," "Talking Richard Clay Wilson Blues") the women in his poems. Finally, both artists exhibit a kind of all-or-nothing romantic extremism (the essence of much good poetry and most good rock and roll) that is majestic in fairly small doses but that can also grow strained and repetitive and cause both figures to lapse into self-parody. Hence, Dylan's uneven work of the past decade, and Johnson's probably mistaken notion that he is now a novelist: since his impressive first novel, *Angels* (1983), Johnson's subsequent works of fiction have been progressively less effective, and his fiction for the most part attempts to recycle notions more convincingly explored in his poetry, a genre which, unfortunately, he now seems to have abandoned.

Johnson's debt to Dylan is perhaps an unusual case, for the gulf between rock and poetry remains a fairly large one. One can't imagine that John Hollander will ever become a diehard fan of The Replacements, any more than Snoop Doggy Dog will base a rap on Elizabeth Bishop's "One Art." James Brown, an artist every bit the equal of the admirable Stanley Kunitz, is unlikely to replace Kunitz as poet laureate. But in an ideal world all these scenarios would be possible. Still, the gulf between rock and poetry is shrinking in some small but significant ways. The laureateship will probably elude James Brown, but thirty years from now—who knows?—it may end up in the hands of an octogenarian from Minnesota named Zimmerman.

(1991)

13.

Large Air: A (Millennial) Notebook

First Century: Romanticism

> *Speculations, whether sad or lively, have a large air about them, they are a convenient way of being helpful or impressive. But we have no right to entertain them. We have refused to be hampered by the past, so we must not profit by the future.*
>
> —*E. M. Forster*

Let's assume that poetry survives. First, of course, it changes. Perhaps it withers; perhaps it is forgotten completely through neglect. (After all, who requires the consolation and challenges of poetry during an era in which the exchange of information—something very different from consolation—has become the sole coin of the realm?) It will likely be buried by some catastrophe or set of catastrophes, though of what sort we cannot know. But it will likely be resurrected as well, like the Gilgamesh tablets pulled crumbling from the Tigris Delta, the scrolls of Nag Hammadi in their frail jars, the longest extant fragment of Archilochos found scribbled on a mummy's shroud. Where the rain of ash fell smoldering down, the excavators make out the library walls. And this one, grinning, holds up his find:

W llace St vens

OPUS POSTHUM S

POEMS PLAYS PROSE

New Ed ion Revi ed En ged Corrected

On it a face: a portly man with neckwear.

Second Century: Local Oracles

> *As we may expect, many local oracles took on a new lease of life in the Hellenic period: Branchidae, Claros, Didymos, Corope in Thessaly, Argos, Emphyre (site of the ominously named "Oracle of the Dead"). In an uncertain world, where men were increasingly loathe to take responsibility for their own decisions and indeed often felt themselves mere puppets, jerked from point to point by the requirements of a fate inscrutable as it was inflexible, divine oracular fiat was one way of having the future mapped out on the individual's behalf. What is fixed by fate could, given especial skills and insights, be predicted. It might not be what one wanted to hear; but forewarned was at least forearmed.*
>
> *—Peter Green*

Hopping on the millennialist bandwagon, *Green Mountains Review* wants to know where poetry will go in the next decade, the next century, the next thousand years. I would like to know, too. But I can scarcely make an educated guess on this subject, let alone indulge in prophecy of the sort that *GMR* seems to want. But poets always at one time or another are tempted to don the prophet's mantle. Prophets, like poets and good car salesmen, are cagey. You must be sincere and convincing, but you can't promise too much, even while appearing to believe mightily in your product. A rational, logical, and well-reasoned approach simply will not do in prophecy, any more than it generally will in poetry.

———

Third Century: Available Selves (1)

> *Poetic knowledge is intuitive (irrevocably personal) knowledge of the origin of the self. Being knowledge, it is non-identical with that origin, but rather, it is a keeping of the self by bespeaking origin. As incarnation and history are stays against apocalypse. The life of the poem is assurance against the end of the world, the opening out of all the secrets.*
>
> *—Allen Grossman*

D: So the world is ending again, and the selves who write the poems are ending too. Is that it?

W: That's the gist of it, yes.

D: Are we of two minds about believing this?

W: Yes, we're of two minds about believing this.

D: But don't you think that people are showing themselves to need poetry more and more? Just about every college, community college, and high school now offers poetry writing courses. And people are writing about subjects that a lot of them couldn't talk about in other ways. Since the advent of the Confessional poets people can write about a whole range of experience that wasn't allowed any literary privilege before: difficult family histories, depression, sexual abuse, bad marriages, addictions—you name it. Isn't it good that we can address these things in poems?

W: Maybe. But don't you think it causes the function of poetry to devolve into something merely therapeutic?

D: But therapy can help people.

W: So can Prozac, Rolfing, and Sufi dancing. Someone else's clumsy self-reckonings aren't necessarily going to be interesting to me. Therapy can help people; poetry can help people. But that doesn't mean that poetry and therapy are one and the same. American poetry is in danger of forgetting this.

D: What do you propose to solve this dilemma?

W: I think we need to write more poems.

Fourth Century: Reading

The book is always recognition of the book.
—Edmund Jabes

We will read in different ways. I can see it already in my students, schooled as their synapses are to the kinetic pulse of video games and the slithering jump cuts of MTV. Narrative, image, music, meter: they all mean something subtly or completely different to generations *Y* and *Z*, and even the associative cascade of surrealism, futurism, and expressionism—methods bred in part because of the influence of the movies—seems preposterously slow to them. We all remember what Walter Benjamin said: "Human sense perception changes with humanity's mode of existence." The painstaking engineering of a Homeric simile or a metaphysical conceit: it is possible that such modes, unfolding with an almost glacial slowness in comparison to the blinding speed of a leitmotif flickering by in a skillfully done TV commercial, may become manners of thought we will not even be able to comprehend without extensive training. Benjamin's Marxism allowed him a certain degree of cultural utopianism: "The history of every art form shows critical epochs in which a certain art form aspires to effects which could be fully obtained only with a changed technical standard, that is to say, a new art form." What I sometimes want to know, however—as someone who writes sonnets and who can't help scanning even the prose poems I read—is what will happen to the old forms.

Fifth Century: Audience (1)

What we have now, as often as not, is a kind of vaudeville.
—Donald Justice, on poetry readings

One of the occupational hazards of being labeled a poet: someone's always asking you what you think of poetry slams, as if this particular blip on the radar screen were the most exciting thing to come about in American poetry since the publication of *Leaves of Grass.* Well, if Whitman claimed that great poetry deserves great audiences, then the pointlessness of poetry slams should be obvious; at slams poems devolve into attempts to pander to an audience of beer- and latte-guzzling rubes in black berets out for a good time—which is fine, but such transactions have little to do with poetry. I doubt if poetry slams will bring about more readers or writers of serious verse, though some slam poets—as performers—will go on to have serious careers. (This is assuming, of course, that slams don't immediately go the way of the hula hoop.) And here's another problem: slams can at least be entertaining, whereas the solemnity of readings sponsored by English departments and writing programs tends to make them about as pleasant as a root-canal session. There are lots of gifted poets who are crushing bores on the podium. (Ashbery on an off night can seem narcoleptic.) And some of the more charismatic readers—Sharon Olds, Carolyn Forché—are figures of questionable poetic abilities. Still, readings have changed the landscape of contemporary poetry: people often discover poetry by attending readings and only thereafter get interested in reading it on the printed page. Some of my graduate students recently lobbied my colleagues and me for classes in oral interpretation, with the notion that some skill upon the vaudeville stage of public readings is an essential aspect of today's poetic career (such as it is).

Sixth Century: Audience (2)

Every man likes the smell of his own farts.
—Icelandic proverb

Readers of poetry today are invariably also writers of it themselves, which is why contemporary poets are seen by many as a club of narcissists (were narcissists *capable* of forming a club). They are seen as a small group of writers who read only themselves, plus some wanna-bes who *aspire* to be writers who read only themselves. They are seen less as a cult than as something akin to baseball card collectors, trekkies, and dirt-bike enthusiasts, eccentrics and hobbyists who have evolved a support system of fanzines, conventions, and sites on the worldwide web, less a community of selves than a gathering of clones. From this outsider's perspective, there is no diversity among poets, who have nothing of interest to say to anyone who dwells outside their tribe, a tribe whose dialect seems all but impossible for outsiders to understand. Visitors to the poets' village come rarely, and do so only to meet their distribution requirements. They can communicate only via the very inadequate phrasebooks supplied by W. W. Norton, Houghton Mifflin, and the University of California Press. *Speken ze Wasteland? Parle vo Red Wheelbarrow?* Or (worse yet) *Habla usted Morrow Anthology of Younger American Poets?*

Seventh Century: Marginalization (1)

But a self-critical poetry, minus the
short-circuiting rhetoric of vatic privilege, might

dissolve the antinomies of marginality that
broke Jack Spicer into uneven lines.
—Bob Perelman

Bob Perelman is one clever guy.
And since marginalization is his subject

he casts his essay in couplets,
each line precisely six words long

so the reader's conscious of margins.
Get it? One of those Derridean

puns the Language writers go on
and on with. Muddled and smug,

brilliant in places but asinine elsewhere,
he is, as I say, one

clever guy. Don't be afraid of
theory, he insists. Study it some

and you too can write smug
gnomic tomes and polemics. And I

admit such writing seems at least
as interesting as the standard-issue-

free-verse-magazine-poem-where-the-
speaker-has-some-little-epiphany-about-

(a) his/her past; (b) his/her present, triggered by
some bland incident in domestic life

"where the meaning of life becomes,"
as Perelman puts it, "visible after

20 or 30 lines." But wait
a minute. Haven't I worked hard

for twenty-some years to make
the self who writes my poems

write them well? The self who
writes my poems may not be

all that clever a guy, but he,
I fear, is all I have,

and I believe this self exists
not as some construct or gesture

determined by cultural force but as
something authentic. (That word authentic—what

do you mean by that? Don't know.)
Do I need to know to know

I need it? I need it.

Eighth Century: Audience (3)

But through all his distress, all the turmoil,
the poetic idea comes and goes insistently;
arrogance and intoxication—that's most likely of course:
arrogance and intoxication are what Dareios must have felt.
—Cavafy

But of course poets hardly consider *themselves* clones of one another, although I suspect that in the deepest recesses of their beings they understand this to be the case, and they combat this knowledge by competitiveness and by absurdly dividing the tiny hamlet that is poetry into even smaller divisions called schools and movements—genteel-sounding equivalents to the Bloods, the Crips, the Gangster Disciples, and the Latin Kings. A puzzling balkanization of American poetry took place in the 1980s, and its consequence is that the new "movements" differ significantly from the various schools of the Modernists, or even from the groups which emerged before the 1960s in the form of Deep Imagism, Confessional poetry, Black Mountain, and the New York School. The earlier movements were based on some particular and thoroughgoingly argued aesthetic positions. But the new schools differ from one another only on some rather petty and trivial points. Strip the Language writers of their theoretical trappings, and they sound like New Formalists. Dialogue between the schools has been replaced by turf wars. We don't read the work of other poets as much as we identify their colors and react according to our training.

Ninth Century: Available Selves (2)

> *To Our Readers:*
>
> *We regret the publication of "Doubled Flowering: From the Notebooks of Araki Yasusada" in our July/August issue. Neither Araki Yasusada nor the three names identified as translators, "Toso Motokiyu," "Okura Kyojin," and "Ojiu Norinaya" are actual persons. The facts in the note "Introducing Araki Yasusada" as well as the "Portrait of Yasusada" are a hoax. . . . Kent Johnson has admitted the above ruse, and has claimed the materials were written by an unnamed American poet whose name he refuses to reveal.*
>
> —*American Poetry Review*

Dear Mr. Yasusada,

I am sorry to hear that you do not exist, for the poems of yours which appeared in *APR* were admired by me, as well as by several of my friends, although I remember asking myself after I read them whether I was moved by them because they were the work of a compelling writer or because they were the work of a Hiroshima survivor. Like many American poets, I sometimes suffer from the notion—at least as old as the Romantics—that authenticity in poetry derives from autobiography rather than from some complicated interaction among self, language, culture, and poetic craft. The fact that you are "merely" literary troubles me, but not because I can't appreciate a well-executed hoax (though you're not as good a hoax as Chatterton's Rowley, Macpherson's Osian, or even W. D. Snodgrass's S. S. Gardons). Although we should know better, readers and writers of poetry tend to see the self which writes a lyric as either someone identical to the writer him/herself or as the speaker of a dramatic monologue, someone playing a role. Stances which question the rigidity of this polarity tend to unsettle us, bizarre as that might seem. Alter egos, personas, the heteroynms of Pessoa: these are the shadowlands of self we'd rather leave unexplored—though a good many theorists have ventured there. I'm reminded of something the expatriate American poet Gustaf Sobin said: "There's no *room* in my poetry for myself."

Yours sincerely,

Michael Weldon

Tenth Century: Marginalization (2)

> *I croon my tears at fifty cents per line.*
>
> —*James Wright*

At a bar with Dean and Michael Weldon to celebrate—the annual royalty check for one of Michael's books arrived this morning: eight dollars and sixty-five cents. It's enough for two pitchers of beer, and we're nearing the bottom of the second. Michael tells us his story about applying for a driver's license—this was in Arizona twenty years ago. In those days, a license had to list its owner's occupation. Feeling particularly aesthetical, Michael wrote LYRIC POET on the application form and sat down to wait for his photo to be developed and his newly laminated license to be placed in his hand. A pair of burly women in buns preparing the licenses peered from their stations, one of them pointing at him and whispering to the other. When the license came, the first thing he noticed was how bad his photo was: eyes closed, he looked like one of those dead CIA agents made up to look animate so that the terrorists can keep the ransom negotiations going. And then on the bottom of the license he read, OCCUPATION: NONE.

Eleventh Century: Silver Ages

> *Time and time again, men have chickened out in the fear of what that hawk, the genius of Poetry, threatens, and surrendered their imaginations to the proprieties and rationalizations of new schools of criticism, grammarians, commonsense philosophers, and arbiters of educated best taste.*
>
> —*Robert Duncan*

They will tell you what poetry is; they will tell you what it should be, declare it dead, and then subject its corpse to their ghoulish necromancies. After all, don't critics and theorists see themselves as the priestly class? And this sanctimoniousness is the same whether the Anointed One is casting down yarrow sticks in Han China or gobbling a still-pumping human heart from an altar on an Olmec pyramid or furiously scribbling notes about a Madonna video in the name of the Most Holy Storm God of Culture Studies.

Of course, the poets whose deaths the critics proclaim (and analyze) are just as sanctimonious about their own practice. Yet a fundamental difference remains: the poets scarcely ever profess to know what a poem is, and thus are subject to a sense of wonder and a kind of weary humility as they sit alone in a room with the English language, waiting for the poems to unscroll. And only at the moment of the poem's emergence do they understand what a poem may be, although this definition is immediately lost to them. They know what a poem is only during the act of writing, like the subject of Luria's *The Man with the Shattered World,* whose head wound deprived him of short-term memory: he could only understand the written word during the act of writing it. The way to define a poem, for a poet, is to write another poem.

Twelfth Century: Writing (Creative) (1)

> *The debate has been carried on with such partisan indignation that different people seem to be talking about radically different things when they talk about creative writing.*
>
> —*D. G. Myers*

The four ages of poetry.

So we will all write the same bad poem for a time; followed by a time in which we all write the same competent but finally mediocre poem; followed by a time in which one or two of us writes a different sort of poem, something astonishing and original, although no one recognizes it at the time and all the attention goes to the more dogged mediocrities, who go on to publish and teach in writing programs; followed by a final stage, in which a few of us will finish with the bad poems, the merely competent poems, the teaching and careerism, and start writing good poems. Does the existence of so many creative writing programs even *affect* this process, which has existed at least since the late Roman Republic? No, save that more people will be trained to write competently if not exactly well. This doesn't seem to do anyone any harm nor, finally, to do any damage to literature.

Thirteenth Century: Academic Discourse (1)

That's like hypnotizing chickens.

—*Iggy Pop*

My friend J. could never understand why he'd gotten the teaching job all those years ago. He'd heard about the other candidates who'd come to campus for the interview, and one was a poet whose work he'd long admired, one of the first poets he'd read when he first became interested in poetry in the 1970s. How could a hiring committee pick J. over the other poet, who by all accounts was as gifted a teacher as he was a writer? Years later, at a party, a slightly pickled colleague finally told him what had happened. The other poet had performed brilliantly during the on-campus interview and at the end of his visit gave a reading, attended mostly by graduate students and—more importantly—by the hiring committee, which in this department was composed mostly of the Suits, the Full Professor types who'd been around since the Pleistocene. The reading was spellbinding, especially a long brooding surrealist elegy. The poet had killed his brother many years before, during a farm accident. The poet was wearing a sport coat, and beneath it a cashmere turtleneck. No podium, he was standing before the Suits and students with only a copy of one of his books in hand. And as he reached the most heartfelt passage of the poem his turtleneck started hiking up above his waist, until the poet's navel and a patch of hair-encrusted middle-aged belly peeked out. The Suits, of course, were aghast, exchanging surreptitious glances. That settled it. The job would go to J., who owes his career to another poet's navel.

Fourteenth Century: Marginalization (3)

Lives, however minor, keep their primitive appeal.
—Randall Jarrell

And yet, what could possibly be *wrong* with the attempt to make the meaning of life "become visible after 20 or 30 lines"? Buson believed he could arrive at this goal in *three lines*—and even in translation we understand that sometimes he attained it.

Fifteenth Century: Writing (Creative) (2)

Once more you will be outraged by my iambs,
which don't deserve it, O my peerless leader.
—Catullus

He fancied himself a kind of bard of the desert, Orpheus crooning along with his lute to the saguaros, his toga picked up at Acme Western Wear. Some of his poems were good in a vaguely Merwinesque way, lots of stones and silence, all shorn of punctuation. He'd read the surrealists, and read them and read them. I was glad he let me study with him, and the routine we'd set up was casual—every other Wednesday I'd drive to his house in the foothills and we'd talk about the poems I'd given him. On my first visit I was met at the door by his wife—"You can find B. out back." He was lugging several breadloaf-sized stones from one end of the yard to the other. "Help me for a minute, will you? I'm building a wall." Three hours later I was still helping him, and after we'd finally called it quits I waited for him in his study while he showered. We discussed my poems for about ten minutes. "I don't see how you ever got into graduate school," he told me. "Your poems are sophomoric, banal, insipid." My only hope, I was told, was to set my alarm clock to go off every two hours during the night and after each ringing spend fifteen minutes doing automatic writing. Then later I was to set the automatic writing into anapestic trimeter. (For some reason, my dreamlife and trisyllabic feet were seen as my only hopes for redemption.) Two weeks of this left me woozy from lack of sleep and with several pages of vaguely metrical gibberish. On my next visit B. was again out in back when I arrived, and again I gamely helped him work on the wall for several hours before our conference began and my utter absence of promise was again remarked upon. Prescription: two hours of automatic writing every day, in a darkened room so I couldn't see the page I was working on. I was then to cast my writing into dactylic tetrameter. Trying to transfer my scribbled-in-the-dark profundities from almost-indecipherable notebook entries to the typewriter was bad enough, but casting them into dactyls proved even more of a challenge. But eventually they were ready, and armed with several pages of them I knocked on B's door. He was out back, beside a still very large pile of stones. He motioned for me to approach. . . .

In B.'s mind I probably proved to him I didn't have what it takes, although I lasted through a couple more sessions of this, finally throwing in the towel after being assigned one half hour of automatic writing while a heavy stone was placed on my chest. It wasn't the stone part that spooked me, as much as my difficulties understanding quantitative meter.

———

Sixteenth Century: Academic Discourse (2)

That all his will, brains and imagination
Are concentrated on a higher station.
He wants to be in the administration.
—*Donald Hall*

Z. in my office after the committee meeting. Z. is a hothead with paranoiac tendencies, and in the meeting he'd had a particularly heated argument with a colleague I very much respect. He's still fuming. I'm trying to calm him down, but nothing seems to work, and finally I come to realize that Z's rage has nothing to do with his disagreement with my colleague. Z. is instead out to get revenge for a perceived slight, for an insult which my colleague dished out to him several years ago and which of course only Z. remembers. We are two tenured adults, the authors of "sensitively rendered" poetry and fiction, yet Z. is starting to sound like a speech in a Cagney movie. "It's about RESPECT! Don't you see?" And now he's enthusiastically quoting some NFL lineman he's heard on the radio. "You can't let 'em screw with you. You've got to spit in their faces. Just spit in their faces!" He repeats this several times. It occurs to me that Z. may be seriously, clinically, insane. What next? Will he start to teach his workshops with an AK-47 at his side, bandoleer stuffed with ammo and grenades? Or will an aneurysm get him first? Neither proves to be the case. Instead, he's kicked upstairs and is now Associate Dean of Something Meaningful Sounding. I'm told he's happy about his new job; it gives him more time to write.

Seventeenth Century: Sincerity (1)

> *In sincerity, writing occurs which is the detail of seeing, of thinking with things as they exist.*
>
> —*Louis Zukofsky*

We tend, in our irony-addled era, to think of sincerity as a mere stance—and as a rather muddled and dubious one at that. But Zukofksy implies that it's something different, a quality of total attentiveness to some aspect of experience or the material world. And I think this state of attentiveness is what best characterizes a successful lyric, in which the tools of language work to halt the progress of time and to blur the differences between the realm of empirical sense and an unseen realm of transcendent possibility. Certain of Rilke's *New Poems* are among the most significant examples of this, a gnostic effort to look so closely at an object or an event that you see through the surfaces to a thing-borne/born *core* which is and isn't corporeal. "Torso of an Archaic Apollo" charts this process, as does "Cadet Portrait of My Father." "The Panther" is about the terror and tragedy of that process being forbidden, hindered.

Eighteenth Century: Sincerity (2)

> *The rhythm—the way sounds move, combine, separate, recombine—is the vehicle for the feeling. . . . And without that inner movement or disturbance, the words, no matter how fetching, remain inert. In this way at least, the dynamics of poetry—and probably of all the arts—are the same as the dynamics of dreaming.*
>
> —*A. Alvarez*

"The eddying of the living soul." That such a state of attentiveness can halt for an instant this eddying: this is not a dewy-eyed mysticism as much as a faith in poetic technique to achieve this end. Tony the other day was discussing the Buddhist concept of *mah*—"the ability to expand or contract time." The emphasis is on *ability*, as if time travel were something that could be achieved through prosodic skill. And it is a skill laden with complexity and ambivalence. Here is Harold Bloom: "Henry Corbain, the great scholar of Iranian Islam, particularly of the Sh'ite Sufis, deplored the gap between sense perception, with its empirical data, and the revolutions or categories of the intellect. From Corbain's point of view, *literal or empirical* sense itself is a metaphor for lack of vision, which seems to me pragmatically true enough. . . ."

Nineteenth Century: Audience (4)

> *[T]he chosen one, the one who is hailed by name.*
>
> —*Osip Mandelstam*

For fifteen years my friend Dave has often been the first person to read my poems. He has probably read and commented upon everything any good that I have written—and how I must have tried his patience over the years! A handful of other friends has played this role as well. "Who is the audience for your poems?" the BBC interviewer asked Berryman. "Five people—well, ten if you count their wives." Leaving the sexism of this remark aside, Berryman is reminding us that the poet's ideal audience is one of trusted intimates, whether real ones or imagined ones, who grow toward intimacy with the writers as they read a poem—a dynamic that Mandelstam's "To the Addressee" likens to finding a message in a bottle. I try to operate according to this principle in part because it permits me to disclose unguardedly my innermost thoughts and feelings, for I can trust my closest friends to accept them. Yet it is a principle, on the other hand, which mandates a certain discretion: enduring friendships don't usually permit excessive self-indulgence. Tact is required, although I suspect that what functions as tact in a good poem has more to do with prosodic issues than with mannerliness of a behavioral sort. This is, I hope, a pretty straightforward premise. It is not a theory (although Bakhtin's notion of the dialogic imagination perhaps resembles it). And it is not a premise which pays much attention to the tactical and strategic elements of poetic discourse that poets of a Marxist bent, such as Thomas McGrath, purport to be guided by. But I stake my continued existence as a poet on a flow of envelopes bulging with poems which get sent off to Dave in Little Rock and to that handful of other friends who are also willing to indulge me and who respond to my poems (as I do to their own) with attentiveness and blue-pencilings. Message in a bottle (SASE enclosed).

Twentieth Century: Mourning

> *I've been telling myself your story for months*
> *and it spreads in the dusk, hushing the streets, and there*
> *you are in the curve of a girl's hand as she lights*
> *her cigarette sheltered beneath the doorway's plaster*
> *cornucopia. . . .*
>
> —*Lynda Hull*

Writing to a friend to thank him for a gift, and I'm reminded of Rilke's essay on dolls: taking the book from the shelf, I find that the doll essay is brimming with Lynda's marginal notes and underlinings. It's over two years since her death, and I make such discoveries all the time; it's like farmers in Flanders and the Somme finding still-live ammunition as they plow their fields, a discovery at once astonishing and dangerous. Amazement and sorrow commingling—it's the feeling you have when meeting dead loved ones in a dream. Even in the dream you're aware that they're gone, but you want the instant of this meeting to continue as long as it can.

My encounter with Lynda through "Reflections on Dolls" is different from all of the others, however, for as I read the essay and Lynda's notes and underlinings, I see the beginnings of one of her last poems, "Street of Crocodiles." Suddenly I recognize passages she's adapted or even taken outright for her poem—"a world in which Destiny and even God Himself have become famous above all because they answer us in silence." And here's the end of the poem,

Maybe I'll call this doll Clio after
the cruelest Muse, blank History, her pages
waiting to fill. Her mouth's perfect bow
parts—as if to cry out, as if surprised, aggrieved

at this world, where Destiny, where God
has grown famous because they answer us with silence.
Her silence swarms packed as the dustmotes
in Poland, how we walked among whispers shriven

from air, lingering remnants, the unbodied shards:
a river tossed by whitecaps before the freshening
spring. A sky foaming jade, cobalt. Yellow fabric
of a dress run through the hands, the full sweet taste

of cream. Pages waiting for their ink, for
everything damned, for everything human & lovely.

As I read the passage in the essay, something like a vision of Lynda arrives—a split second in which I seem to be looking over her shoulder while she sprawls on the old chaise lounge in her study (her "fainting couch," she called it) furiously underlining the Rilke, notebook open beside her. It is a vision in the truest sense, for it seems intensely real—and in an instant is gone. For this second or two, though, I feel *inside* her writing process, yet this sense of intimacy is replaced immediately by a sort of dread, an awareness of erasure and dissembling, for I'm trying to reckon all the other sources of "Street of Crocodiles," and with each thing added to the list my sense of union with Lynda slips farther away: the doll from turn-of-the-century Poland she kept on her desk, its cracked celluloid forehead and, where the hair had fallen away, "a Star of David [that] spikes between the doll's initials"; her visit to Poland with her mother, and her meeting with relatives long thought dead; the visit to Auschwitz. And all of the poem's other sources: the nightmare animations of the Brothers Quay, Mengele's experiments with the Auschwitz twins, "the steam hammering pipes" in our apartment. Everything is ruins—each piece intensely called up in my mind but none joined together except as relentlessly haunting fragments of a single loss. And it takes the better part of a day for me to come back to myself. And I come back in a way that should be of no surprise. I read aloud "Street of Crocodiles." And then I read it again.

———

Twenty-First Century: Small Engine, Large Air

To give a single new word, never before spoken and impossible to enunciate.

—Hart Crane

Memory of the first place I lived during college. With a dozen or so of my friends I'd rented a large old house in St. Paul, and though it's twenty-five years ago I still remember the address—25 South Fairview, now the parking lot of a bank. We'd rented the place from a lawyer, who promptly sold the property to the auto repair shop next door, whose owners allowed us to stay on, provided they could use the basement to repair small engines. Equipment was moved in, the basement door padlocked, and each morning we'd wake to the grate and screech of the "small engines" being fixed. Then, shortly before the first snowfall, we woke to find someone pulling down the hedge that circled the yard. The repair shop would henceforth be using the yard for parking cars, the ones awaiting repair and the larger number of junkers being stored for their parts. They packed them in like sardines, in strict rows, until there might have been two hundred of them lodged bumper to bumper to bumper in the yard, or what was left of the yard. A January night, blindingly cold in the way that only Minnesota winters can be—maybe thirty below—and several of us have been up late smoking pot, and my friend Mark suggests we read aloud from a translation of the *Centuries* of Nostradamus. "He predicted everything," Mark was saying. "The French Revolution, both world wars, Hiroshima, space travel, the next thousand years." And so for an hour or two we take turns reading the strange, cryptic, apocalyptic gibberish of Nostradamus, a Sun Ra album playing in the background. And then the sound begins, an incessant high-pitched wail. At first we think it's coming from Sun Ra, but it lasts long after the album finishes. We walk out to the porch to investigate and come to realize that the cold has set one of the parking-lot car horns off. Three of us bundle into parkas and begin to wander the lot, hoping to find the right car and shut it up. They're packed so tightly that we can't move between them, but instead scurry over the snow-covered hoods and trunks. A single new word, impossible to enunciate, and it keeps repeating its one-note wail, the decapitated head of Orpheus, still wailing, still shrieking, and no one able to shut it off. Back and forth along the hoods we trudge, trying to find the source. For years I wanted to put this in a poem, but I could never find the context.

(1996)

14.

Mercantile Eyes: Travel Poems and Tourist Poems

Let me offer a few snapshots from my travels that comment metaphorically on my subject, the situation that confronts the American poet when he or she voyages into foreign cultures. First, let me show you the Gran Via in Madrid, stretching graciously from a fountain showing Neptune rising triumphant in his carriage from the sea, meant to commemorate Spain's mastery over the sea routes, toward the imperial complex; it's a royal parade route in a city built as a capital for the Castilian kings. Today its swarming Baroque buildings are blackened from Madrid's endless clamor of traffic, and soot-faced cherubim frolic over tacky flamenco palaces and restaurants posting *menus turisticas.* Palazzos transformed into movie palaces trumpet the latest Hollywood schmaltz—*Police Academy 3, A Nightmare on Elm Street, Troop Beverly Hills.* Gran Via is also graced by the world's most elegant McDonald's, a building that once housed one of the nation's largest banks. A marble and brass interior swooping with balconies houses the familiar counter and a menu board offering Big Mac and McPollo sandwiches. These are not a conqueror's grand monuments, but they vividly and uncomfortably illustrate the Americanization that's occurred in Spain at an accelerated rate since Franco's death.

Another scene: Plock, a small city northwest of Warsaw where, last fall, my mother was reunited with the remnants of her family. We are sitting in a small, sparsely furnished room overflowing with people weeping and embracing, and through the lavish shush and murmur of Polish I hear a familiar theme song. On a small black and white a waterfall flickers and opening credits roll. It's *Twin Peaks,* David Lynch's violent and surreally American foray into TV drama. The episode is badly dubbed, so that the English is still audible a second before the Polish—more like one of those U.N. simultaneous translations. Amidst bitter talk of the Soviet regime, we learn that one of my cousins has just been hired on at the new Levi Strauss plant in town. The Poles are very ambivalent about the inroads these American imports are already making in their country, and so am I, the American traveler nibbling at the hand-picked mushrooms placed before us, sipping the home-pressed cherry juice. Earlier that day we'd eaten a restaurant meal that would cost the average Pole a month's wages.

Once again, I found myself reminded that this is the American century, as the nineteenth century was the British. Beginning in the late 1700s, the concept of the grand tour was initiated. With British power in the ascendency, flocks of tourists crossed the Channel to travel the Continent and go beyond to even more exotic places. Think of those crass or hapless or moonstruck Victorians (familiar from Merchant-Ivory films), laden with trunks, guidebooks, and a parcel of misapprehensions, all of it seasoned with a dose of xenophobia. The aim of these tourists, even those traveling under the aegis of "science," was essentially encyclopedic—the accumulation of souvenirs, charming experiences, sketches, plunder, knowledge, cultural artifacts. (One only has to visit the Victoria and Albert or the British Museum to get the point.) I'm talking about a form of colonialism, or exploitation. Among the tourist flocks we also see literary voyagers—the likes of Shelley, Byron, Coleridge, and the young Wordsworth, for whom travel mapped an inner journey as well as a passionate engagement with foreign landscapes. In a broad sense, then, one might draw a distinction, as Bowles does in *The Sheltering Sky,* between the *tourist,* whose impulse is largely acquisitive, that of a consumer and bystander, and the *traveler,* whose impulse is to witness, a standpoint perhaps more receptive, more self-questioning, more ambivalent and ironic. A traveler's viewpoint, then, might be called more poetic in the sense that it is about the process of discovery and is transformative. Travel can give us back to ourselves different, changed in the way that the speaker of Rilke's "Archaic Torso of Apollo" so urgently admonishes.

I don't mean to be crudely reductive or to establish easy dichotomies. All of us have been tourists and travelers by turns. Shelley himself, the anarchistic anti-imperialist, could whine and behave with imperious patronization toward the Italians among whom he had exiled himself. Nor do I mean to be simplistic about the act of traveling, which is a complex and laden experience. The root of travel, as William Matthews reminds us, is *travail,* work.[1] Complex motives set us voyaging: curiosity, the need for change, escapism, the impulse to self-exile, the urge to find new perspectives, or a longing that is almost erotic—the desire for the experience of otherness. We are seeking here, though, to examine not behavior but vision realized through writing and to look at the pitfalls and risks attendant in writing about foreign places and people, to isolate strategies that seem useful in writing the successful poem of travel.

In this century we have become the heirs of the tradition of the writerly grand tour. Particularly since World War II, American artists have swarmed abroad in unprecedented numbers, and their "thematic colonization" of the rest of the world has been abundantly evident. Part of this results from an increase in grant and fellowship money, a benefit of postwar affluence. Guggenheim fellowships have been available since the 1920s, but beginning in the 1950s awards such as the Prix de Rome, the Amy Lowell Fellowship (which stipulates the recipient engage in foreign travel), and Fulbright and NEA fellowships have afforded writers the chance to "widen their horizons."

Elizabeth Bishop, Robert Lowell, James Wright, Richard Howard, Anthony Hecht, Adrienne Rich, W. S. Merwin, Richard Wilbur, and John Ashbery, among lesser lights, all spent time abroad in the fifties, and naturally the poems spun out, some distinguished, many more not. The era heralded a plethora of bad, merely shallow "Roman fountain" poems. Here's Henry James commenting on the seduction of the flimsily rendered exotic: "Our observation of any foreign land is extremely superficial." Auden, writing on the difficulty of travel as a subject, notes the manner in which it "restricts freedom of invention while [offering] the lure of journalism, of superficial typewriter-thumping." Many of these poems were written, as Robert Von Hallberg notes in *American Poetry and Culture,* by writers "simply glad for the chance to write descriptive poetry," as were poems impelled by a vague social impulse, hence a number of character sketches, typically focusing on stereotypical European "virtues."[2]

Unconsciously or not, Americans were powered by an urge, according to Von Hallberg, to "assume the custodianship of European cultural traditions as militarily and economically the U.S. had taken responsibility for the postwar recovery."[3] The issue rose as early as 1944, when Eisenhower warned his military commanders to "move cautiously around the monuments and cultural centers which symbolize to the world all that we are fighting to preserve." So we see in these travel poems, and in the poems that continue to be written, the old proprietary stance; poem after poem is an act of appropriation, and as Von Hallberg comments, some of the poets could not help but see Europe figuratively as a museum with themselves as custodians. Writers establish their authority over their subjects in a variety of ways, among them "reading" monuments and experiences "for analogies to the moral life of the individual"—as parables, in essence—or, as currently fashionable jargon would have it, reading them as "texts."[4] Another favored stance is for the speaker to exempt him or herself from mere touristhood, to assume that the American poet abroad is somehow above the run-of-the-mill, often in fact more fit than the natives to appreciate the surrounding bounty, typically speaking *for* rather than *about* the subject. The pitfall of this stance runs through the whole English and American tradition of travel poems.

Edward Said, in his book *Orientalism,* speaks about this kind of imperialism in regard to early Middle Eastern scholars whose "inauguration of orientalism . . . established the figure of the Orientalist as a central authority *for* the Orient, [and] . . . put into cultural circulation a form of discursive currency by whose presence the Orient would henceforth be *spoken for.*"[5]

Of course many writers from the 1950s onward sensed this connection between tourism and imperialism, and the best poems admit uncertainty, admit that "empires run on rapine, and poets follow empires—the plunder sometimes being imaginative."[6] Think, for instance, of Bishop's superb collection *Questions of Travel,* in which the poet herself is implicated in the exploitation of Brazil along with the conquistadors she evokes in "Brazil, January 1, 1502." Both Bishop and Lowell, in Von Hallberg's assessment, "wrote with a sense of imperial doom" during the optimistic fifties, an awareness all of us most likely hold in our own troubled present. Furthermore, "American poets are usually aware, painfully so, of being the unacknowledged representatives of national culture, of vulgarity, wealth, and power, and implicated in the expansion of empire"—hence my complicated sense of shame, guilt, and anger at the panorama of the Gran Via or the encounter in my Polish cousin's sitting room.[7]

In Poland, that country where the most savage events of modern times transpired, I was acutely aware that the United States was a major player in all three of the century's most pivotal events: World Wars I and II and the development of the bomb. Furthermore, one might venture that the United States has profited economically from these cataclysms while remaining relatively unscathed and has emerged as a culture with the means of spreading its influence across the globe. So, in essence, the victims of history have been anybody but Americans. The poet-traveler abroad cannot escape the vivid evidence of our insidious presence, our influence in even very remote areas or in those newly open to the "West." It seems, then, that this awareness is part of the baggage we carry along with our blue jeans and toothpaste.

Perhaps the best commentary on this has come from non-American artists. In *Kings of the Road,* Wim Wenders's searing parody of a road movie, two young Germans—an itinerant projector repairman and the hitchhiker he picks up—travel through West Germany in a massive American-built RV. The odyssey becomes a search for the hitchhiker's past, an ultimately frustrated journey of reconciliation, retrieval, and forgiveness. The two end up in an abandoned East German border patrol post that the hitchhiker recalls from a youthful weekend: it is the place where he first made love. Slashed all over the walls is Yank graffiti, territorial marks of American presence. The hitchhiker says, "Now the Americans have everything." In essence, the vandalism is the appropriation of more than a place, an emblem; it is the appropriation of memory, the past. It's a perfect act by a mass culture that all too often seems hell-bent on a kind of endless and oblivious self-erasure as well as a gratuitous assertion of its continuing power.

Earlier I mentioned that travel can give the traveler back to him or herself changed. I'd like to let the Polish poet Adam Zagajewski conjure a night in America from the point of view of a foreigner. A universal experience of all tourists/travelers is alienation, a vertiginous response to the strangeness, the otherness, of the visited place that causes heightened perception and intensity of vision but also a phantasmagorical dislocation. The self, too, becomes other. "Watching *Shoah* in a Hotel Room in America" is set in that most impersonal of places, an American hotel room:

> There are nights as soft as fur on a foal
> but we prefer chess or card playing. Here,
> some hotel guests sing "Happy Birthday"
> as the one-eyed TV nonchalantly shuffles its images.
> The trees of my childhood have crossed an ocean
> to greet me coolly from the screen.
> Polish peasants engage with a Jesuitical zest
> in theological disputes: only the Jews are silent,
> exhausted by their long dying.
> The rivers of the voyages of my youth flow
> cautiously over the distant, unfamiliar continent.
> Hay wagons haul not hay, but hair,
> their axles squeaking under the feathery weight.
> We are innocent, the pines claim.
> The SS officers are haggard and old,
> doctors struggle to save them their hearts, livers, consciences.
> It's late, the insinuations of drowsiness have me.
> I'd sleep, but my neighbors
> choir "Happy Birthday" still louder:
> louder than the dying Jews.
> Huge trucks transport stars from the firmament,
> gloomy trains go by in the rain.
> I am innocent, Mozart repents;
> only the aspen, as usual, trembles,
> prepared to confess all its crimes.
> The Czech Jews sing the national anthem: "Where is my home . . ."
> There is no home, houses burn, the cold gas whistles within.
> I grow more innocent, sleepy.
> The TV reassures me: both of us

are beyond suspicion.
The birthday is nosier.
The shoes of Auschwitz, in pyramids
high as the sky, groan faintly:
Alas we outlived mankind, now
let us sleep, sleep:
we have nowhere to go.[8]

It's a shattering poem, and much of its relentless force issues from its ironic restraint, from the strategies the poet uses to create a sense of alienated dislocation. Everything arrives mediated. The "one-eyed TV nonchalantly shuffles its images," a chilling description of the medium's monstrous dispassion as it flickers Claude Lanzmann's epic documentary on the Holocaust. The Americans' singing of "Happy Birthday" is filtered through the wall; all are distanced from "the [night] soft as fur on a foal" outside the hotel. Zagajewski makes skillful use of personification throughout to increase the poem's phantasmagorical quality, its fluid sense of historical time and reality. The televised images fuse with the poet's memories of his native country and become disturbingly animate: "The trees of my childhood have crossed an ocean / to greet me coolly from the screen." Later, "the pines," "the aspen," and "the shoes of Auschwitz," through an unsettling displacement, introduce the key terms of the poem's argument: the issues of culpability and what constitutes humanity. The poet makes powerful use of the idea of silence: these "Polish peasants engage with . . . zest / in theological disputes," but the victims, the Jews, "are silent," a reverberant absence. In travel one turns in on one's past, one's memories: as the speaker watches *Shoah,* the Polish scenes collide with the blank Americanscape and those oblivious singers to create a palimpsest.

Through ironic undercutting of lyricism with savage imagery, Zagajewski interrogates the concept of "innocence." Look again at this violated pastoral passage: "The rivers . . . of my youth flow /cautiously over the distant, unfamiliar continent. / Hay wagons haul not hay, but hair, / their axles squeaking under the feathery weight." Auschwitz, which has been preserved as an eloquent museum, is thirty miles from Krakow, where the poet grew up. Those "haggard and old" SS officers, attempting in the film to salve their "consciences," had stored in warehouses mountains of hair and clothes and shoes. In great bins at the camp one can still see this. There are rows of poplar and aspen at the perimeter of the camp, planted by prisoners and meant to screen what was going on inside.

The poem reenacts in microcosm how the world chose ignorance, chose to screen itself from the realities of the Final Solution. Those "innocent" Americans foolishly celebrating; the "innocent" speaker; even Mozart, the paradigm of Austrian artistic achievement—all deny culpability: "The TV reassures me: both of us / are beyond suspicion." His descent into sleep occurs while the Jews ask, "Where is my home"; while "the cold gas whistles," disturbingly echoing the victims' poisonous passage into terminal sleep. Through the poet's use of "innocence," he ironically explores guilt. We know that his sleep will be one burdened by the tortured dream of history. It is the "shoes of Auschwitz" that "groan faintly" the last word, a statement that poses a question: if they have "outlived mankind" what kind of humanity is left? Where does one go after such knowledge? In this poem of travel, then, through the use of irony, ambiguity, and self-confrontation, everyone is implicated.

To again quote Von Hallberg, Zagajewski has indeed "read" experience "for analogies to the mortal life of the individual."[9] But even within the grimly anaesthetizing abstraction of the Holocaust on a hotel-room TV screen, Zagajewski seeks to reaffirm a sense of the most abject horror, a horror that is finally resistant to the forces which seek to abstract it. The Holocaust, he reminds us, is not merely another text; it cannot be deconstructed. Perhaps one of the reasons why Zagajewski's poem is so effective is that it claims no implicit control over its subjects, nor even anything more than a very provisional understanding of them; the speaker can no more turn off the chorus of drunken revelers singing "Happy Birthday" than he can turn away from the grisly footage of the Auschwitz victims' shoes. Zagajewski, born in 1945, is not himself a Holocaust survivor, yet his poem is informed by a complex sense of history, both personal and public, that is perhaps unavailable to most of his American contemporaries.

How is travel treated by current American poets? *The Morrow Anthology of Younger American Poets* offers a partial but somewhat distressing answer. The 105 figures it represents, all born between 1940 and 1955, are Zagajewski's exact contemporaries, and to judge from the selections they do a lot of traveling. Twenty-eight of the poets have among their selections poems that have foreign settings or that discuss foreign travel.[10] Predictably, they favor Italy and France over most other locales, as a sampling of some of the poems' openings suggests: "A hot, bright day, late June. The bus from Rome / passed a seaside town" (Rika Lesser); "The natives [of Champagne] . . . have given up their backyards / and are happy where we cannot see them" (Rita Dove); "Although you mention Venice, / keeping it on your tongue like a fruit pit / and I say yes, perhaps Bucharest, neither of us / really knows" (Carolyn Forché); "Driving, driven / the driven sun, the surf- / slicked autostrada, glare / more slippery then ice . . . / Geneva to L'Aquila in ten hours" (Nicholas Christopher); "in Gubbio, an Umbrian city / the most purely medieval in Italy" (Daniel Halpern). It goes without saying that none of these openings is particularly promising. Halpern seems afflicted with a case of Arthur Frommer–speak, and although Dove begins by implying an intriguing connection between the speaker and the Champagne "natives," her language is quite pedestrian. But stylistic limitations are only part of the problem. The real difficulties of the poems are embedded in what we might call their perspectives: Lesser looks out the window of a bus; Christopher is speeding down the boot of Italy (in an Alfa-Romeo, presumably); Forché is in a train compartment, having met a mysterious stranger out of central casting. None of this trio is *within* a landscape as much as passing through it. If travel offers us a text, these poets take the Evelyn Wood approach to reading it, and none seems to question this process.

Perhaps the inevitable consequence of such superficiality is to simplify the issues implicit in travel poetry even further. Why go overseas to exploit foreign culture when it can be more easily and cheaply written about at home? Isn't the studio backlot perfectly adequate? The *Morrow Anthology*'s selection of Michael Blumenthal's poetry contains a competently written love poem set in Assisi ("This morning, in Assisi, I woke / and looked into my wife's face / and thought of St. Francis," he begins). But more telling is the poem that precedes it, "Today I Am Envying the Glorious Mexicans."[11]

The title is also its first line, and the speaker's envy becomes the subject of the twenty-two-line poem, which is written in a loose pentameter. The speaker envies the "glorious" inhabitants of Mexico who siesta beneath their sombreros beside "unambiguous" cacti. He envies a pair of imagined Mexican lovers, who are awaiting a liaison in the moonlight. He envies grass, which he compares to "the green whiskers of God." His catalogue of envies eventually takes on a somewhat magical realist turn—the "singing" dead and the genitalia of flowers are listed, and the poem eventually transforms itself into a kind of loopy prayer; the speaker implores the almighty to let him live a bit longer, so that he can learn to emulate his Mexicans' and flowers' lack of purpose. His goal seems to be a sort of giddy self-forgetfulness. "I want to be the perfect madman," he tells us, "without reflection," capable of "babbling" on endlessly about himself. Fortunately, the poem begins to wind down at this point and concludes with a sort of smiley-face trope—something about "sangria" and "the happy earth."

Although I am not sure the poem achieves the speaker's goal of becoming the perfect madman, his other goal, of being "without reflection," has been consummately attained. One needn't be rabidly PC to see that the poem's view of the "glorious Mexicans" is a reprehensible stereotype—happy, indolent Panchos and Ciscos, dozing in sombreros beneath the midday sun, slugging tequila beneath the saguaros. True, there's a certain element of self-mockery in the poem's tone, which is complimented further by the flourishes of Nerudaesque surrealism—"the singing dead," "the green whiskers of God." Yet Blumenthal's self-mockery does not extend to any sort of questioning of the stereotypes he has exploited. His envy of the Mexicans is a sort of yuppie update of the cult of the noble savage, and it is hard to believe that such reactionary sentiments could be expressed in a poem published as recently as the mid-1980s.

Yet the poem's willingness to traffic in stereotypes is in some ways less troubling than a more subtle problem. Where, we have to ask, do the glorious Mexicans come from? Do they arise from a memory that the speaker has half-forgotten and that is now suddenly released? Is he remembering an actual visit to Mexico, or has he discovered the motif through armchair travel, from Weston's Mexican photos of the 1930s, for example? Our only clue to this enigma is that we are told the event is occurring "today." Is our speaker *in* Mexico as he writes the poem then, back in his hotel room after having scavenged the countryside for local color? Any of these explanations is, of course, possible, but the most likely explanation is that the Mexicans come from none of these sources, that they were conjured by the speaker as he sought to crank out his daily quota of poem. Creative writing teachers are fond of repeating the truism that any subject is a proper one for a poem, and in many instances this claim is valid. But poems should also incorporate into their structure some element that attempts to analyze the poet's motives for writing about a subject. Poems without this quality run the risk of treating subject matter in the way that conquistadors and Visigoths treated plunder. Blumenthal may claim to envy his glorious Mexicans, but his true allegiance is to Cortez and Pizarro.

Perhaps an important requirement for any good travel poem is that it must, even more than other sorts of poems, build a recognition of the gap between motive and subject matter into its very structure. As an impetus of self-questioning, the alienation inherent in travel is at least as strong a catalyst as are those forces we associate with self-interrogation. Travel causes us to look into ourselves just as uncomfortably as do guilt, regret, and a recognition of aging. Travel is more an act of self-reckoning than of diversion. Blumenthal and several other poets represented in the *Morrow Anthology* seem too preoccupied—either with getting to the trattoria in the next Umbrian town or with finishing the next poem—to acknowledge this.

But even those of us who acknowledge the complexities and self-annihilating dangers of travel often have a difficult time balancing these concerns with the seductive appeal of the exotic. A case in point is Mary Jo

Salter's Lamont-winning *Unfinished Painting.* Many of the poems describe a period of living in Japan and show a true sympathy with the culture, one strong enough to overcome some of Salter's exasperating poetic mannerisms, not the least of which is a tendency to wield form and wit like machetes. Here are two regrettable quatrains that open a poem about Chernobyl: "Once upon a time / the word alone was scary. / Now, quainter than this rhyme / it's the headline of a story / long yellowed in the news. / The streets were hosed in Kiev / and Poles took more shampoos. / The evacuees were brave. . . ."[11] The poem I would like to focus upon is better than this, but its failings are ultimately more interesting than its strengths. "I Lose You for an Instant" carries the subtitle, "Guilen, China," and its opening is animated and engaging:

The sun's at last soaking up
the rut-puddled street, and hundreds
of age-old unoiled bicycles
together like thunder rip

over the hump of bridge.
Out of the blue, in another
military-mud-
green jeep conveying

what looks like body bags
until one spills (just rice)
or heaps of gravel (why?)
it's a mystery

nobody can unravel
tons of it from nowhere
and deposited in the most
God-forsaken spots. . . .[13]

Despite some clumsy gestures—the bikes on the bridge compared to thunder, for example—the opening does a good job of conveying both the scene and the speaker's sense of uncertainty within it. The parentheses and asides give a kind of querulous immediacy to the descriptions, as do the short lines and the incidental rhyming. Salter carries on in this fashion for a few more stanzas and then introduces some information that considerably complicates the poem:

I'm standing on the bridge
and under the black coat

packed that I might blend
into the bleakness I expected, am

five months pregnant.
I've dragged you all the way to China
(you dragging all the bags)
because I've been afraid

our days of exhilarating frights
are drawing to an end.
I'm scared alright. . . .

The speaker's confession of impending change in her life—of "our days of exhilarating frights / . . . drawing to an end"—now gives way to a purer sort of vulnerability. She is alone, pregnant, and the husband's errand has lost him in a crowd that is now seen as more threatening than picturesque. In the city's bustle she is nonchalantly ignored by the bicycle-pedaling crowd, but this in several ways intensifies her sense of desolation.

ten

minutes I've stood here
round-eyed, round-bellied foreigner
whom nobody seems to mind.
It's just occurred to me

that I have both our passports
and you have all our money. . . .

This is the moment of the poem's dramatic and thematic reckoning. It is an affecting scene, rich with implication. Salter captures the traveler's simultaneous experience of alienation and wonder, contrasts the West's sense of individualism and privacy with the East's collectivism, and creates a fair amount of narrative suspense. Will the husband return? What will the speaker do if he is lost? The poem's resolution of these issues promises to be exciting. Unfortunately, the conclusion of the poem is overwrought and formulaic.

You will come back. And time
though it promises to fill

full the brave new world
with gravel, will deliver us
a daughter—as it braids another
river from a glossy fall

of rain, and chooses to preserve
as lovelier than the often
painted mountains of Guilen
so steep they ought

to come to pencil-points.
High parentheses
(enclosing that lost
instant), they rise mis-

shapen in my eyes.

Salter's almost-Pavlovian wittiness, which has been kept admirably in check up to this point, now overwhelms the poem. Salter chooses to end with an archly descriptive flourish rather than to explore the situation's more promising implications, which she even appears to refute. The poem's sense of immediacy is obliterated when we are told that its first two-thirds are merely a flashback, an aside. The poem's final parenthetical remark—"(enclosing that lost / instant)"—takes a device that had earlier been used quite effectively and reduces it to a crass typographical pun. Salter's use of the pencil conceit near the end of the poem is also revealing. While Salter could hardly be labeled a Language poet, the implicit message of the conclusion is one of Language poetry's main precepts: this is not a poem about content and experience, she tells us, but about "writing."

At that richly frictional moment in "I Lose You for an Instant" when a personal and cultural collision occurs, Salter ice-skates away, settling for superficial knowledge of her subject rather than a deeper involvement. Ultimately, the poem simply exploits the experience for the sake of a dubious technical execise instead of mining that experience for self-confrontation. Let's turn now to Elizabeth Bishop's "Over 2,000 Illustrations and a Complete Concordance," which confronts a similar issue: tourist experience versus a more intense, troubling, and mysterious traveler's experience.

The poem dislocates the reader immediately by entering into a dialogue that implies a comparison: "This should have been our travels: / serious, engravable." The poet then describes plates in what is probably one of those Victorian travel books, where all the images are somewhat romanticized, abstracted, or sanitized:

The Seven Wonders of the World are tired
and a touch familiar, but the other scenes,
innumerable, though equally sad and still

are foreign. Often the squatting Arab,
or group of Arabs, plotting, probably,
against our Christian Empire,
while one apart, with outstretched arm and hand
points to the Tomb, the Pit, the Sepulcher.[14]

The opening, which with light irony undercuts its playful tone with the capitalized references to Tomb, Pit, and Sepulcher, establishes the terms the poem will negotiate: that otherness infused with fear the "foreign" can engender, notions of power both sacred and secular, the facing off of East and West, and mortality. And whereas Salter somehow turns life into "art," Bishop questions that tidy transformation.

Granted a page alone or a page made up
of several scenes arranged in cattycornered rectangles
or circles set on stippled gray,
granted a grim lunette,
caught in the toils of an initial letter,
when dwelt upon, they all resolve themselves.

Perspective and resolution are possible through representation in a way perhaps impossible in actual experience. Bishop continues to sound more deeply; this is not someone whose gaze consists of snapshots from a train: "The eye drops, weighted, through the lines / the burin made, the lines that move apart / like ripples above sand, / dispersing storms, God's spreading fingerprint, / and painfully, finally, that ignite / in watery prismatic white-and-blue."

The black and white images in the travel book conjure living-color memories of actual travel—the Narrows at St. John's; St. Peter's; "Mexico," where "the dead man lay / in a blue arcade; the dead volcanoes / glistened like Easter lilies. / The jukebox went on playing 'Ay, Jalisco!'" These are a tourist's light observations: no galvanizing transformation here—those "volcanoes," although they look like "Easter lilies," are as "dead" as the man in the arcade. So what makes this poem a traveler's poem? Like the visual sounding in the second stanza, the poet goes again for depth in what becomes an anguished self-confrontation (though, granted, Bishop insists throughout the poem on "we"). The perceiver's emotion bleeds through in her details and in her relentless questioning. The modesty of this point of view is typical of Bishop, and typically canny, reflecting that powerfully disturbing element in travel of self-erasure and uncertainty. So while this poem may at first strike the reader as more impersonal than the Salter or Blumenthal poems, it is profoundly more honest and revealing.

The tone radically changes near the end of the middle stanza, when the poet sees "what frightened [her] most of all" (here is the sole deviation from the first person plural—she says "frightened me"), a desacralized tomb that is

> one of a group under a keyhole-arched baldaquin
> open to every wind from the pink desert.
> An open, gritty, marble trough, carved solid
> with exhortation, yellowed
> as scattered cattle-teeth;
> half-filled with dust, not even the dust
> of the poor prophet paynim who once lay there.

She undercuts this moment as if trying to back away from where she must go next: "In a smart burnoose [the guide] looked on amused." Von Hallberg in mentioning this poem notes—and this is something the fastidious Bishop would have known—that "Khadour . . . is an Islamic figure of immortality who was the protector of mariners and river travelers."[15] But here Bishop's imagining of the death leaves him "amused" at this outsider; it's a subtle indictment of the traveler's lightness or superficiality that the poem examines, the "infant sight" of the poem's famously ambiguous last line. Here is the poem's passionately visionary closure:

> Everything only connected by "and" and "and."
> Open the book. (The gilt rubs off the edges
> of the pages and pollinates the fingertips.)
> Open the heavy book. Why couldn't we have seen
> this old Nativity while we were at it?
> —the dark ajar, the rocks breaking with light,
> an undisturbed, unbreathing flame,
> colorless, sparkless, freely fed on straw,
> and, lulled within, a family with pets,
> —and looked and looked our infant sight away.

Everything connects in a chain—images and experiences, travel, memory, death, the desire for transformation—all linked by those conjunctions but eluding a kind of design, some ultimate fusing with the object of desire. The imperative to herself to "Open the book" is also a challenge to the reader, the traveler. The journeying of the traveler becomes a mapping of an interior landscape, a project for which there is no easy resolution.

I fear that in exploring these issues I too have succumbed to the easy dualities that we so often rely upon when discussing literary works—tourist poems versus travel poems; looking versus seeing; the worldly Europeans of

Henry James novels versus the rough earnestness of his Americans; the Old World's valorization of culture versus the New World's more pernicious valorization of materialism. Yet the fact remains that nearly all poems of travel imply such dualities; that the enduring works of the genre seek not just to explore these dualities but to obliterate them by breaking through their boundaries. And it is often at these borders between states—at these borders both metaphorical *and* national—where the best poetry becomes possible. To exist for a time at these junctions and margins is of course risky business, for it entails uncertainty. (Why do the guards look so closely at our passports? Why was the woman before us called into the back room?) At such crossings we experience the moment when, as Jarrell's "The Orient Express" would have it, "a questioning precariousness / comes over everything." And it is this very precariousness that must precede the moment of gnosis, when we have "looked our infant sight away." Yet to state the issues in this way is a bit grandiose, and the truest travelers are, like the poems of Bishop, self-effacing. The best written and most beautiful travel book I know of is Aspley Cherry-Garrard's unpromisingly titled *The Worst Journey in the World.* Cherry-Garrard, who used inheritance to pay for a place in Scott's final arctic expedition, had the dubious honor of discovering the frozen bodies of Scott and his companions. While remaining behind at the base camp while Scott and his party set out to conquer the Pole, Cherry-Garrard and two associates planned a shorter expedition of less ostensibly heroic implications: a week-long excursion to a nearby ice floe to obtain some emperor penguin eggs for scientific study. The trip in fact took nearly two months, and Cherry-Garrard and his party suffered unbelievable privations, returning to base camp frostbitten, snow-blind, starved, and nearly toothless because of scurvy. This harrowing journey, recounted in the deadpan fashion so typical of British travel writing, occupies a good portion of Cherry-Garrard's six-hundred-page memoir. But it is only near the end that Cherry-Garrard succumbs to the urge to philosophize, and at the close he offers a bit of advice to all prospective travelers: "You will have your reward, as long as all you want is a penguin egg."[16]

(co-authored with Lynda Hull, 1992)

15.

Magi-in-Residence: An Alchemy of Poetic Ruin

For eighteen months the monks will tour the West, performing a variety of sacred Tibetan chants, dances, and music. It's billed as "The Mystical Arts of Tibet" and is a little reminiscent of old-fashioned traveling circuses. The monks will come to your town, remain in residence for a week at whatever organization has paid to host them, and help to satisfy the current American rage for All-Things-Tibetan. They come with a pedigree, for they are all associated with the Lobelang Monastery in Dharmsala, home of the Dalai Lama and the Tibetan government in exile, and are bankrolled by the actor Richard Gere, who seems to want to do for the Dalai Lama and his minions what the Beatles did many years ago for the Maharishi. To see the nine monks in action might lead you to conclude that monastic life in Tibet is anything but retiring: the monks put in long days as they attend to the sacred and to the commerce involved in selling it. They spend several days building a sand mandala; it's the size of a large dining-room table, the colored sands deposited on their grid one grain at a time. They talk to schoolchildren and the media, but their showpiece is a three-hour performance of the aforementioned mystical arts. Garbed in saffron and purple robes and wearing plumed saffron hats that look like something sported by centurions in a gladiator movie, the monks chant and play traditional Tibetan instruments and later present a number of ceremonial dances. A properly trained Tibetan vocalist can emit three tones simultaneously, and the effect this produces is unearthly; the chants seem not to issue from the monks' throats but from everywhere in the room at once. The low tone, with its eerily resonant pulsations, seems like nothing that could emerge from a human body. On the one hand it sounds spacey and electronic—like something made by a theremin or an early model of synthesizer—and on the other atavistic, reminding you of the rolling-thunder croak of a didgeridoo. It seems both the majestic perfection of an ancient craft and the harnessing of a force of nature, distant thunder somehow trapped like a genie in the lungs and expelled. Later, during the intermission, these same monks will sell T-shirts, prayer wheels, and small Tibetan flags in the lobby. Later still, when the monks come to the end of their residency, they will dismantle the mandala they have so painstakingly constructed, place its colored sands in a canvas bag, and carry it in a procession to the nearest lake or river, where the sand will be poured into the waters to the accompaniment of more music and chanting. The forces of good which have been magically embodied in the mandala will thus be dispersed into the world.

Being a "monk-in-residence" is no doubt quite different from being a "poet-in-residence," though neither occupation is a very common one. But for a brief time this week the tiny Vermont town of Johnson could boast of both a set of monks-in-residence and a poet-in-residence. The monks have been brought in by Johnson State, the small liberal arts college whose campus sits on the top of the hill overlooking this Green Mountain village, and I am the poet in question, in residence for a week at the Vermont Studio Center, a colony for the arts which sits below the campus along the river, in a converted flour mill. Here I'll give a talk, confer with some of the poets who have been given studio space here, and present a reading of my poems. My life during my stay here is probably more monastic than that of the monks. I spend most of my time working in my studio or taking walks, no mandala to construct, no sacred dances or chants to perform, and certainly no T-shirts to peddle. On my walks I've now and again encountered one or another of the monks, who smile cheerfully when we pass but who also look chilly in the crisp air of Vermont September: the robes and flip-flops may be all right for Dharmsala, but not for New England on the eve of first frost. Yesterday was the end of the monks' stay in Johnson, so the mandala was dismantled, its sand conveyed with pomp and ceremony to the river beside the Studio Center. The monks looked even more out of place than usual as they marched down School Street in their robes and miters, playing cymbals and trumpets as they passed the Mobil station and the shop that sells maple syrup; they were followed by a crowd of a few dozen students, professors, and families with kids hoisted on their parents' shoulders. The eldest monk opened the bag of colored sand—which looked for all the world like bath salts—and it spiraled to the water; the chanting continued for a few minutes, and thus the waters of the Lamoille River had been magically blessed, the mandala dispersed within them. The monks took off their hats and called it a day, and the poet-in-residence returned to his studio, happy to have shared in this blessing but having no magic of his own, neither white nor black nor sympathetic, no voodoo, no mojo, no oracle bones.

Poetry, after all, has grown far removed from the magical. In a century in which the aesthetics of verse have sought to follow the good Dr. Williams's assertion that a poem is nothing more than a machine made of words, and which in more recent years has come to be dominated by the aesthetic nihilism of post-structuralist theory (a manner of thought which is surely hermetic but never occultist), it is hard to even say *what* poetry is concerned with anymore, save that it is about language and that language itself should never be trusted. Slippery; indeterminate; tongue-tied by cant and forked-tongued through its intended, unintended, and manifold falsehoods; language is a bad material from which to build anything. A machine made of words? Perhaps, but in all likelihood we don't know how to work the thing; the owner's manual has been misplaced, and wasn't it a lemon from the very start? Bad machines and incompetent mechanics: this is the state, we're told, to which poetry and poets have arrived. And the obsolescence of both is fast approaching. "Poetry" is becoming one of those quaintly neglected words that carry with them a sweetly Victorian mustiness. It sits upon a shelf with the Sublime; with Meadows (pronounced to emphasize the trochee); with curling irons, sincerity, and antimaccasars. Even "Modern poetry," that term which in the era of the New Critics had a distinctly triumphalist import, now belongs to the contemporary idiom only in the way that 8-tracks, black and white TVs and 45-rpm singles bespeak modernity—to utter such words is to evoke a charmingly inane nostalgia. Now we have text and cybertext, now we have "writing," now we have "language," and language must be seen not as a gift from Apollo or the muses but as the tool of some malevolent trickster, a Pan, a Coyote, a Loki, a Derrida. The only thing he's here for is to fuck with our heads. Ah, how the mighty have fallen.

Now, to have your head scrambled up is not always a bad thing, but no one should be mind-fucked all the time. Questions of "agency" arise: why must language be the psychosurgeon and we his patients, subjected to his bone saw and trepannings? And why must we volunteer, again and again, to let his anesthesia put us under? Was there ever a time when poets were the psychosurgeons, and language lay beneath us on the gurney? How often we poets have longed to believe that such an age once existed and that we might somehow regain our rightful place as magi, as Rimbaud's alchemists of the word. This longing was of course exceedingly acute among the Romantics and their Symbolist successors, whose antirationalism fostered a sometimes fanatical interest in the occult. Blake and Baudelaire were Swedenborgians. Rimbaud, Blok, and Nerval devotees of alchemy and the writings of Hermes Trismegistus. You might even link to this movement Joseph Smith, whom Harold Bloom regards as the greatest American visionary after Whitman—golden tablets, apparitions in the wood, the Urim and Thummim; it's far more sexy than Pope or the French Encyclopedists. And in the twentieth century we have Yeats and Merrill. The astringencies of Modernism, we're told, brought an end to most of this wackiness. And yet, as Timothy Materer contends in his *Modernist Alchemy: Poetry and the Occult,* mystical and occultist systems have left their stamp on a goodly number of twentieth-century poets beyond the obvious examples of Yeats and Merrill. Materer devotes chapters to H. D., Duncan, Plath, Hughes, and even—astonishingly—to Pound and Eliot.[1] Now, for a poet to be intrigued by the occult is one thing; for a poet to *believe* in it is quite another. Merrill was famously evasive when interviewers tried to get him to say that he believed his Ouija-board voices actually derived from the spirit world. And when Yeats, in *A Vision,* asks his spirit guides why they have contacted him, they reply that they have done so in order to give him "new metaphors for his poetry." This seems to suggest that the elaborate cosmological system outlined in the book must ultimately be little more than a tool to aid poetic composition and thus no more mystical than a thesaurus, a rhyming dictionary, or a spell-check program.

Yet even in the face of their own skepticism, poets have never really ceased their striving to become alchemists of the word, nor ever abandoned a nostalgia for the worldview of animism, which Freud in his *Totem And Taboo* argues will always exert a powerful influence—or spell—on human thinking. Animism, the notion that the universe is populated by "innumerable beings both benevolent and malignant," who control both the forces of nature and human destiny, continues to exert a seductive appeal over us all.[2] Scientific rationalism and more sophisticated religious systems, based as they are upon a belief in the limitations of human knowledge and understanding, are to Freud less "consistent and exhaustive" systems. Animism offers the atavistic reassurance of "a truly complete explanation of the universe."[3] The sky gods, demons, and spirits who exist in the world of animism may be fickle, but such a system is predicated upon the notion that these beings can be understood and even mastered. More importantly still, the realm of art is seen by Freud as one of the few remaining aspects of modern civilization which grants authority to the animistic world view: "People speak with justice of 'the magic of art' and compare artists to magicians."[4] Materer convincingly extends this analogy:

> The artist draws on the primitive feelings found in animism just as the magician draws on them to demonstrate a power over spirits. But there is a second and even closer affinity between magic and art: both work through the association of ideas. For example, the destruction of a carven shape of a person will stand for the destruction of that very person, or the anointing of a knife will alleviate the pain of a wound made by that knife. In this association of ideas, Freud identifies two principles—similarity (as in the carving) and contiguity (as in the

> weapon); in literary art, the principles would be termed *metaphor* and *metonymy.* The artist is thus linked with the shaman. And magic with literary technique—just as an occultist would wish.[5]

You can see the appeal here: who'd want to fiddle with Lacan and Foucault when you could instead cast spells, call up the dead, and lay your enemies low with a couple of well-chosen needle stabs into the voodoo doll? It is not for nothing that a good poem is said to be "spellbinding." Nor is it inaccurate to say that the great elegies, from Archilochos's lamentation for his companions lost at sea to Bishop's bittersweet strophes for her friend Robert Lowell in "North Haven," seek to resurrect their subjects, if only fleetingly, and surely the searing invective of a Catullus or Brecht can be said to work a kind of voodoo. Magical thinking can thus be seen not merely as a symptom of obsessive-compulsive disorders, treatable by Wellbutrin or Prozac, but instead as a powerful component of poetic motivation and technique, which manifests itself in some surprising places in twentieth-century poetry, ranging far beyond the examples given in Materer's book. You see it in the lapidary surrealism of the Deep Image poetry of the sixties and seventies, where totemistic and shamanistic situations and imagery abound: Galway Kinnell turns into a bear; Robert Bly entitles a poem "A Man Locked Inside an Oak"; and Merwin give us an effort called "Words for a Totem Animal." Stephen Dunn offers up a long poem entitled "Sympathetic Magic," a title coopted later by Michael Blumenthal for a first book. Poems such as these were often fueled by a kind of atavistic metonymy deriving from ethnopoetics. Many Deep Image lyrics are little more than effete retoolings of the shaman spells and Native American chants collected by Jerome Rothenberg in his influential anthology, *Technicians of the Sacred.* Here is Charles Simic's "Fear" in its entirety:

> Fear passes from man to man
> Unknowing,
> As one leaf passes its shudder
> to another.
>
> All at once the whole tree is trembling
> And there is no sign of the wind.[6]

Such efforts seem dated now, but even Language poets such as Charles Bernstein have been known to profess a fascination with the nomenclature of magic and mythopoetics such as those expressed in "Fear." In an essay entitled "The Artifice of Absorption"—which first carries on a lengthy rant against that bugbear of the Language writers, "official verse culture"—

Bernstein calls for a "self-canceling rather than a self-conscious" poetry and tosses out words such as "spellbinding" and "spellweaving" to make his case, drawing an interesting link between the hypnotic cadences of shaman drummers, who use their instruments to inaugurate a trance, and the propulsive insistence of three-chord rock and roll.[7] Bernstein also makes reference to a book which for a number of years has been a favorite of mine, *The Greek Magical Papyri in Translation, Including the Demotic Spells.* [8] It is a book of *truly* atavistic poetry, much more interesting than your average Deep Image lyric or Language poem. These spells, chants, prayers, and hymns from Greco-Roman Egypt are of course practical in their design rather than aesthetic, formulated to send precognitive dreams, make someone fall in love with you, afflict your enemy with insomnia, make your rival's pecker fall off, or allow you to cross the Nile on a crocodile's back. In them prosody is a tool for magic and vice versa, and thus we read them with nostalgic envy, as a representation of what Barthes calls "the corporeal exteriorization of discourse." We also read them palimpsistically, seeing both the exoticism of the papyri themselves and a similar exoticism deriving from their function as arcane academic texts. What is more weird and magical, the notion of bringing bad luck upon your enemy by inscribing a spell "on a pot of smoked fish . . . with a bronze stylus" or the fact that two millennia later such a formula would appear in a fifty-five-dollar hardback, in which the translator must not only seek to render accurately the spell and its instructions but also line breaks, lacunae caused because the text is fragmentary, drawings which accompany the text, and the hocus-pocus which forms a major portion of many of the spells? How do you translate Coptic and Demotic nonsense words into English? (Or, in some cases in the book, first into German, and *then* into English?) It gets curiouser and curiouser. But also curiously beautiful:

> *Love-spell of attraction through wakefulness:* Take the eyes of a bat and release it alive, and take / a piece of unbaked dough or unmelted wax and mold a little dog; and put the right eye of the bat into the little dog, implanting also in the same way the left one in the left. And take a needle, thread it with the magical material and / stick it through the eyes of the little dog, so that the magical material is visible. And put the dog into a new drinking vessel, attach a papyrus strip to it and seal it with your own ring which has crocodiles with the backs of their heads attached, and / deposit it at a crossroad after you have marked the spot so that, should you wish to recover it, you can find it.
>
> *Spell written on the papyrus strip:* I abjure you three times by Hekate PHORPHORBA BAIBO PHORBORBA, that she, NN, lose the fire in her eye or even / lie awake with nothing on her mind except me, NN alone. I adjure

> by Kore, who has become the Goddess of Three Roads and who is the true mother of . . . (whom you wish), PHORBIA BRIMO NEREATO DAMON BRIMON SEDNA / DARDAR, All-seeing one, IOPE, make her, NN, lie awake for me through all [eternity].[9]

Curiously beautiful, but also curiously modern. Is this some formerly untranslated text by Tristan Tzara? To break down the barrier between art and life, to create from word or paint a version of sympathetic magic, was of course one of the major goals of the Surrealist and the Abstract Expressionist movements. The right words or the right actions, when rendered with the right sort of improvisational zeal, would open a door to the absolute as surely as a soothsayer's spell. Harold Rosenberg, in christening Pollock and his associates the "American Action Painters," bestows upon words such as "action" and "gesture" a mystical force. "The act-painting," he writes, " is of the same metaphysical substance as the artist's existence. The new painting has broken down every distinction between art and life."[10] Rosenberg's existentialist zeal, like the clumsily oracular musings of the Deep Imagists, seems a bit naïve to us today. But is it possible to preserve some of this particular form of ardor while at the same time not succumbing to its simplicities? The bifurcated and pentimentoed reading which the *Magical Papyri* demands may offer us some answers, answers which are explored in an even more intriguing way in the late Armand Schwerner's exquisite and strange long sequence, *The Tablets.*

Schwerner's sequence alleges to present a series of translations of twenty-seven Sumerian cuneiform tablets inscribed with religious texts, chants, songs, and ritual and lyric poems, few written by the same scribe or author, and thus representing a motley of styles and concerns. Individual tablets can veer from the liturgical to the scatological without warning, and many of them are "incomplete" thanks to damaged texts, untranslatable passages, corrupt transcriptions by their original "scribes," and so forth. So many gaps in the "original" texts exist that Schwerner must use a series of typographical symbols to indicate not only when such moments occur but why: plus signs, for example, indicate a missing passage, ellipses a passage that is untranslatable, a question mark encased in parentheses a footnoted variant reading of a word. The tablets parody the conventions of academic translation of ancient texts such as those represented in *The Greek Magical Papyri* but also allude slyly to post-structuralism; they are texts under erasure, examples of what Derrida calls "a play of traces." This makes them sound rather highfalutin, but such is not the case. They're often quite funny and risqué. Here is Tablet V:

is the man bigger than a fly's wing?   what pleasure!
is he much bigger than a fly's wing?   what pleasure!
is his hard penis ten times a fly's wing?   what pleasure!
is his red penis fifteen times a fly's wing?   what [pleasure!]
is his mighty penis fifty times a fly's wing?   what pleasure!
does his penis vibrate like a fly's wing?   what terrific pleasure!
is his arm four and a half times a strong penis?   . . . . .a great arm
is his arm two hundred-twenty-five times a fly's wing   in the shape of
petified wood

is his body three times his great arm?   what pleasure!
is his body thirteen times his red penis?   what pleasure!
is his body three-hundred-thirty-six-times a big
fly's body?   what pleasure!

does he touch his body with pleasure?   what pleasure!
does she count fly's wings throughout the night?   what pleasure!
is her vulva tipped with spring color?   what terrific pleasure!
does he move behind in her?   let us have rain!
does she vibrate like the wheel on the axle?   let us have rain! what pleasure!
let us call a fly's half-wing *kra*   lay a *kra* on this bull's horn
let us call a fly's half-wing *kra*   lay another *kra* on this bull's horn
let us call a fly's half-wing *kra*   lay another *kra* on this bull's horn
let us call a fly's half-wing *kra*   lay another *kra* on this bull's horn
let us call a fly's half-wing *kra*   hold the bull down quiet
let us call a fly's half-wing *kra*   lay another *kra* on this bull's horn
look, the bull's horn is more
than six *kra*   hold down the bull's head
let us call the man's red penis *pro*   lay a *pro* on this cow's vulva
let us call the man's red penis *pro*   lay another *pro* on this cow's vulva
let us call the man's red penis *pro*   lay another *pro* on this cow's vulva
look, the cow's vulva is five *kra*   what pleasure!
look, the cow's vulva is almost
three *pro*   what terrific pleasure!
pro kra kra pro kra kra kra pro   *kra* what pleasure! *pro* what pleasure!
the man's sacrificed hand is more
than one *pro*   this twig is more than one *pro*
the man's aching head is forty *kra*
round   this great melon is forty *kra* round
the man's sick groin is three *pro*   feel this lamb shank, three *pro*
let's sacrifice this twig   what a pleasure!
let's sacrifice this great melon   what a pleasure!
let's sacrifice this shank   what a terrific pleasure!

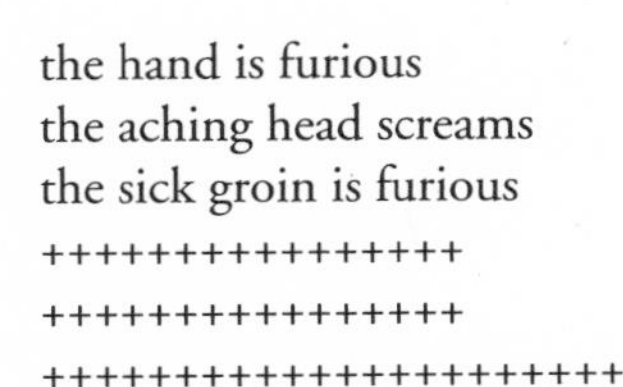
the hand is furious
the aching head screams
the sick groin is furious
+++++++++++++++
+++++++++++++++
+++++++++++++++++++++

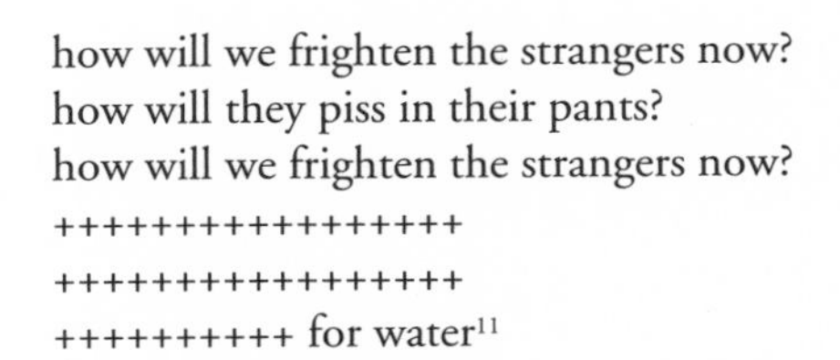
how will we frighten the strangers now?
how will they piss in their pants?
how will we frighten the strangers now?
++++++++++++++++
++++++++++++++++
++++++++++ for water[11]

The conceit of *The Tablets* allows for a roominess which is familiar to us from twentieth-century long poems in the mode of the *Cantos* and *Paterson*—the materials which work their way into the poem can be extremely diverse. Schwerner at one point offers a long list of them: "Incunabula—devotional and mystical texts, hagiography, musical printing, fake literature, homiletics, juristics, history and fictionalized history, satire, poetry, romances, travel books, herbals. . . ."[12] But on the other hand, perplexing gaps, conundrums, and puzzles remain in both the text itself and in our ability to conceptualize the intended meanings of their imaginary originals. This technique derives not exclusively from the aesthetics of modernist fragmentation and collage, however, but also from Schwerner's understanding of authentic cuneiform tablets. In the "Tablet Journals," which are an appendix to the volume, he quotes this passage by the Assryiologist R. Labat: "The great literary tablets of Ashur, Ninevah and Uruk feature little holes, either triangular or round. Appearing randomly on the various parts of the tablet, they may occasionally fill one or two entire lines. Most often they seem uniquely destined to decorate any spaces not occupied by writing."[13] Anything can make its way into the poem, from a hypothetical reconstruction of the musical notation of a chant to "psychotic rant" to charts and diagrams which seem to derive from the kabbala. Yet Schwerner resists any impulse to narrativize or ascribe rigid meanings to the tablets: the lacunae are rarely explained away, and many of the words and phrases he presents are amended by footnotes which offer synonyms and variant translations, some of which are hilarious in their context—is the word "hair" or is it "beginning"? "Penishole/Vagina" or "whirlpool"? "Stony Shit" or "lentil soup"?

But what is it about *The Tablets* that makes it more than eccentric parody? Two things strike me. First, there remains Schwerner's stubborn insistence that within the fragmentation, paradox, and inaccessibility of his imaginary tablets, there remains an essence, a form of pure and exact expression which can be retained even in "translation." It is an essence which can be glimpsed only fleetingly, in the manner in which "being" is perceived by Heidegger—as soon as it is identified, it begins to recede and change. Yet Schwerner implies that such glimpses of the essential can occur more frequently and urgently when they are foregrounded within the collage-making, genre-hopping, and conjecturalism of his poems. Thus, *The Tablets* employ their modernism not in order to replicate objective reality through description, in the manner of Williams, but in order to transcend the objective or to revert to a mystical animism in which word and object, sign and signifier cannot be divided. To achieve this goal Schwerner must first divest himself of concepts of linear structure and received form, even as he pays homage to them through parody. Early in the process of writing the sequence, Schwerner sketched out its rationale: "the modern, accidental form of Sumero-Akkadian tablets provided me with a usable poetic structure. They offered, among other things, ways out of closure—which I find increasingly onerous—as well as the expansion of the constricting girdle of English syntax. They also invited phonetic improvisation . . . made me feel comfortable in recreating the animistic . . . & [enabled] me to put in holes wherever I want. . . ."[14]

Because of these holes, these slits in the arras formed by scholarly pedantry, we can glimpse something of the animistic character of the imagined originals of each tablet. Beneath the curtain we can perceive a consciousness which assumes that language and writing are fluid forces, occult forces. Schwerner does not teach us to read cuneiform as much as he allows us to imagine the state of consciousness which can write and read it, one far different from the consciousness which reads present-day alphabetic writing, one in which fixed meaning and the rigid bifurcation of thought into abstract and concrete terminology does not so easily arise. If you wanted to employ theoretical cant, you could say that Schwerner interrogates the logocentric worldview. But it's more interesting than that, and Schwerner has done his research by doing more than parroting the bromides of deconstruction. While Sumerian began as a logogrammatical system (i.e., one in which a written sign stands for a whole word), it soon began to incorporate phonetic representation as well. This innovation was a hugely significant one, as Jared Diamond points out in his *Guns, Germs, and Steel:* "Perhaps the most important single step in the whole history of writing was the Sumerians' introduction of phonetic representation, initially by writing an abstract noun (which could not be readily drawn as a picture) by means of a sign for a depictable noun which had the same phonetic pronunciation. For instance, it's easy to draw a recognizable picture of *arrow,* hard to draw a recognizable picture of *life.* The resulting ambiguity was resolved by the addition of a silent sign called a determinative, to indicate the category of nouns to which the intended object belonged. Linguists term this decisive innovation, which also underlies puns today, the rebus principle."[15] The expressive system of Sumerian, as Diamond envisions it, is thus one that occupies a cusp between an archaic approach to written thought, in which words were evoked through pictures, and the largely phonetic system of alphabetic writing. "Sumerian writing seems to consist," says Diamond, "of a complex mixture of three types of signs: logograms, referring to a whole word or name; phonetic signs, used in effect for spelling syllables, letters, grammatical elements, or parts of words; and determinatives, which were not pronounced, but used to resolve ambiguities."[16] The poetic possibilities of this "complex mixture" are what most attract Schwerner; it becomes for him a system in which many of the sophisticated expressive possibilities of alphabetic writing can coexist with a sense of the numinous and even totemic possibilities of words. Here words can both stand for a thing and also be that thing, and it is context which determines when one or the other of these possibilities occurs. Schwerner can of course only suggest this sort of worldview, imagine it through the lens of contemporary thinking, and render it in the form of his parody of academic scholarship, but this tack works to underscore the poignancy of his struggle, his desire to reconstruct, however partially, a lost mode of thought—a lost mode which has much in common with all that we hope poetry can be. Schwerner's Sumerian scribes and characters, such as the "Blind Artificer," are all alchemists of the word.

And the narrator of *The Tablets,* a figure Schwerner labels the scholar-translator, is a would-be alchemist of the word. Perhaps even more so than the tablets themselves, his characterization represents the gravity and impassioned urgency of Schwerner's intentions in the poem. For much of the sequence the scholar-translator remains torn between his desire to render an accurate scholarly translation of the tablets and his willingness to be transformed by his study of them, to allow himself to inhabit their mythopoetic and occultic modes of thought. Like an isolated colonial trader who has long resided in the tropics, he finds himself going native, a process which both attracts and repels him. The asides, footnotes, and explanations which the scholar-translator appends to individual tablets grow increasingly lengthy and self-revealing, until at last they point to his surrender to the consciousness which the tablets represent. Like the enthnomusicologist narrator of Carpentier's novel of the Amazon, *The Lost Steps,* he must undertake a mythic regression in order to arrive at self-knowledge. Schwerner is careful to avoid making this process smack of cheesy Jungian clichés, however. Although he never diminishes the pathos of the scholar-translator's struggle, Schwerner tends to present it in comic fashion, as in this note which follows Tablet VIII:

> The reader who has followed the course of these tablets to this point may find, upon looking back to Tablet I particularly, that I have been

responsible for occasional jocose invention rather than strict archaeological findings. I now regret my earlier flippancy—an attitude characteristic of beginnings, a manifestation of the resistance a man feels when he faces the probability of a terrific demand upon his life energy. Looking back myself to that first terrific meeting with these ancient poems, I can still sense the desire to keep them to myself all the while I was straining to produce these translations—desperately pushing to make available what I so wanted to keep secret and inviolable.

> In addition I am worried that I may have mistranslated part of the preceding Tablet, a combination of dialogue and narrative. How unsteady the ground I am plowing, walking on, measuring, trying to get the measure of. . . . There is a growing ambiguity in this work of mine, but I'm not sure where it lies. Some days I do not doubt that the ambiguity is inherent in the language of the Tablets themselves; at other times I worry myself sick over the possibility that *I* am the variable giving rise to ambiguities. . . .[17]

By the time we reach the final two Tablets, XXVI and XXVII, the voice of the scholar-translator dominates the writing, and instead of "pure" translations of the tablets we are offered some fifty pages of an utterly unclassifiable document which is partly a Borgesian parody of an academic paper; partly the application of a software program designed to replicate the logograms, pictographs, and determinatives of cuneiform; and partly the journal entries and diary notations of the scholar-translator in his old age, when his musings have taken on a distinctly bardic tone while at the same time always veering back to a semblance of scholarly jargon. It becomes a strange jackalope of a text, brooding and pedantic by turns. Imagine a work which is equal parts a fragmented version of the Book of Ecclesiastes, pages torn from Dostoevsky or Kierkegaard, and a lengthy E-mail composed by your most bilious and stodgy English department colleague. Here is a paragraph from the beginning of Tablet XXVI.

> As I age and my eyes weaken I do not read fewer books, but I finish a smaller proportion of the ones I take on. How different from the way I ate books in the greed and ever-new abandonments of adolescence and early manhood. Did the Old Ones, like me in my dawn, live in the revivifying newness of discovery? The history of my mind besieged by 5,000 years of written documents is the history by turns of a weary and oppressed animal and that of a repeated and sometimes galling insistence on confronting and mastering the unabsorbable. And their minds? And what about their consciousness, they who are perhaps, in the Way of mind, our coevals in one lightning blink of 5,000 years. . . .[18]

There is nothing to indicate that Tablet XXVII was meant to bring the poem to a close. Although it is the final section of the elegantly produced National Poetry Foundation edition of the sequence which appeared last year, my hunch is that, in the tradition of Modernist long poems such as Zukofsky's *A,* Olson's *Maximus,* and McGrath's *Letter to an Imaginary Friend,* the poem cannot end in any strict sense—it simply has its plug pulled upon the occasion of the author's death. Even so, the present version of the poem ends with a gesture of cautious transcendence, followed by its erasure. Yet the poem's final lines—appearing in what must be a twenty-five-point typeface, more appropriate for a poster than for a book page—suggest stasis rather than nullity, a resonant oneness rather than vacancy or silence. Schwerner brings us to this moment by employing his characteristic imagery of evisceration, digging, and consumption, while at the same time fusing such images with gestures which are markedly sacramental, even eucharistic: the Body and the Blood are consumed, and language is the paten and the chalice from which they are offered, language "the sentence of the eater," "the sweet macerated word-mash." Here is the passage which closes Tablet XXVI:

> so this world is the one
> it constitutes our food language-food we eat and we are
> translatable let's say equidistant from every point or we are
>
> a bloody loin of soul like them that's all right language-cannibal bait

. . . BUILDING AND DREAMED ; INTO THE JOY
~~PLACELESSNESS~~[19]

We are translatable, which is to say there exists for us the possibility of a mystical union with the world through language. We may become what Schwerner in an earlier passage of this tablet calls "the not-two." From our building and dreaming we thus may create for ourselves a "placelessness," a term which, by virtue of the line that is slashed through it, can no longer be read as a word but instead must be seen as Schwerner's neologistic symbol of timelessness, transcendence, the paradoxical ecstatic state in which one is everywhere but nowhere at once—it is Schwerner's version of the skewed figure eight which represents infinity or of alchemy's similar depiction of infinity as a snake which swallows its tail. It is meant to be neither a word nor a logogram nor a pictograph, but each of these things at once. And thus, like the spells and incantation of the Greek papyri, the properties of Schwerner's neologism are magical—insofar as magic is a power which permits us to recast our conceptions of reality, time, or location. When we arrive at "placelessness," we can exist, as shamans are said to exist, in more than one place at a single time. Schwerner is reminding us of something crucial which our culture has for the most part forgotten—that words may possess properties which can be described as supernatural and that to create a poem is to believe in our ability to guide and master such properties, to craft them. This is why Tess Gallagher makes the claim that a good poem is a kind of "time machine" and why Seamus Heaney talks of poetry "as divination . . . as revelation of the self to the self, as restoration of the culture to itself."[20] Poems, he insists—using language strikingly akin to that of Schwerner—are "elements of continuity, with the aura and authenticity of archaeological finds, where the buried shard has an importance that is not obliterated by the buried city. . . ."[21]

To unearth the shard, the crumbling tablet, the beads of the necklace whose catgut string has long returned to dust. And to each of these shards has been granted the power of speech; each is a revenant whose voice rises up from debris and broken statuary. A romantic notion, surely, but also a grimly austere one, for the underground city from which these ghosts have risen is truly gone; these fragments cannot easily be "shored against our ruins," for they utter a brittle cacophony. None of them can speak to us in sentences, and the buried polis shall never be restored in the way that Eliot believed it might be, or as Mandelstam did when he defined Acmeism as "nostalgia for world culture." Heaney's metaphor is soberingly explicit: the buried city shall never rise again, and we may read it—and by extension read ourselves—only by first amassing a bewildering aphasic heap of shards—some inscribed with pieces of a sacred text; others with human bones, whose marrow was long ago sucked clean by jackals and pariah dogs. Within this wreckage and detritus it is easy for the word to be lost to us entirely and for the coprolite to be mistaken for a jewel. And yet we excavate, digging down into the myriad layers, each of which contains its own unfathomable city. Heaney and Schwerner, like so many of their postmodernist peers, must walk among the excavation trenches; they cannot inhabit the towers and parapets of their High Modernist forebears. It is in a basement that George Oppen locates himself in the principal section of his great ars poetica, "Of Being Numerous":

> I want to talk of rooms and of what they look out on and of basements, the rough walls bearing the marks of the forms, the old marks of wood in the concrete, such solitude as we know—
>
> and the swept floors. Someone, a workman, bearing about him, feeling about him that peculiar word like a dishonored fatherhood has

swept this solitary floor, this profoundly hidden floor—such solitude as we know.

One must not come to feel that he has a thousand threads in his hands,
He must somehow see the one thing;
This is the level of art
There are other levels
But there is no other level of art.[22]

The level of art lies below. How may these shards be translatable, how can they turn into "the one thing" when the city from which they come is a confused necropolis? When the language we unearth is dead, its cadences lost or at best deeply hidden within the breakage? This question has been asked repeatedly by the essential poets of the last half century, by figures as different from one another as Milosz and Ashbery. But no poet of the later twentieth century has asked them with quite the urgency of Paul Celan. Celan understands the tragic difficulty of such questions, and his attempts at answering them make for a notoriously hermetic poetry. Yet to some degree his response to our condition of brokenness is a militantly straightforward one: we may read the shards only by making a language of the shards. He builds an aesthetic from our brokenness, and from this he seeks to glimpse, however fleetingly, Schwerner's "one thing," Heaney's "aura and authenticity," Oppen's "level of art." We may glimpse this moment rather than dwell in it, and to do so requires the abandonment of all the traditional blandishments and consolations we have previously sought in verse, all the "lies of mere neat poetry," as Frank Bidart so chillingly expresses it in one of his early poems.

From ruin Celan proceeds, and from the ruins he sifts the materials for his terse, compacted stanzas. From ruin he both draws his language and refines it: the screen though which language must be sifted so that it may finally emerge from the myriad fragments of cry and stammer and be fashioned into phrases and sentences. This process of sifting, of shaking the debris of language over a screen in the way that an archaeologist might sift a patch of rubble in an excavation site, is in fact the prevailing metaphor of one of Celan's most haunting poems. In German it is called "Sprachgitter," and it is the title poem of Celan's third collection, published in 1959. The term is an archaic one, and maddeningly ambiguous: you can translate it as "language mesh," implying a sieve or net, through which language may be trapped—or from which language may be shut out. (The fences of the labor camps, where Celan's family lost their lives, are always a part of his metaphorical universe, even though the Holocaust is rarely evoked in an explicit fashion.) Michael Hamburger chooses this wording in his translation of the poem. But the term can also be rendered in English as "speech-grille," the mesh partition through which the nuns of a cloistered order are allowed to speak to visitors. Celan's mother-in-law in fact joined such an order after she was widowed: the Celans would visit her there. Partly because of this biographical fact, "Speech-Grille" is the title which Joel Felstiner, Celan's biographer, chooses in his rendition of the poem. Like the English word "cleave," "Sprachgitter" embraces contradictory meanings. As Anne Carson writes, "Does Celan use *gitter* to imply passage, blockage, or salvaging of speech? Mesh can do all of these. Celan may mean all of these."[23] And truly this may be the case, as we can see from Michael Hamburger's translation. Oblique as the poem may be, its central dramatic situation is unmistakable—two people are gazing upon one another through bars. Here is the poem in its entirety:

Language Mesh

Eye's roundness between the bars.

Vibratile monad eyelid
propels itself upward,
releases a glance.

Iris, swimmer, dreamless and dreary:
the sky, heart-gray, must be near.

Athwart, in the iron holder,
the smoking splinter.
By its sense of light
you divine the soul.

(If I were like you. If you were like me.
Do we not stand
under *one* trade wind?
We are strangers.)

The flagstones. On them,
close to each other, the two
heart-gray puddles:
two
mouthsfull of silence.[24]

This seems to be a mutual stare of great intensity—the mouths and eyes of the couple appear to fuse, although they do not speak to one another. Yet this metamorphosis does little to bridge the distance between the two faces, even as their gazing in the torch-light "divine[s] the soul." The closure of the poem suggests vacant eyes and gaping mouths which appear to feed upon the void. And yet the poem's final gesture, in keeping with its ambivalent title, is mysterious and supple, suggesting that the void may somehow have been overcome. As Felstiner suggests, "'Speech-Grille'" ends on an estrangement . . . that almost suggests communion."[25] Perhaps it is only after the sieving and refining which occurs when language is drawn through the mesh that *the one thing* can be recognized.

Vacancy and wholeness at once: paradoxes such as these abound in Celan's work, and it is customary to attribute their existence in part to the terrible personal and historical upheavals which afflicted him. An exile, a Holocaust survivor, hospitalized on several occasions after mental breakdowns, and finally a suicide, Celan often seems to write from a need for self-concealment rather than from a desire for self-revelation; the poems can seem a form of camouflage or protective coloring. He coins confounding neologisms and abandons complete sentences in favor of fragments, abruptly canceled asides, and non sequiturs. The poems seem not to defy meaning as much as to withhold it from us, presenting it in shards or in a jumble. (It comes as no surprise to us that Paul Celan is a pen name, an anagram of his given name, Paul Ancel.) And yet, as in "Language Mesh," Celan's most baffling passages can suddenly be punctuated by ones of astonishing clarity and emotional directness.

I wonder if Celan's desire to withhold comprehensible meanings from us stems not from a mistrust of language but from a reverence for it which is as strange but also as deeply abiding as that of Schwerner. The tongue may be "embabeled," as a coinage from one of his later poems would have it, but the work of poetry is for him a project of reconstructing the word's prelapsarian clarity: "we are translatable," he insists. Tellingly, Celan published translations of Shakespeare, Dickinson, and Mandelstam, and was deeply influenced by the mystical traditions of kabbala and alchemy, seeing in them, I suspect, metaphors for his project of linguistic restoration. Yet this process is regarded by Celan as a hugely difficult endeavor, demanding both an excavation of the ruins and the breakage of our "confounded" speech and the labor to create a form of scripture from its shards. As Felstiner puts it, "Celan's verse seems to be assembling fragments of a shattered vessel."[26] In a poem entitled "Alchemical," the alembic cooks only silence, and its fuel may well be crematorium fire. Yet, within this terrible refining conflagration, perhaps it is the Godhead whom we glimpse. Here are the poem's concluding stanzas:

> Silence, cooked like gold, in
> charred, charred hands
> Fingers, insubstantial as smoke. Like crests, crests of air
> around—
>
> Great, gray one. Wake-
> less.
> Re-
> gal one.[27]

Like so many of Celan's poems, "Alchemical" proceeds by contradiction, by Keatsian contraries. Yet to see in his writing the easy romantic dichotomies of negative capability is to demean the gravity and the breadth of his project. Celan is "translatable," yet his poems defy explication. Suffice it to say that he asks that the broken world be restored and that the devices he employs to achieve this end can veer from lamentation and prayer to alchemy and sympathetic magic. Yet magic has always been a form of prayer, a plea for the agency and benevolence of an inattentive god. And Celan's pleas are like those of no other supplicant. Perhaps this is why his poems can haunt us as they do. I first read the following poem twenty years ago, and in succeeding years I doubt if a month has gone by in which I haven't returned to it. It contains the same prayerful ardor of the greatest of George Herbert's poems, the same agonized appraisal of the difficulties of grace. And yet grace, it seems to me, is the state to which the poem arrives:

> *SO MANY CONSTELLATIONS* that
> are held out to us. I was,
> when I looked at you—when?—
> outside by
> the other worlds.
>
> O these ways, galactic.
> O this hour, that weighed
> nights over for us into
> the burden of our names. It is,
> I know, not true
> that we lived, there moved,
> blindly, no more than a breath between
> there and not-there, and at times
> our eyes whirred comet-like

toward things extinguished, in chasms,
and where they had burned out,
splendid with teats, stood Time
on which already grew up
and down and away all that
is or was or will be—

I know.
I know and you know, we knew,
we did not know, we
were there, after all, and not there
and at times when
only the void stood between us we got
all the way to each other.[28]

Hatshepsut's mortuary temple is partly hewn from the rocks of the Theban hillside, a stone's throw from the Valley of the Kings. Hatshepsut herself is not buried in the Valley of the Kings, however. The resting place of Tut and the various Rameses is, after all, a men's club, and it was regarded as unseemly to allow the only female pharaoh to rest there. So her tomb, pillaged by grave robbers countless generations ago, sits not far from her temple. The tomb is not open to the public these days, and our stay at the temple, once one of the most visited sites on the Nile's West Bank, will be short and unsettling, thanks to the presence of dozens of Egyptian army personnel, who patrol the tomb environs with unslung AK-47s. There's an armored car parked at the ticket gate, and in its turret stands a helmeted figure who scans the horizon with binoculars. Since the massacre last year, Hatshepsut's temple has been an armed camp. Some fifty European tourists were killed here last fall, most of them by Muslim fundamentalist terrorists—but others were caught in the crossfire when the military and the tourist police stormed the site, thereby granting the terrorists their wish for martyrdom. So troops in mirrored sunglasses guard the site, watching you watch them, their lenses throwing your own image back at you. They stand at attention beneath the temple pillars, shaded from the morning sun. The area is also pocked with excavation pits. For several decades a team of Polish archaeologists has dug at this site. You can see them rise and descend their ladders, faces covered with dust and sweat. And as you circle the temple grounds—circle gingerly, for the atmosphere is far too tense to permit you to stroll—you hear in the distance a mixture of Arabic, Polish, Japanese, and English, and from a pit a static-ridden radio blares the Eagles singing "Hotel

California" ("such a lonely, lonely place"). Our guide, for the second time, has warned a member of our tour group not to take photos of guards: it is forbidden for security reasons. And here, past the porticos of the temple courtyard, we come to the famous murals which record the trading expedition sent by Hatshepsut to the Land of Punt—an exotic distant country for the Egyptians, far down the Red Sea coast in modern-day Somalia, where three thousand years later Arthur Rimbaud would voyage to trade in guns and slaves, having abandoned forever his attempts to alchemize the word. The murals, some still bearing faint traces of paint, show Egyptian triremes being loaded down with goods—baskets of incense, chained slaves, the hides of hippos and leopards. And beyond them our guide picks out the profiled figure of Hatshepsut herself and points to the face, which had been chiseled away at the command of her successor, Thutmose III. Pharaohs were god-kings, after all; to set oneself up as a god-queen was to commit an unpardonable sacrilege. And thus to chip away her face was not to him an act of vandalism but one of sympathetic magic. Destroy the face and you destroy her memory, destroy as well her immortal soul. Our guide points also to the smooth eroded place where Hatshepsut's cartouche—her name in hieroglyphics—stood. This too was chiseled away, for the Egyptians regarded the soul as inhering also within every written character of a pharaoh's name. So beside the erased cartouche of Hatshepsut was placed the cartouche of Thutmose, which itself was chiseled away sometime in the early Christian era, when Coptic monks erected a monastery here, worshiping their own version of logos. For in the beginning was the Word, not the cartouche and not, surely, the names and faces of pagan kings and queens. To the right of all this, in a random pattern against the pillars and the temple walls, are the fresh scars of bullet holes. Someone has circled each one with chalk.

(1999)

Notes

Chapter 1

Generations "I": The Future of Autobiographical Poetry

1. *Poetry* (March 1995).
2. Jimmy Carter, *Always a Reckoning* (New York: Random House, 1993), p. 103.
3. J. D. McClatchy, *White Paper* (New York: Columbia University Press, 1989), p. 16.
4. Alan Williamson, *Eloquence and Mere Life* (Ann Arbor: University of Michigan Press, 1994), p. 161.
5. Majorie Perloff, *Radical Artifice: Writing Poetry in the Age of Media* (Chicago: University of Chicago Press, 1991), p. 38.
6. Perloff, p. 50.
7. Mary Kinzie, *The Cure of Poetry in an Age of Prose* (Chicago: University of Chicago Press, 1993), p. 56.
8. Kinzie, p. 54.
9. Kinzie, p. 56.
10. Williamson, p. 163.
11. Alan Shapiro, *In Praise of the Impure* (Evanston: Northwestern University Press/Triquarterly Books, 1993), p. 41.
12. Bruce Weigl, *What Saves Us* (Evanston: Northwestern University Press/Triquarterly Books, 1992), p. 68.
13. Robert Lowell, *Day by Day* (New York: Farrar, Straus, and Giroux, 1977), p. 127.
14. Susan Mitchell, *Rapture* (New York: HarperCollins, 1992), p. 14.

Chapter 2

Some Kind of Statement, One Ear Showing: Social Poetry and Its Problems

1. The best account of Bull's career is James Adams's *Bull's Eye* (New York: Times Books, 1992).
2. Nazim Hikmet, *Nazim Hikmet: Selected Poetry,* trans. Randy Blasing and Mutlu Konuk (New York: Persea Books, 1986), p. 90.
3. Terence Des Pres, *The Writer in the World: Essays 1973–1987* (New York: Viking, 1991), p. 34.
4. Walter Benjamin, *Illuminations* (New York: Schocken Books, 1968), p. 242.
5. Robert Conquest, *Stalin: Breaker Of Nations* (London: Penguin, 1991), p. 203.
6. Carolyn Forché, ed., *Against Forgetting: Twentieth Century Poetry of Witness* (New York: W. W. Norton, 1993).
7. John Bayley, "Night Mail," *New York Review of Books* (24 June 1993), p. 20.
8. Daniel Weissbort, ed., *The Poetry of Survival: Post-War Poets of Central and Eastern Europe* (London: Penguin, 1991); Kerry Flatley and Chris Wallace-Crabbe, eds. *From the Republic of Conscience: An International Anthology of Poetry* (Fredonia, New York: White Pine Press, 1992).
9. Carolyn Forché, introduction to *Against Forgetting: Twentieth Century Poetry of Witness* (New York: W. W. Norton, 1993), pp. 29–30.
10. Forché, introduction, p. 31.

11. Miklos Radnóti, "Letter to My Wife," in *Against Forgetting: Twentieth Century Poetry of Witness,* ed. Carolyn Forché (New York: W. W. Norton, 1993), p. 370.

12. Jonathan Holden, *Style and Authenticity in Postmodern Poetry* (Columbia: University of Missouri Press, 1986), p. 80.

13. Holden, p. 91.

14. Benjamin, p. 241.

15. Alan Shapiro, *In Praise of the Impure: Poetry and the Ethical Imagination* (Evanston: Triquarterly Books/Northwestern University Press, 1993), p. 27.

16. Carolyn Forché, *The Country Between Us* (New York: Harper and Row, 1982), p. 16.

17. Wislawa Szymborska, "Writing a Curriculum Vitae." *Quarterly Review of Literature* 6 (1982), pp. 17–18.

18. David Wojahn, *Mystery Train* (Pittsburgh: University of Pittsburgh Press, 1990), p. 46.

Chapter 3
Ferality and Strange Good Fortune: Notes on Teaching and Writing

1. Dana Gioia, *Can Poetry Matter?: Essays on Poetry and American Culture* (St. Paul: Graywolf Press, 1992), p. 10.

2. D. G. Myers, *The Elephants Teach: Creative Writing Since 1880* (Englewood Cliffs: Prentice-Hall, 1996), p. 9.

3. Gioia, p. 136.

4. Quoted in Charles Bernstein, *A Poetics* (Cambridge: Harvard University Press, 1992), p. 93.

5. Osip Mandelstam, *The Noise of Time,* trans. Clarence Brown (Princeton: Princeton University Press, 1965), p. 114.

6. Lynda Hull, *The Only World* (New York: HarperCollins, 1995), pp. 8–9.

7. Lynda Hull, *Ghost Money* (Iowa City: University of Iowa Press, 1991), pp. 6–7.

Chapter 4
The State You Are Entering: Depression and Contemporary Poetry

1. U.S. Department of Health and Human Services, "Plain Talk About Depression" (Rockville, Maryland: Government Printing Office, 1989), p. 1.

2. Roy Porter, *A Social History of Madness* (New York: Dutton, 1989), p. 94.

3. Quoted in Porter, p. 81.

4. Porter, p. 79.

5. Ivor Guerney, *Selected Poems,* ed. P. J. Kavanagh (New York: Oxford University Press, 1990), p. 82.

6. Jeffrey Meyers, *Manic Power: Robert Lowell and His Circle* (New York: Arbor House, 1987), p. 19.

7. Theodore Roethke, *Selected Letters,* ed. Ralph J. Mills (Seattle: University of Washington Press, 1968), p. 116.

8. Roethke, *Letters,* p. 220–21.

9. Theodore Roethke, *Collected Poems* (New York: Doubleday, 1966), p. 257.

10. John Berryman, *Collected Poems 1937–1971,* ed. Charles Thornbury (New York: Farrar, Straus, and Giroux, 1989), p. 208.

11. Anne Sexton, *Selected Poems,* ed. Diane Wood Middlebrook and Diana Hume George (Boston: Houghton Mifflin, 1988), p. 76.

12. Randall Jarrell, *Letters,* ed. Mary Jarrell (Boston: Houghton Mifflin, 1985), p. 501; Ian Hamilton, *Robert Lowell: A Biography* (New York: Farrar, Straus, and Giroux, 1982), p. 209.

13. William Styron, *Darkness Visible: A Memoir of Madness* (New York: Random House, 1990), p. 47.

14. Robert Lowell, *Robert Lowell's Poems: A Selection,* ed. Jonathan Raban (London: Faber and Faber, 1974), p. 67.

15. Richard Hugo, *Making Certain It Goes On: Collected Poems* (New York: W. W. Norton, 1984), p. 216.

16. Hugo, p. 237.

17. Julia Kristeva, *Black Sun: Depression and Melancholia,* trans. Leon S. Roudiez (New York: Columbia University Press, 1989), p. 5.

18. Frederick Seidel, *These Days* (New York: Alfred A. Knopf, 1989), p. 18.

Chapter 5

A Cavalier and Doomed Lot: James L. White, a Memoir

1. James L. White, *The Salt Ecstacies* (St. Paul: Graywolf Press, 1981), p. 23.

2. Elizabeth Frank, *Louise Bogan: A Portrait* (New York: Alfred A. Knopf, 1985), p. 325.

3. David Kalstone, *Becoming a Poet* (New York: Farrar, Straus, and Giroux, 1989), p. 88.

4. Michael Heller, "Mentoring," *Ohio Review* 45 (Winter 1990), p. 49.

5. White, p. 9.

6. White, p. 20.

7. White, p. 42.

Chapter 6

"Mad Means Something": Anger, Invective, and the Period Style

1. Catullus, *The Poems of Catullus,* trans. Charles Martin (Baltimore: Johns Hopkins University Press, 1990), p. 135.

2. Martial, *Martial: The Epigrams,* trans. James Michie (New York: Penguin, 1978), p. 68.

3. Celia Farber, "Antihero: An Interview with Camile Paglia, Part 2," *Spin* (October 1991), p. 88.

4. David Wojahn, *Glassworks* (Pittsburgh: University of Pittsburgh Press, 1987), p. 10.

5. Anne Wright, foreword to *Two Citizens,* by James Wright, rev. ed. (Fredonia, New York: White Pine Press, 1988), p. 2.

6. Anne Wright, p. 3.

7. James Wright, *Two Citizens,* rev. ed. (Fredonia, New York: White Pine Press, 1988), p. 5.

8. Sharon Olds, *The Gold Cell* (New York: Alfred A. Knopf, 1987), p. 23.

9. Mark Doty, *Bethlehem in Broad Daylight* (Boston: Godine, 1991), p. 34.

Chapter 7
Without a Deep Delight: Neo-Narrative Poetry and Its Problems

1. Mark Jarman and Robert McDowell, *The Reaper Essays* (Brownsville, Oregon: Story Line Press, 1996), p. 34.

2. Jonathan Holden, *Style and Authenticity in Postmodern Poetry* (Columbia: University of Missouri Press, 1986), p. 31.

3. David St. John, *Study for the World's Body: New and Selected Poems* (New York: HarperCollins, 1994), p. 54.

4. Vikram Seth, *The Golden Gate* (New York: Random House, 1986), p. 54.

5. Robert Hass, *Human Wishes* (New York: Ecco Press, 1989), p. 32.

6. Holden, p. 33.

7. Richard Tillinghast, *Our Flag Was Still There* (Middletown, Connecticut: Wesleyan University Press, 1984), p. 5.

8. William Matthews, *Selected Poems and Translations 1969–1991* (Boston: Houghton Mifflin, 1991), p. 103.

9. Jack Myers and Michael Simms, *The Longman Dictionary of Poetic Terms* (White Plains, New York: Longman, 1989), p. 119.

10. Jarman and McDowell, p. 111.

11. Robert McDowell, *Quiet Money* (New York: Henry Holt, 1987), p. 14.

12. Susan Mitchell, *Rapture* (New York: HarperCollins, 1992), p. 38.

Chapter 8
Weldon Kees: A Photo and Two Afterlives

1. Louise J. Kaplan, *The Family Romance of the Imposter Poet Thomas Chatterton* (New York: Atheneum, 1988), p. 75.

2. Mark Ford, "The Least Deceived," *Times Literary Supplement* (9 April 1993), p. 10.

3. Larry Levis, *The Dollmaker's Ghost* (New York: Dutton, 1981), p. 42.

4. Simon Armitage, *Kid* (London: Faber and Faber, 1992), p. 13.

5. Kathleen West, "Imperfect Monorhyme After Lines by Weldon Kees," *Prairie Schooner* (Spring 1996), p. 65.

6. John McKernan, "When the Ghost of Weldon Kees Visited," *Paris Review* (Spring 1995), p. 58.

7. Donald Justice, introduction to *The Collected Poems of Weldon Kees,* by Weldon Kees, rev. ed. (Lincoln: University of Nebraska Press, 1975), p. ix.

8. David Wojahn, *Icehouse Lights* (New Haven: Yale University Press, 1982), pp. 38–39.

9. Howard Nemerov, introduction to *Weldon Kees: Reviews and Essays, 1936–55,* ed. James Reidel (Ann Arbor: University of Michigan Press, 1988), p. 3.

Chapter 9
Snodgrass's Borrowed Dog: S. S. Gardons and "Remains"

1. Richard Avedon, "Borrowed Dogs," *Grand Street* 7, no. 1 (Autumn 1987), p. 53.

2. Jeffrey Meyers, *Manic Power: Robert Lowell and His Circle* (New York: Arbor House, 1987), p. 23.

3. A. Poulin Jr., foreword to *Remains: A Sequence of Poems,* by W. D. Snodgrass (Brockport, New York: BOA Editions, 1985), unpaged.

4. Poulin.

5. Louise J. Kaplan, *The Family Romance of the Imposter Poet Thomas Chatterton* (New York: Athenum, 1988), p. 75.

6. Kaplan, pp. 115–16.

7. W. D. Snodgrass, *Selected Poems, 1957–1987* (New York: Soho Press, 1987), p. 28. All subsequent quotations from the poetry have been taken from this volume.

8. Donald Hall and Hayden Carruth, jacket notes to *Heart's Needle,* by W. D. Snodgrass (1959; New York: Alfred A. Knopf, 1983).

9. W. D. Snodgrass, "Tact and the Poet's Force," in *Radical Pursuit: Critical Essays and Lectures* (New York: Harper and Row 1975), p. 22.

Chapter 10

Illegible Due to Blotching: Poetic Authenticity and Its Discontents

1. Ed Brown, "Does *Birthday Letters* Spell M-O-V-I-E?" *Poets and Writers Magazine* 26, no. 3 (May/June 1998), p. 12.

2. J. D'Agostino and C. Geary, "Ariel Photograph: Hughes Sings His Blues at Last," *Vanity Fair* (May 1998), p. 59.

3. Wilfred Olsen, "Poetic Injustice: How the Cold War Wrote Poetry and Invented a Laureate," *The Observer* (7 June 1999), sec. 1, pp. 1, 13–15. Details relating to the Hughes-Plath hoax derive from Olsen's account.

4. Charles Bernstein, "My Turn: A Column," *National Review* (14 June 1999), p. 33.

5. Paul Cullum, "The Beverly Hillbillies," in *Museum of Broadcast Communications Encyclopedia of Television,* vol. 1, ed. Horace Newcomb and Noelle Watson (Chicago: Fitzroy Dearborn, 1997), p. 176.

6. Michel Foucault, "What Is an Author?" in *A Foucault Reader,* ed. Paul Rabinow (New York: Pantheon, 1984), p. 116.

7. Hugh Kenner, *The Counterfeiters: An Historical Comedy,* 2nd ed. (Baltimore: Johns Hopkins University Press, 1985), p. 20.

8. Araki Yasusada, *Doubled Flowering: From the Notebooks of Araki Yasusada,* ed. and trans. Tosa Motokiyu, Ojiu Norinaga, and Okura Kyojin (New York: Roof Books, 1997), p. 10. Subsequently cited as *Doubled Flowering.*

9. Quoted in Marjorie Perloff, "In Search of the Authentic Other," *Boston Review* 22, no. 2 (Spring 1997), p. 26.

10. Perloff, p. 29.

11. *American Poetry Review* (September/October 1996), p. 14.

12. Emily Nussbaum, "Turning Japanese: The Hiroshima Poetry Hoax," *Lingua Franca* 6, no. 10 (November 1996), p. 84.

13. Quoted in Nussbaum, p. 82.

14. Juliana Chang et al., "Displacements," *Boston Review* 22, nos. 3–4 (Summer 1997), p. 34.

15. Perloff, p. 27.

16. Quoted in Nussbaum, p. 83.

17. Dean Young, "Go Ahead and Make My Day (Anusmundi Series #5)," *The New Criterion* 15, no. 3 (September 1997), p. 43.

18. Arthur Vogelsang, "Dear Editor," *Boston Review* 22, nos. 3–4 (Summer 1997), p. 34.

19. Eliot Weinberger, "Three Footnotes," *Boston Review* 22, nos. 3–4 (Summer 1997), p. 37.

20. Kent Johnson and Javier Alvarez, "A Few Words on Araki Yasusada and Tosa Motokiyu," in *Doubled Flowering,* pp. 123–33.

21. Quoted in Jon Silkin, "Yasusada Revisited: Letter from Jon Silkin," *Poetry Review* 87, no. 3 (Autumn 1997), p. 44.

22. Kent Johnson, "From the Daybook of Ogiwara Miyamora," *Ironwood* 15, no. 2 (Autumn 1987), pp. 187–91.

23. *Doubled Flowering,* p. 15.

24. *Doubled Flowering,* p. 18.

25. Ted Hughes, *Birthday Letters* (London: Faber and Faber, 1998), pp. 87–88.

26. Charles Simic, "Our Scandal," *Boston Review* 22, nos. 3–4 (Summer 1997), p. 32.

27. Kenner, p. 83.

Chapter 11

John Flanders on the Anxious Highway: First Books and the Politics of Poetry

1. Richard Yates, *The Easter Parade* (New York: Delacorte, 1975), p. 1.

2. Yates, p. 85.

3. Yates, p. 143.

4. Craig Arnold, *Shells* (New Haven: Yale University Press, 1999), pp. 5–6.

5. George Bradley, introduction to *The Yale Younger Poets Anthology,* ed. George Bradley (New Haven: Yale University Press, 1998), p. lxxxvi.

6. Robert Hass, preface to *Field Guide,* intro. Stanley Kunitz, 2nd ed. (New Haven: Yale University Press, 1998), p. viii.

7. Jeff Clark, *The Little Door Slides Back* (Los Angeles: Sun and Moon Press, 1996), 71

8. Clark, p. 56.

9. Talvikki Ansel, *In Fragments, In Streams,* intro. James Dickey (New Haven: Yale University Press, 1997), p. 25.

10. Ansel, p. 55.

11. Hart Crane, *O My Land, My Friends: The Selected Letters of Hart Crane,* ed. Langdon Hammer and Brom Weber (New York: Four Walls Eight Windows Press, 1997), p. 405.

12. Wallace Stevens, "A Note on the Text," in *Collected Poetry and Prose,* ed. Frank Kermode and Joan Richardson (New York: Library of America, 1998), p. 970.

Chapter 12

Like a Rolling Incognito Lounge: Rock and Roll and American Poetry

1. Peter Guralnick, *Feel Like Going Home: Portraits in Blues and Rock and Roll* (New York: Harper and Row, 1989), p. 174.

2. For an engaging discussion of the L.A. poetry and punk scene, see David E. James, "Poetry/Punk/Production: Some Recent Writing From L.A.," in *Postmodernism and Its Discontents: Theories, Practices,* ed. E. Ann Kaplan (London: Verso Books, 1988), pp. 163–86.

3. William Matthews, *A Happy Childhood* (Boston: Houghton Mifflin, 1983), pp. 46–47.

4. Thom Gunn, *The Passages of Joy* (New York: Farrar, Straus, and Giroux, 1982), p. 48.

5. Mark Halliday, *Little Star* (New York: William Morrow, 1987), p. 14

6. David Rivard, *Torque* (Pittsburgh: University of Pittsburgh Press, 1988), pp. 34–35.

7. *Sonora Review* 5 (1983), pp. 96–98.

8. Bob Dylan, *Lyrics: 1962–1985* (New York: Alfred A. Knopf, 1985), p. 471.

9. Denis Johnson, *The Incognito Lounge* (New York: Random House, 1982), p. 78.

10. Denis Johnson, *The Veil* (New York: Alfred A. Knopf, 1987), p. 50.

11. Lynda Hull and David Wojahn, "The Kind of Light I'm Seeing: An Interview with Denis Johnson," *Ironwood* 25 (Spring 1985), p. 40.

12. Johnson, *Incognito Lounge,* p. 61.

13. Dylan, *Lyrics,* p. 177.

14. Dylan, *Lyrics,* p. 223.

15. Johnson, *Incognito Lounge,* pp. 3–8.

16. Dylan, *Lyrics,* pp. 228–29.

17. Johnson, *Incognito Lounge,* p. 8.

Chapter 14

Mercantile Eyes: Travel Poems and Tourist Poems

1. William Matthews, *Curiosities* (Ann Arbor: University of Michigan Press, 1989), p. 159.

2. Robert Von Hallberg, *American Poetry and Culture, 1945–1980* (Cambridge: Harvard University Press, 1985), p. 64.

3. Von Hallberg, p. 71.

4. Von Hallberg, p. 72.

5. Edward Said, *Orientalism* (New York: Pantheon Books, 1978), p. 122.

6. Von Hallberg, p. 80.

7. Von Hallberg, p. 83.

8. Adam Zagajewski, *Canvas* (New York: Farrar, Straus, and Giroux, 1991), pp. 46–47.

9. Von Hallberg, p. 76.

10. David Bottoms and David Smith, eds., *The Morrow Anthology of Younger American Poets* (New York: William Morrow, 1985).

11. Michael Blumenthal, "Today I Am Envying the Glorious Mexicans," in *The Morrow Anthology of Younger Poets,* ed. David Bottoms and David Smith (New York: William Morrow, 1985), p. 95.

12. Mary Jo Salter, *Unfinished Painting* (New York: Alfred A. Knopf, 1989), p. 54.

13. Salter, pp. 47–48.

14. Elizabeth Bishop, *The Complete Poems, 1927–1979* (New York: Farrar, Straus, and Giroux, 1983), p. 57.

15. Von Hallberg, p. 82.

16. Aspley Cherry-Garrard, *The Worst Journey in the World* (New York: Carroll and Graf, 1989), p. 643.

Chapter 15

Magi-in-Residence: An Alchemy of Poetic Ruin

1. Timothy Materer, *Modernist Alchemy: Poetry and the Occult* (Ithaca: Cornell University Press, 1995).

2. Sigmund Freud, *Totem and Taboo,* trans. James Strachey (New York: W. W. Norton, 1950), p. 77.

3. Freud, p. 79.

4. Quoted in Materer, p. 11.

5. Materer, p. 11.

6. Charles Simic, *Selected Poems, 1963–1983* (London: Secker and Warburg, 1986), p. 19.

7. Charles Bernstein, *A Poetics* (Cambridge: Harvard University Press, 1992). pp. 44–49.

8. Hans Dieter Betz, ed., *The Greek Magical Papyri in English Translation, Including the Demotic Spells,* vol. 1, *Texts,* 2nd ed. (Chicago: University of Chicago Press, 1992).

9. Betz, pp. 95–96.

10. Quoted in Carter Ratcliff, *The Fate of a Gesture: Jackson Pollack and Postwar American Art* (New York: Farrar, Straus, and Giroux, 1996), p. 108.

11. Armand Schwerner, *The Tablets* (Orono, Maine: National Poetry Foundation, 1999), pp. 23–24.

12. Schwerner, p. 155.

13. Schwerner, p. 156.

14. Quoted in Jerome Rothenberg and Pierre Joris, eds., *Poems For the Millennium: The University of California Book of Modern and Postmodern Poetry,* vol. 1 (Berkeley, University of California Press, 1995), p. 778.

15. Jared Diamond, *Guns, Germs, and Steel: The Fates of Human Society* (New York: W. W. Norton, 1997), p. 220.

16. Diamond, pp. 221–22.

17. Schwerner, pp. 31–32.

18. Schwerner, p. 70.

19. Schwerner, p. 123.

20. Seamus Heaney, *Preoccupations: Selected Prose 1968–1978* (New York: Farrar, Straus, and Giroux, 1980), p. 41.

21. Heaney, p. 41.

22. George Oppen, *Collected Poems* (New York: New Directions, 1976), p. 168.

23. Anne Carson, *An Economy of the Unlost* (Princeton: Princeton University Press, 1999), p. 23.

24. Paul Celan, *Poems,* trans. Michael Hamburger (New York: Persea Books, 1980), p. 105.

25. Joel Felstiner, *Paul Celan: Poet, Survivor, Jew* (New Haven: Yale University Press, 1995), p. 108.

26. Felstiner, p. 236.

27. Celan, *Poems,* pp. 147–49.

28. Celan, *Poems,* pp. 135–36.

Index